EXISTENTIAL PERSPECTIV
THERAPY

To our husbands, Digby and Stephen, and the children, step-children, foster children and grandchildren who enrich our physical, personal, social and spiritual worlds.

Existential Perspectives on Relationship Therapy

Edited by

Emmy van Deurzen and Susan Iacovou

palgrave
macmillan

First published 2013 by
PALGRAVE MACMILLAN

Palgrave Macmillan in the UK is an imprint of Macmillan Publishers Limited,
registered in England, company number 785998, of Houndmills, Basingstoke,
Hampshire RG21 6XS.

Palgrave Macmillan in the US is a division of St Martin's Press LLC,
175 Fifth Avenue, New York, NY 10010.

Palgrave Macmillan is the global academic imprint of the above companies
and has companies and representatives throughout the world.

Palgrave® and Macmillan® are registered trademarks in the United States,
the United Kingdom, Europe and other countries.

ISBN 978–0–230–36209–3

This book is printed on paper suitable for recycling and made from fully
managed and sustained forest sources. Logging, pulping and manufacturing
processes are expected to conform to the environmental regulations of the
country of origin.

A catalogue record for this book is available from the British Library.

A catalog record for this book is available from the Library of Congress.

Printed and bound in the UK by Charlesworth Press, Wakefield.

Contents

Figures and Table

Figures

Table

Acknowledgements

'If I have seen further it is by standing on the shoulders of giants.'
Bernard of Chartres

From an existential point of view, we are inseparable from those with whom we share the world and therefore our individual ideas are to a large extent derived from others. We therefore owe a great debt of gratitude to all those who have influenced our thinking over the years. In a more concrete and direct manner in editing this book we have been much inspired by working with others to weave together a fabric of existential relationship work. If we had co-authored the book it would have been a very different book, than the one that emerged from the contributions of so many authors and different experiences and points of view. This has been a liberating process, creating something greater than we could have conceived by working alone. We are extremely grateful to the seasoned existential therapists who have written chapters for this volume, especially for the commitment with which they approached the task of breaking new ground in existential therapy and for the patience and good humour they demonstrated through out the long process from conception to publication.

The real credit for this book, however, lies with those who came before – from Socrates to Buddha, Aristotle to Jaspers, Kierkegaard to Sartre and Camus to Nietzsche. These are the true giants upon whose words of wisdom we have relied and to whom we are most indebted. We hope that this work does justice to what has come before, while offering something of value to what is yet to come.

Emmy van Deurzen and Susan Iacovou
Sheffield and Manchester, July 2013.

Notes on Contributors

The editors

Emmy van Deurzen has worked with couples for over 35 years and has been a therapist since 1973. She established existential psychotherapy in the UK, founded the Society for Existential Analysis and Regent's College School of Psychotherapy and Counselling and was the first chair of the United Kingdom Council for Psychotherapy (UKCP). She has written or edited a dozen books and she lectures worldwide. She is the Principal of the New School of Psychotherapy and Counselling (NSPC) in London and a fellow of the British Psychological Society (BPS), the UKCP and the British Association for Counselling and Psychotherapy (BACP). In spite of this she prefers to think of herself as a philosopher and an artist.

Susan Iacovou is a UKCP accredited existential therapist and psychologist with a private practice in Cheshire and has a particular interest in existential therapy with couples and families. She has published widely and has a forthcoming book on key points and techniques in existential therapy. Susan teaches on a range of psychotherapy Doctorate and Masters' courses, and was a Research Associate on the European Funded Continuing Education in Psychotherapy Project, which was designed to improve access to quality psychotherapy training across Europe. Susan received an MA in Psychology from Edinburgh University and will shortly complete her Doctorate in Existential Counselling Psychology with the New School of Psychotherapy and Counselling.

The contributors

Martin Adams is a psychotherapist and supervisor in private practice and he is also a lecturer and clinical supervisor at Regent's College and the New School of Psychotherapy and Counselling, both in London. He has worked in a variety of psychiatric, NHS, statutory and voluntary agencies. He has written and researched on subjects such as death, addiction, phenomenology, supervision and human development all from an existential perspective and is the author of *A Concise Introduction to Existential Counselling* (Sage, 2013), and co-author with Emmy van Deurzen of *Skills in Existential Counselling and Psychotherapy* (Sage, 2011). He is also a sculptor.

Meg Barker is a senior lecturer in psychology at the Open University and a UKCP accredited existential therapist working in sex and relationship counselling. Meg has published co-edited collections on non-monogamies and sadomasochism with Darren Langdridge and the two of them also co-edit the journal *Psychology & Sexuality* with Taylor and Francis. Meg's research has been published in many journals and books culminating recently in a general audience book on relationships called *Rewriting the Rules* (www. rewriting-the-rules.com). Meg regularly provides training for practitioners on gender, sexuality and relationships, and has a forthcoming book on these topics with Christina Richards as well as a single-authored book on mindfulness.

Golnar Bayat is a UKCP registered existential psychotherapist and BACP Snr. Accredited Counsellor working in private practice in York. As a bilingual therapist, she has worked extensively with clients from different cultures and developed a special interest in highlighting issues arising from cross-cultural therapeutic relationships between therapists and clients belonging to black and minority ethnic groups. She is currently a therapist, supervisor, trainer and consultant in the field of cross-cultural counselling with a particular focus on the underlying assumptions inherent in psychotherapeutic theories that create barriers to delivery of counselling and psychotherapy to minority groups living in Britain.

Betty Cannon is a licensed psychologist who has worked with individuals, couples and groups in Boulder, Colorado, for over 30 years. She is president of the Boulder Psychotherapy Institute, which trains mental health professionals in Applied Existential Psychotherapy (AEP). AEP interlaces the insights of contemporary existential and psychodynamic approaches with interventions inspired by Gestalt and other experiential therapies. Dr Cannon is its founder. She is the author of numerous chapters, articles, and an internationally recognized book on existential therapy, *Sartre and Psychoanalysis*. She is a member of the editorial boards of three professional journals and an internationally known lecturer and workshop presenter.

Maria Clark works as an existential psychotherapist and supervisor in private practice specializing in working relationally with couples. She co-founded the Australasian Existential Society in 1997. Her background in education and special education supports her existential approach to psychotherapy as it creates a greater understanding of the complexity and uniqueness of learning, meaning and relationships with others.

Simon du Plock is Head of Post-Qualification Doctorates at the Metanoia Institute, London where he leads the Doctorate in Psychotherapy by Professional Studies and the Doctorate in Psychotherapy by Public Works, both joint programmes with Middlesex University. He is a UKCP accredited Psychotherapist, a BPS and HPC Chartered Counselling Psychologist, and a Foundation Member with Senior Practitioner Status of the BPS Register of Psychologists Specialising in Psychotherapy. He maintains a clinical practice in existential psychotherapy and academic and clinical supervision, and lectures internationally, most frequently in Russia and the Baltic States. He has edited *Existential Analysis*, the journal of the UK Society for Existential Analysis, since 1993.

Mark Jepson is a counselling psychologist specializing in work with couples. Mark graduated from Manchester University with a Masters degree in sociology in 1980, and followed that with three years working as a research fellow at Brunel and Loughborough Universities. He subsequently worked for 25 years as a management consultant, helping organizations in Europe and the US improve their inter-organizational relationships. Mark started a second career as a couples' counsellor in 1995, gaining a degree in psychology in 2005, and completing his doctorate in counselling psychology in 2010. He currently works as a relationship therapist in private practice and for a relationship counselling charity.

Darren Langdridge is Head of the Department of Psychology at the Open University, UK, Honorary Professor of Psychology at Aalborg University, Denmark and a UKCP accredited existential psychotherapist working in private practice. His research and writing has focused on the critical application of ideas from phenomenological and hermeneutic philosophy to social psychology and psychotherapy within the substantive context of the social scientific study of sexualities. He is co-editor of the journal *Psychology & Sexuality* and his books include *Existential Counselling and Psychotherapy* (Sage, 2012) and *Phenomenological Psychology: Theory, Research and Method* (Pearson Education, 2007).

Dmitry Leontiev is Professor of Psychology, Lomonosov Moscow State University, head of the research lab of positive psychology and quality of life studies at the Higher School of Economics, Moscow and the founder and the head of the Institute of Existential Psychology and Life Enhancement (EXPLIEN) in Moscow. He strives to integrate the existentialist approach to human personality with the cultural-historical activity theory approach and with synergetic views on human self-regulation and self-organization. The author of numerous publications in the psychology of personality and motivation, theory and history of psychology, psychology of art and empirical aesthetics, Dmitry is a former recipient of the Promotional Award of the Victor Frankl Foundation of the city of Vienna (2004).

Jacky Lewis is an existential therapist and clinical supervisor with many years' experience working as an accredited mediator in a variety of conflict situations. She has been a visiting faculty tutor at both Regent's College SPC and at the NSPC in London. Jacky has taken existential ideas into the legal and corporate arena and developed them into professional training courses. She is an external CPD trainer for both the Solicitors Regulatory Authority and the Bar Standards Board. Jacky has a busy general, employment and divorce mediation practice and is often consulted to help separating couples devise co-parenting contact arrangements for their children. She is a Collaborative Law Family Consultant.

Reed Lindberg is a licensed professional counsellor who works primarily with couples in Boulder, Colorado. He refers to his work as Relationship, Sex and Romance Counselling: An Existential Approach. He has practised for nearly 25 years. Reed is managing director of the Boulder Psychotherapy Institute, which trains mental health professionals in Applied Existential Psychotherapy (AEP). AEP interlaces the insights of contemporary existential and psychodynamic approaches with interventions inspired by Gestalt and other experiential therapies. He is currently co-authoring a book on AEP with Betty Cannon and Robyn Chauvin. He is the person to contact about international outreach for the Institute.

Jyoti Nanda is a Chartered Psychologist and an Associate Fellow of the BPS, an HPC Registered Counselling Psychologist, a UKCP Registered Existential Psychotherapist and is a BACP Senior Accredited Practitioner and Supervisor. She is on the Visiting Faculty at Regent's College and is in Private Practice seeing individuals, couples and groups. A long-term practitioner of meditation in more than one tradition, her published work in peer reviewed journals focuses on an embodied integration of mindfulness and existential therapy. Jyoti has lived, studied and worked in India and the UK, and travelled widely. She brings a wide world-view in her therapeutic work, and sees clients across different cultures.

Donna Christina Savery is an Existential and Creative Therapist working in both private practice in Windsor and London, and for a mental health charity. Her therapy work draws significantly upon her creative background and uses story, myth, literature, music, art, symbols, play and drama alongside more traditional 'talking therapies'. She is a founder member and workshop leader of a CPPD group for therapists and counsellors, taking both a facilitating and strategic role. Donna is an experienced lecturer, speaker and group therapist, as well as an avid researcher. She lives in Windsor and is currently working on a book on Narcissus and Echo.

Chris Scalzo is a UKCP registered existential psychotherapist, currently working full time in the NHS, as a therapist, supervisor and manager of a specialist Child and Adolescent Mental Health Service. He has previously lectured and taught post-MA psychologists in training on existential psychotherapy and has published philosophically based articles in the journal *Existential Analysis* as well as written for the BACP about his therapeutic practice with children and families. He is author of the book *Therapy with Children: An Existential Perspective* (Karnac, 2010).

Naomi Stadlen realized when she met Anthony Stadlen, now her husband, and they had children how little was understood about how we relate. Today she works as an existential psychotherapist specializing in seeing mothers and parent couples. Her two books are *What Mothers Do – Especially When it Looks Like Nothing* (Piatkus, 2004) and *How Mothers Love – and How Relationships Are Born* (Piatkus, 2011). She teaches and supervises at the New School of Psychotherapy and Counselling. She runs Mothers Talking, discussion meetings for mothers, at the Active Birth Centre and at Born. She is a breastfeeding counsellor for La Leche League.

Alison Strasser is the Director of the Centre for Existential Practice in Sydney and has been instrumental in creating existential curricula for a variety of counselling and psychotherapy trainings in Australia. She is a practising psychotherapist, coach and supervisor with an emphasis on working relationally with her clients. Her doctorate focussed on unravelling the process of supervision which led to a framework for teaching supervisors. Alison is co-author of *Existential Time-Limited Therapy* (1997) and was the founder of the Australasian Existential Society.

Digby Tantam is a Psychiatrist, Chartered Psychologist and Psychotherapist. He has been an Honorary Consultant Psychiatrist since 1983 and Honorary Consultant Psychotherapist in the National Health Service since 1990. He has been providing an assessment clinic for people with autism since 1980. He is an Emeritus Professor with the University of Sheffield, and Honorary Visiting Senior Research Fellow with the University of Cambridge. A Director of the Septimus group of companies, he is Deputy Principal of NSPC. He is the author of *Psychotherapy and Counselling Practice*, published in 2002 by Cambridge University Press, *Can the world afford Asperger syndrome?* and *Autism Spectrum Disorders through the Life Span* with Jessica Kingsley in 2011 and 2012, 9 other books and 160 scientific publications.

Karen Weixel-Dixon is a psychotherapist, mediator, supervisor and trainer in the fields of psychotherapy, mediation and coaching. Her paradigm is described as existential-phenomenological and she has a special interest in how people engage with temporality. She maintains practices and delivers seminars in the UK and in France, her current country of residence.

Lilian C. J. Wong received her PhD in Counselling Psychology from the University of British Columbia. She served as Psycho-educational Consultant and School Psychologist for several school boards in Ontario and British Columbia. She was Associate Professor and Clinical Coordinator for School Counselling in the Graduate Program in Counselling Psychology at Trinity Western University, and Associate Professor of Psychology at Tyndale University College. She is co-editor of the *Handbook of Multicultural Perspectives on Stress and Coping* (Springer, 2006) and *The Positive Psychology of Meaning and Spirituality* (Purpose Research, 2007). She is President of the Meaning-Centered Counselling Institute, and Co-Chair of Supervision and Training Section, Society of Counseling Psychology, APA.

Paul T. P. Wong received his PhD from the University of Toronto in Psychology. He has held professorial positions at Trent University, the University of Toronto, Trinity Western University and Tyndale University College. He is a registered clinical psychologist in Ontario. His meaning-centred counselling and therapy has gained worldwide recognition. He is the President of the International Network on Personal Meaning (www.meaning.ca), and International Society for Existential Psychology and Psychotherapy. He is also editor of the *International Journal of Existential Psychology and Psychotherapy*.

Setting the Scene: Relatedness from an Existential Perspective

EMMY VAN DEURZEN AND SUSAN IACOVOU

Existential philosophers recognize the centrality of relationship to human existence and they have argued convincingly that individuality is secondary to relationship, as we are always in relation and are shaped and defined by the very relationships we have:

> We are never but an aspect, an element, a part of a wider context. We are one of the channels through which life flows. We are a vessel through which life manifests. As such we are always in relation, always in context, always connected to what is around us, always defined by what we associate with. Relationship is essential to our very survival and inspires everything we do. (Deurzen, 1997: 95)

Although the primordial nature of relationship in human existence is a central tenet of existential thinking, there has been little written (see Tantam and Deurzen, 2005) about how this translates into the practice of existential therapy with people facing challenges in their relationships. Nevertheless most existential therapists implicitly work with relationships, as these are so fundamental to an existential way of considering the world. This book has gathered together the reflections and experiences of leading existential relationship therapists from across the globe, in order to document existential relationship practice. In good existential tradition, each of the authors who have contributed to this text has their own view of an existential way of working with relationships. Each gives preference to the particular existential philosophers and practitioners who have inspired them and influenced their therapeutic work with clients in relationship. The way that the book roams across centuries of existential wisdom, highlights the multiple and varied strands of this rich and enlightening tradition. And yet, in spite of its obvious diversity the book also identifies and explores common values and general principles of existential relationship therapy. These core themes and propositions emerge from within the pages of each chapter and are explicitly woven together in the final chapter, which contains a coherent yet flexible and open-ended model of existential relationship practice.

To set the scene, this introduction provides you with a broad overview of those aspects of existential philosophy that are most relevant to working with people in relationships. Readers already familiar with existential ideas will recognize much of what we have to say here as we introduce the core themes that will be referred to and built upon throughout the book. The philosophy outlined here forms the skeleton framework, which authors will bring to life in various ways. It is the philosophical angle that is shared, while the practice remains free and individual.

Philosophical background to existential relationship therapy

The breadth and depth of existential philosophical thought is staggering and contains a plethora of perspectives on all aspects of human existence, making it difficult to summarize the key foundational tenets. One way of approaching the challenge of establishing a philosophical basis for existential relationship therapy is to turn to the most vocal existential philosophers who have spoken about relationships and learn from their writing. Let us look briefly at what Kierkegaard, Nietzsche, Heidegger, Sartre, Buber, Jaspers and Levinas tell us about living with others.

Kierkegaard

> Most people are subjective toward themselves and objective toward all others, frightfully objective sometimes – but the task is precisely to be objective toward oneself and subjective toward all others. (Kierkegaard, 1998: 72)

Kierkegaard was wary of close relationships and lived his life in relative solitude disdaining, but also carefully describing the effects of human relations on the individual. He famously spoke about the crowd as misleading people into things they would not do if they thought for themselves, as individuals, about what they wanted to achieve and be. The youngest of seven children, Kierkegaard grew up in a blended family – his father was a wealthy businessman and, on the death of his first wife, married the family maid (Kierkegaard's mother). He was a dominant and punitive father and husband, and Kierkegaard's experiences growing up in such a family may have influenced his philosophy and his life choices. He never married and broke off his engagement to Regina Olsen, the girl he continued to love, in preference for a life of solitude and devotion to his writing. As psychotherapists we may recognize a similar stance to relatedness in some of our clients, who may come to us having decided that the costs of relationships far outweigh their benefits. In doing so, of course, they are still taking a stance to their being in the world with others and we can help them reflect on this stance. Even isolation is still a way of relating, as even the hermit in his hut in the forest is making a statement about his relatedness to others.

In his book *Works of Love* (1998), Kierkegaard implores us to create a loving relationship to God, or to whatever image we may have of eternity. A relationship to anything else, be it a job, a possession or another person has to come from our clear individuality as it reflects on itself and reaches out to eternity. Only then will any love we pursue be the love for the most ultimate of ideas or objectives rather than a self-serving love, which mistakes its object in another. Again, we often find clients in relationship therapy who have lost sight of themselves, their individuality and their sense of ultimate purpose, and have attempted to merge with the significant other in their life, something Kierkegaard is quick to warn us against. Existential relationship therapy will usually encourage partners to take stock of their outlook, their values and the things that really matter to them and that they may try to obtain from their relationship rather than finding them individually in the first instance. Kierkegaard's admonition of learning to be objective about oneself is helpful in this respect. His proposal of becoming able to be subjective about others is equally helpful in reminding us to teach partners to imagine putting themselves into each other's position.

Nietzsche

> It is not a lack of love, but a lack of friendship that makes unhappy marriages. (Nietzsche, 1985: 37)

Like Kierkegaard, Nietzsche spoke of the bad effects of following the lead of others (what he called the herd mentality – Nietzsche, 1973) where we do what others do, frightened to stand out or take any risks. Unlike Kierkegaard, however, he focused on facing up to the realities of the world (rather than a world beyond) and proposed that the most well-being could be had from staying clear of the overwhelming influences of other people and by safeguarding one's personal space and separate existence. Perhaps in recognition of the challenges inherent in being with others, he was to later describe a relationship – that between himself and the composer Wagner (Nietzsche, 1985) – as his greatest achievement. Nietzsche was no happier in love than Kierkegaard and yet he has much to teach those who work with couples, as all partners need to learn to take enough personal space and time to stand strongly in their own sense of dignity and individuality. Love and relationship can be much improved if we first learn to love ourselves and also to love our lives, taking responsibility for what we make of our lives ourselves, rather than holding others responsible for it.

Heidegger

Heidegger's view was that we are taken over by the world before we become capable of starting to be aware of it and that similarly we are taken over by others before we can start to differentiate ourselves and learn to be for ourselves instead of for the other (Heidegger, 1927). He agreed with Levinas (1999a) that 'the other' has priority in our lives, but also connected our relationship as fallen with others to the idea of inauthentic being, whereas authentic being requires us to come into our own and learn to be aware of the limits of our existence and stand alone in the face of death.

While Heidegger did not think we could ever be only authentic, he clearly believed it important for us to take the time to be separate from others and think for ourselves about life. In doing so we realize that we are always in relation.

> *Authentic Being-one's Self* does not rest upon an exceptional condition of the subject, a condition that has been detached from the 'they'; *it is rather an existentiell modification of the 'they' – of the 'they' as an essential existentiale.* (Heidegger, 1927: 130)

We cannot escape from others as the 'they' is part of ourselves and so we have to learn to modulate our existence between being with others and being for ourselves. Those who work with couples can attest to the regularity with which this tension between meeting our own needs and addressing our own priorities on the one hand and putting the needs and priorities of others with whom we are in relationship before our own on the other hand, is an issue.

Sartre

Sartre famously declared 'hell is other people' (Sartre, 1949: 57) and observed that we punish each other automatically by observing and critiquing each other for all the ways in which we ourselves fall short. Human beings, he thought, were essentially trying to be free consciousness whilst reducing others to the state of objects, in order to win over them and control them. We feel shame in the face of the other's look and expect to be judged and found deficient. Consequentially we try to outsmart each other and compete with each other for dominance. If we control the other, we feel safe from their judgement. And yet, the dialectic of the master and the slave, tells us that even the master becomes slave to the slave and has to work hard to maintain the slave's devotion. The slave also holds power. Allowing ourselves to be submissive and controlled by another can not only yield safety but also a sense of being needed. The choice between oppressing the other sadistically or submitting ourselves masochistically to be used by the other can only be avoided by trying to escape from the other's gaze and withdrawing from competition all together. All of these familiar moves exhibit themselves in couple relationships. In later life, Sartre's views were a lot more positive and optimistic as he acknowledged the possibility and desirability of reciprocity and cooperation in relationships as a way to get on with others for the overall good, working towards a common project. This hinged on the idea of generosity, which is an important way of emptying ourselves of fake possessions and identities. Since we cannot ever really possess our selves or our lives, to be generous with what we have is the key to good human relations. As we give away, so we feel more in tune with what we really are, that is, nothing. As we become emptied we become ready to receive in return. When, in mutuality, we give to each other we never run out of what we need.

There is no doubt that the later Sartre inspires hope and belief in the possibility of good relations between partners. Simone de Beauvoir might not quite have agreed with this, however, as she was very aware that in relationships not everyone is equal, which leads easily to one person feeling entitled to more power than another. She observed how women often become 'the other' to the man – someone who is secondary, dispensable and replaceable and at the mercy of the other's initiative (de Beauvoir, 2011). She undoubtedly influenced Sartre's change of outlook over the years as she took the view early on that we needed to work with others rather than against them and that true collaboration, where each partner provides something for the other and contributes something to the relationship is essential. She thought this was inevitable in order to achieve shared power as none of us can really accomplish anything without the collaboration and enthusiasm of others.

Sartre's and de Beauvoir's work reminds us as relationship therapists of the human desire to possess someone else, to merge with them – to find our missing other half and to struggle with this until we find a better way forward. Sartre spoke of this search for:

> ...something that was not always bound to the sex life and that at that moment caused each of us to be himself at the very depths of himself. (Sartre in Chaine, 1978: 116)

He also reminded us, however, of the need to allow the other freedom within the relationship as we want our partner to love us freely. Since we are also frightened that if we give them the space to do so they will choose to leave us, we have to find the strength to re-commit to a relationship on a daily basis and not expect promises that are premature and cannot be kept. We see these dynamics at play in many relationships plagued with jealousy, anxiety and insecurity. Existential work with relationships favours the search for freedom in each partner so that they can come together with a mutual commitment to being with the other rather than by feeling constricted or obliged to be together.

Buber

As Buber showed with such panache, we can never say I, without implying 'It' or 'You' (Buber, 1970). We are always in relation. No man or woman is an island and no one can live without addressing others or being addressed by them. We do, however, have a choice over how we take others into account, and opinions in psychology and philosophy vary over how we should do this. Our lives are embedded in our relationships to other people whether we like this or not. In addition, the way in which we relate to our selves, our environment, our own bodies, the natural world and the ideas and values we hold about our universe profoundly affects the way in which we approach others.

Our expectations of relationships form the background to the partnerships we form.

For Buber, human life finds its meaning in relationships. He distinguished between I-Thou (sometimes translated as I-You) and I-It forms of relating. In I-Thou moments we are truly *with* the other person. We are not trying to get something from them, nor are we trying to understand them or study them. In these moments we are fully open to the totality of the other, enabling the other to be completely themselves and this allows us to becoming ourselves, in the fullness of who we are. I-It moments, on the other hand, occur when we relate to the other as someone 'out there', separate from us, making them into an object or an It. When we do this we only see part of the person and we become stunted and less than we can be ourselves as well. In relating to the other as an object we objectify ourselves as well. Of course we cannot always be in I-Thou mode – the practicalities of life demand that we relate to people in the I-It mode a lot of the time. However, a life, or a relationship devoid of I-Thou relating is an impoverished one, according to Buber. Clients who routinely relate to their partners in fixed ways, objectifying them as 'selfish' or 'needy', for example, miss out on the opportunity to truly encounter them. And for Buber, human existence is about encounter:

> Without It, a human being cannot live. But whoever lives only with It, is not human. (Buber, 1970)

Jaspers

Jaspers was perplexed and frustrated by what he saw as people's 'rigid inaccessibility' (Jaspers, 1941) to others, by which he meant our unwillingness to listen and truly hear each other, the frequency with which we put barriers up against open and honest communication and the way in which we often resist any form of closeness or connection. For him, true connection comes from a meeting of true selves in which each person is receptive to the beliefs, ideas and reasoning of the other. He exhorted us to be ready to enter into genuine encounter with others and emphasized the rewards available to those who give up self-deception and open themselves to the glory of other human beings. He renounced solitude and self-sufficiency as a way of being, describing it as impoverished, and was keen to remind us that:

> The individual cannot become human by himself. Self-being is only real in communication with another self-being. Alone, I sink into gloomy isolation – only in community with others can I be revealed in the act of mutual discovery. My own freedom can only exist if the other is also free. Isolated or self-isolating Being remains mere potentiality or disappears into nothingness. (Jaspers, 1941: 17)

Finally, Jaspers also encouraged us not to shy away from what others think of us and want us to be, as without this information we cannot decide what we ourselves are and want to be. As relationship therapists, we can help partners explore their perceptions of each other and guide their attempts to make sense of the perceptions of the other in the context of how they see themselves and want to be seen. Such an exploration is often eye opening and mind blowing. Partners in a relationship, when facilitated by an existential relationship therapist in exploring their own and each other's way of being, often have a sudden realization of never having properly seen or known each other, nor even themselves.

Levinas

In his book *Totality and Infinity* (1999a) Levinas showed the phenomenon of being face to face with another, in the encounter, to be primordial because it reveals the other in his alterity, in his or her difference to ourselves. He argued that the other is prior to ourselves. This is not intended to frighten us with the other's difference but rather to help us recognize the other's need as well as their willingness and capacity to be gentle with us and recognize our need in turn. Levinas describes our subjectivity as formed by and through our subjection to the other (Levinas, 1999b). The other founds our being and gives it direction. He emphasizes the non-symmetrical relationship between us and the Other – a relationship in which we are responsible for the Other but cannot tell if the Other will take the same care of us. We cannot make them take this care, indeed it is not our concern, we can only be responsible for our own solicitude towards them.

> ... I am responsible for the Other without waiting for reciprocity, were I to die for it. Reciprocity is his affair. It is precisely insofar as the relation between the Other and me is not reciprocal that I am subjection to the Other; and I am 'subject' essentially in this sense. It is I who support all ... The I always has one responsibility more than all the others. (Levinas, 1999a: 33)

Levinas points out that if we attempt to master or change the form of a relationship then we attempt to meet with the other on our own terms and therefore enter into what he describes as a relationship to totality, in which we abuse the other in the very act of trying to enter into a relationship with them. As relationship therapists, we regularly encounter clients who attempt to shape their relationships with their partners in these ways, when, Levinas would suggest, they should be trying to connect with, discover or resonate with them instead. It is a sobering reminder of the need for each partner to take responsibility for their care of the other and to not wait to be given to before they begin to give.

Phenomenology as it underpins existential relationship therapy

> The method of phenomenology is to go back to things themselves. (Husserl, 1967)

Our scene setting for this book would be incomplete without a mention of phenomenology and its basic premises as they inform existential therapeutic work in general. When working with couples or other less traditional relationship formats, existential therapists are faced with the challenge of understanding and working with the worldviews, values and beliefs of two or more individuals, as well as the philosophy of relationship held by each.

Phenomenology is best understood by reference to the ideas of Edmund Husserl (1859–1938). Husserl was a trained mathematician who sought to establish the essence or core of concepts in science. He describes this fascination as something that arose in childhood when he was given a penknife as a gift. He was determined to make it as perfect as he could before he used it, and ended up sharpening it until there was hardly any blade left. Husserl wanted to do the same with concepts or ideas. As the quote above illustrates, he was convinced that phenomenology would allow the observer 'to go back to the things themselves' – to focus so intently on something that it revealed all there was to reveal. Husserl's ideas were expanded upon by Martin Heidegger (1889–1976) who gave them an existential twist by establishing human experience as a concept in its own right and focusing on the interpretation of meaning in human experience.

Put simply, phenomenology in the therapeutic setting encourages a focus on people's lived experience – how they encounter the world, how it appears to them and what it means to them. We all experience the world – we see, hear, imagine, want, feel and do. And when we experience the world in these ways, we are always experiencing (or are conscious of) *something*. We see a car, we imagine a beach, we want a drink. This is important to phenomenologists because it reflects a fundamental principle – the idea that our minds are instruments for making connections with the world and can function only in relation to the world (Deurzen, 2010). There is no subject-object split, as Descartes most famously claimed. Instead our self is intimately connected, indeed unified with the things of which we are conscious. Not only that, we create our own meanings out of our connections and these in turn influence how we relate to the world and to things or people in the world. If, as therapists, we are to truly appreciate and get to grips with how our clients experience the world, we need to reveal these connections and meanings and help our clients recognize, explore and accept or modify them. To do this we use a number of fundamental phenomenological attitudes to guide our work:

- A stance of curiosity, openness and questioning as we seek to set aside our own bias, composed of our assumptions, values and beliefs, to view what the client is saying without attributing meanings of our own and to come anew to what they are telling us. Husserl described this as the epoché, literally suspension, but often referred to as bracketing, reflecting the fact that we cannot un-know our usual attitudes, bias and interpretations but we can recognize them and then place them in metaphorical brackets, so that we will deal with them separately from the object of our intentionality. Of course we can never remove our own bias, our particular perspective on the world. Our bias is our edge and it helps us frame the world and formulate opinions on it. We can never suspend our biased views entirely, but we can become increasingly aware of how they might influence our understanding of the client. And of course when we work with clients in relationships we can encourage them to take a similar stance when listening to their partners' stories – to recognize the internal chatter they experience in response to what their partners say and find a way to listen with curiosity and openness instead (see Deurzen, 2010; Deurzen and Hanaway, 2012).

- A focus on description, exploration and meaning (Husserl, 2012). Rather than jumping to conclusions about our clients' worldviews and attributing meanings to their way of computing their ideas, we ask them to describe their own meanings as fully as possible. We encourage both partners to describe their experience in as much detail as they can (rather than trying to explain or understand it) and may ask them what a particular concept means to them, or how they experience it. At this stage we are helping them resist the urge to interpret their own experiences, to hypothesize or theorize or explain their motivations or the origins of their experience. We help them to stay with the lived experiences as they actually are and become much more familiar with their own views and take on the world. Often this process is difficult in relationship work as one or other of the partners seeks to leap in and explain things or even fix things before they are properly described. As existential relationship therapists our role is to maintain an open space for the process and resist attempts to foreclose it prematurely. This is often facilitated by the practice of working separately with each partner, initially in a private session and after this in front of the other partner, without the other interrupting or contradicting.
- The horizontalization of information gathered is about setting each partner's experience against the background and perspective of their own world. We resist the temptation of giving some aspects of the client's experience precedence over others and initially equalize the importance of everything they need to say or explore. In other words we try to regard every aspect of their story as equally important and stop assuming that certain aspects are key and that we already know which threads to follow and which to abandon. Once again this may be challenging when working with couples who may think that they know what is key in their own or their partner's story and may find it difficult to attend equally to all aspects of what they are experiencing or hearing. To explore the social, cultural and ideological context of each partner's story and worldview is usually extremely productive. They discover new angles to their own experience and uncover aspects of their partner they never knew about. This exploration immediately changes the perspective each partner has on their own as well as on the other's outlook and difficulties. Of course it is crucial that the therapist shows complete respect for each partner during this exploration and demands the same from each partner for the other's exploration.

Only when we feel that each client has laid bare all the layers of their story, and described them in all the detail that they needed to go into, do we begin to work with the partners in tentatively uncovering the meanings inherent in their preoccupations and current troubles. These meanings are left to emerge naturally from the process, rather than being dragged out into the open through some structured questioning process or by reference to any therapeutic theory or dogma. Existential therapists help people to find their own meanings rather than imposing meanings and interpretations on them. Clients are free to articulate themselves in their own language and in doing so make their own connections to the wider context. As therapists we take the role of 'perpetual beginners' (Moran, 2005: 62), making us 'less likely to think we already know' (Orange, 2009: 4) and helping us to stay committed to the idea that understanding is, in and of itself, therapeutic. Thus the existential relationship therapist signals to the partners in the relationship that being in relationship can be done in an open-minded and mutually accepting manner and that the reciprocity of finding understanding is an adventure well worth embarking on. It is often an adventure that pays great dividends when getting to know an other we never knew before and had never troubled ourselves to truly find out about and understand.

The book's structure

And so, though each of the therapists writing the following chapters will come to their task in a different manner, they will, as you will see, do so with this same phenomenological stance and this same existential project. They all agree that existential relationship therapy is an important form of therapy, since relationships are elemental and we can never be fully separate from others, in the same way in which we can never live without a physical world to dwell in. We are always embedded in a context, in a situation, and in a world we share with others. Even when we are on our own our thoughts and feelings are marked by their relationship to others. It makes sense, then, to have a form of therapy that enables us to be better at being in relationship.

Most of us are acutely aware of our fundamental interdependence with others, and know that we cannot survive without getting on with those around us. We can never live completely according to our own lights, but have to take others into account. Each person's life is fundamentally embedded in a social and cultural sphere that both makes demands of us and offers sustenance, comfort and support. Growing up in a family or within another group of reference, we learn to belong with others and to seek out other human beings who are akin to us and who want to belong with us. Together we create new relationships, outside of the family of origin and we hope to be able to thrive and feel safe in this new intimacy. We seek out others to establish a 'home', a place where we feel comfort and ease, a place where we feel we can be ourselves and at peace. When this 'home' becomes a place of strife, where miscommunication, misunderstanding and betrayal invade the sanctuary of our relationship, we may be overwhelmed with feelings of grief, hurt and anger. At this point we may seek out a relationship therapist to help us make sense of it all.

As you will discover by reading this book, relationship work is a fundamentally existential activity and working with couples elucidates other forms of existential therapy as well. In Part I, the chapters focus on the core aspects of existence and their impact on relationships and on the issues couples bring to therapy, with a focus on how awareness of existential theories and concepts can enrich the practice of relationship therapy. Part II addresses the skills, knowledge and methods that therapists need if they are to work existentially with relationships where there are particular presenting issues (such as violence or grief) or where clients are experiencing certain scenarios (including living in blended families or with a partner with Asperger Syndrome). In both parts of the book the chapters are based around case studies and the practical application of existential relationship therapy. For those interested in particular issues, individual chapters can be read on a stand-alone basis; however, as with most books that seek to establish the foundation stones of a body of knowledge, the whole is greater than the sum of the parts and the greatest benefit comes from reading it in its entirety. We hope that you are inspired by what you find.

References

Buber, M. (1970) *I Thou*, trans. W. Kaufmann, New York: Charles Scribner's Sons.

Chaine, C. (1978) 'A conversation about sex and women with Jean-Paul Sartre', *Playboy*, January, 116.

de Beauvoir, S. (2011) *The Second Sex*, New York: Vintage.

Deurzen, E. van (1997) *Everyday Mysteries: Existential Dimensions of Psychotherapy*, London: Routledge.

Deurzen, E. van (2010) *Everyday Mysteries*, 2nd edn, London: Routledge.

Deurzen, E. van and Hanaway, M. (eds) (2012) *Existential Perspectives on Coaching*, London: Palgrave Macmillan.

Heidegger, M. (1962 [1927]) *Being and Time*, trans. J. Macquarrie and E. S. Robinson, London: Harper and Row.

Husserl, E. (1967) *Cartesian Meditations*, trans. D. Cairns, The Hague: Nijhoff.

Husserl, E. (2012) *Ideas: General Introduction to Pure Phenomenology*, London: Routledge.

Jaspers, K. (1941) *On my Philosophy*, in W. Kaufman (ed.), *Existentialism from Dostoyevsky to Sartre*, New York: Meridian.

Kierkegaard, S. (1998) *Works of Love*, in H. V. Hong and E. H. Hong (eds), *Kierkegaard's Writings*, Vol. 16, Princeton, NJ: Princeton University Press.

Levinas, E. (1999a) *Totality and Infinity*, trans. A. Lingis, Pittsburgh, PA: Duquesne University Press.

Levinas, E. (1999b) *Otherwise than Being or Beyond Essence*, Pittsburgh, PA: Duquesne University Press.

Moran, D. (2005) *Edmund Husserl: Founder of Phenomenology (Key Contemporary Thinkers)*, London: Polity Press.

Nietzsche, F. (1973) *The Will to Power in Science, Nature, Society and Art*, New York: Random House.

Nietzsche, F. (1985) *The Nietzsche-Wagner Correspondence*, New York: Liveright.

Orange, D. M. (2009) *Thinking for Clinicians: Philosophical Resources for Contemporary Psychoanalysis and the Humanistic Psychotherapies,* London: Routledge.

Sartre, J.-P. (1949) *No Exit and Three Other Plays*, London and New York: Vintage Books.

Tantam, D. and Deurzen, E. van (2005) 'Relationships', in E. van Deurzen and C. Arnold-Baker (eds), *Existential Perspectives on Human Issues*, Basingstoke: Palgrave Macmillan.

PART I

ADDRESSING THE CHALLENGES
OF RELATEDNESS IN EXISTENTIAL
RELATIONSHIP THERAPY

CHAPTER 1

The Challenge of Human Relations and Relationship Therapy: To Live and to Love

EMMY VAN DEURZEN

Introduction

Existential relationship therapy is based in dialogue. Partners are invited to explore what it means to them to live with another person in a loving way. They are encouraged to face their conflicts, doubts, fears and sense of failure. Relationships get better to the extent that we learn to calmly and confidently consider the contradictions, dilemmas and difficulties that inevitably arise in loving another person. While sharing some core assumptions about what it means to exist in the world and to be in relationship, each existential therapist tends to shape and fine-tune her own unique way of working with clients.

In this chapter I will describe my personal way of working with couples, which has evolved over four decades of reflective practice. Invariably, my objective is to help each person to get better at being close to the other by learning to respect, understand, value and love both self and other in a new way. In this process all aspects of life come into focus as partners become increasingly able to find their way across the divide, exploring the paradox of distance and intimacy, getting to know themselves and speaking about what matters to them most deeply.

What is love?

The crux of the matter is always the idea we have of love and the way this clashes with our actual experience of it. People come together because they love each other or believe they can learn to love each other. Their troubles begin when they realize that there are many different ways of loving and many layers of love in the world. When people find that to fall in love is one thing but to build a loving relationship quite another, they often give up or fall out of love. Lowering the expectations we have of each other and starting from scratch in discovering what is possible in living with an other are a good start to any existential relationship therapy. Partners need to accept that loving and living together is inevitably shot through with disappointments and problems. Though at the outset of the work they may feel that they are not loved enough, they may come to realize that they have also not been very expert at doing the loving. Many existential authors have written about intimate relationships and love. The classic existential texts on the subject are still invaluable (see, for instance, Fromm, 1995; May, 1969; Solomon and Higgins, 1991; Deurzen, 1998).

As human beings get better at understanding and formulating their experience of loving and being loved new ideas are being added and new insights are gained. Each of us sooner or later discovers the limits of love, even as we hope for a love that is deep and strong. To love another person is to be dedicated to knowing and valuing the other for what they are and can be, allowing them to live as fully and freely as possible, keeping their welfare at heart, as our own, in a full, attentive and uncompromising way. But this does not mean we can forget to look after our own well-being, for we cannot love unless we love ourselves first. Nor should we become complacent about the risks inherent in taking advantage of the other's good will and availability, or indeed the risk we take when we allow ourselves to be taken advantage of. Love is the movement towards the other in the spirit of care, affection, commitment, generosity, kindness, intimacy, tenderness and attachment. But it is not blind. When love is blind, it is not love but craving for something that might save us from ourselves. Such craving may lead to love but it is not love in and of itself. Love is hard earned and continuously tested and tried through the challenges of life. It needs to be learnt and requires active engagement.

The paradox is that in order to truly love someone, you first have to learn to love yourself and that if you want to find real closeness with another you have to be able to affirm your freedom. If you want to live in peace with another, you have to be willing to face up to the conflicts between you. If you want to learn to communicate you have to learn to be in silence together and listen. If you want love to flourish you must recognize that love is a way of being as well as a feeling and that the feeling is fleeting and will wax and wane, whereas the attitude and active process of being loving is something that requires consistency, continuity and dedication. For it to thrive it also requires reciprocity.

What is existential relationship therapy?

Existential relationship therapists demonstrate a loving way of being through their attentive, fair and frank attitude towards both partners. They show the importance of matching a loving way of being with a wise, considered and considerate way of being. But they do not avoid confrontation, and they model the courage to be truthful and challenging in a respectful manner. They also show an optimistic view of human relationships by expecting (and sometimes predicting) difficulties whilst always stimulating and valuing the partners' ability to deal with them creatively.

The start of every piece of relationship work is that of establishing where each of the partners in that relationship has come from, where they currently find themselves and where they see themselves going. We listen to the story each partner tells us and explore it from a number of different perspectives. By constantly checking each narrative from different angles, a natural process of verification is set into motion and new facets of the old stories are shown up, engaging partners afresh with each other. Partners will soon get the hang of this and start being far more open to different possible interpretations of reality, no longer feeling marred or hampered by their difference or by the old chestnuts that previously frustrated or bored them. They become encouraged to look at each other with curiosity and may even have a sense of exhilaration at the possibilities this opens up. This is one fantastic advantage of the phenomenological way of working: each aspect of what is under consideration has multiple angles and many doors through which to enter into new knowledge and new understanding.

Existential therapy uncovers the life expectations and values that each partner entered the relationship with and establishes how each had hoped that the other might help them to achieve these objectives and projects and where they feel this is failing. What this means in raw terms is that the therapist listens out for where the pain is, tracing how each partner feels hurt and identifying where their secret longing is. It is important to make each partner feel safe enough to speak from the heart, without attacking or reproaching but without holding back for fear of retaliation. We help them to bring their hopes and longings out of their darkness and into the light. What is it that makes them feel overlooked, or offended or upset or taken for granted or exploited? If you can hear what the partner cannot yet hear and bring it out into the open and if you can translate and give voice to what has been left unsaid, something entirely new will come into the room and the relationship that was shut tight, will slowly start to open.

Quite often the therapy is purely about helping people to find the concepts and the words to communicate their experience, helping them to stop fighting and start describing their sorrow and fear and begin to search for common ground. In this process it is important to pay attention to the way in which partners tend to place responsibility for disappointments in the other. As in individual therapy, each partner needs encouragement to find the strength to start seeing their own role in creating the misunderstandings and disenchantments. This is never about accusations of pathology or pointing of fingers, but always about helping partners to bridge their lack of insight or understanding about both self and other. As soon as a person feels enabled to take responsibility for what is going wrong, they can also take charge of what can be put right.

My starting point with relationship work

I began working with couples in the early seventies, when my ex-husband Jean Pierre Fabre (a psychiatrist, who was to become a psychoanalyst) and myself worked together in the Psychotherapeutic Centre, la Candelie, in Agen, in the

South West of France. We worked together, with couples that were deeply troubled and confused in relation to the attempted suicide of the wife. Marriage in France in the early seventies was a very patriarchal institution in which men were dominant. Both partners in the twelve couples we worked with at that time, without exception, viewed the wife's suicide attempt as a failure on her part. The husbands (several of them agricultural workers) typically considered their wife to be a domestic animal they had acquired and found to be defective. The husbands often dealt with their own despair over having failed to find the right woman to support their hard work on the land by acting aggressively to try to punish their wife or by abandoning her and taking on a lover, or drinking with their friends or otherwise withdrawing from the relationship and getting on with some hobby or task. They frequently felt deep shame at their wive's suicide attempts. The women behaved in a broadly submissive manner, many of them feeling incompetent and incapable, using terms like 'I am soiled goods' or 'I am no good' or 'I am nothing but a disappointment to my husband'. But the despair in both partners was normally dismissed by the psychiatric system as secondary to the 'attention seeking behaviour' of the wife. My direct contact with these women showed me that they were indeed seeking urgent attention and were desperate to find someone who would listen to their story and understand their plight and who could help them find some self-esteem, some hope and a reason to live in their own right. When I began to listen to the men, separately at first, I heard equally great despair in them. Though they were generally more strong-minded and angry rather than just desperate, several of them came to the edge of sanity and suicide themselves. I was shocked by the massive amount of misunderstanding and despondency about relationships that seemed to abound in both the men and the women and was determined to learn from it and tackle it in a philosophical rather than a medical manner.

Work with the husbands involved listening questioningly to their sense of failure, showing them they could release themselves from their suffering by giving up a worldview that forced them to see their wives as dysfunctional live-stock or badly made vehicles. It involved helping them appreciate their wife's sensitivity, her capacity for other things than keeping the house or minding the kids, the geese or the cows. With the women it often involved releasing them from a bitter sense of their malfunction: this could often be achieved by inviting them to think about themselves and their talents and abilities anew. Sexuality and religion invariably played an important role in these discussions. The women were frequently bound by catholic ideas about not being allowed to use birth control. The men were often hugely sexually frustrated and angry about having no sex at home and then being reproached for seeking it elsewhere. Some of the women had just given in to their husbands' sexual demands, without any enjoyment and then had secret abortions, which they would feel terrifically guilty about. Many of the women bought into the assumption that they should be a good wife, mother and partner in the household (which often meant playing a secondary, supporting role on the farm or in the husband's business) and satisfy the husband's sexual needs as well.

Whenever they defaulted on any of these perceived duties, they began to feel incompetent and second rate. The women who had attempted suicide, without exception, felt deficient and condemned by their husbands for not being able to cope with all these demands. They felt impotent and bad for not being able to cope with absences, infidelities and unwanted sexual practices that damaged them whilst also struggling to raise their children almost single-handedly as their husbands dealt with farming issues or with other demanding jobs such as that of travelling salesman. Having been caught in a vicious circle of negative feedback and self-reproach they became embittered and gave up on life. They felt flawed and defective. And so too did their husbands, for having chosen the wrong wife, or for being unable to push their woman a bit harder or cajole her into obedience.

The first thing I learnt from working in this context was that interpreting other people's difficulties through a theoretical model was not a very useful method for progressing. Applying psychoanalytic concepts would alienate these people and make them feel even worse about themselves. They felt offended and incapacitated by any suggestion that they were unable to cope and generally did not really want to be hospitalized or medicated. They just wanted to find a better way forward. They did not want expensive divorces. They did not want to lose their children or be the outcast in their community for having been in the psychiatric hospital.

The second thing I learnt was that each partner needed to feel equally important and fairly heard. Both partners had suffered greatly by the time they came to talk about their relationship to a psychologist and they often felt great shame at their failure to manage their family life. I began to see that assuring them of their ability to make sense of what had gone wrong was most important. In existential terms they needed someone to put things into perspective and to enable them to feel they were both in the right and that it did not have to be a fight to the death between them. They could both come out with their heads held high, if they could only just agree that it was life that was difficult and wrong and that they needed each other to make it all work out.

The third thing I learnt was that conflict was an inevitable part of relationships and an aspect of human relations that people are afraid of and try to avoid. My own tendency was, and is, towards peace making, even if it means fitting in and swallowing your pride. I learnt that this is not good enough and that people can and should demand more than that from life. We need to learn to stand up for ourselves and have our voice heard before we accommodate to the other voice. I realized that partners got much stronger as soon as they allowed each other to have and express different views without blaming each other for these different departure points.

And finally, the fourth thing I learnt was that couples were rarely aware of their own worldviews and way of being. Many people find it very difficult to begin to formulate or even imagine why they feel the way they do. Some do not even want to name their feelings, as they think of these as a nuisance. Even when they do speak about their situation they often have little real grasp of what they believe and value and what they assume as given or take for granted. I realized how important it was to show each partner what the other partner felt and dreaded and hoped for in private, creating a space where they were able to speak freely and with confidence of being understood.

My way of practising existential relationship therapy

Based on these insights, I developed an existential method of working with couples in crisis and I have taught this to most of my supervisees and students over the years.

This method consists of making couple therapy into a form of individual therapy, where, rather than making the couple the issue or allowing the dispute to take over the therapeutic space, each partner is addressed as a separate individual who is entitled to some understanding and support. It is all about people taking responsibility for what they contribute to the situation they are in, both in negative and in positive terms. First, I see partners separately for at least two one-hour sessions each before attempting any joint work. I then continue this personal therapy with each of the partners in front of the other partner, with a focus on the failing relationship. This means that I see couples in double sessions, where I work with each of the partners as if they were still on their own with me, asking the other partner to sit through this session quietly with no response being made at all until the end. Of course it is very important to stop any aggression or accusations and to bring the therapy firmly back to a personal focus so that the listening partner can have trust in the fact that the therapist is not siding against them.

There is a space for feedback at the end of each twenty minutes of private work and this gradually lengthens, so that both partners learn slowly to hear each other out instead of arguing and disputing each other's perspectives. They learn to hear each other and value being heard, rather than jumping in and becoming worried they will not be understood. I treat the couple therapy rather like a counselling training session, teaching each partner listening and observing skills before they start making interventions with each other. Of course this means that I impose a discipline to which we stick until the partners are ready to take over. I assume that my authority as arbiter and facilitator will be respected. If it is not, I cannot work with the couple, but this has never been a problem as couples are desperate for a safe framework in which to start over. In the first few weeks I ask each of the partners only two things after they have listened to their partner in silence: 'what was it like to listen to your partner's story and to allow yourself to feel what they feel?' and 'what have you learnt about each other today and how might you take this forward?' Sometimes as I ask these questions I summarize what I have heard in a simpler, more dramatic and pithy way, emphasizing the suffering or the conflict. More often than not people rise to their partner's genuine upset and sadness and they find it helps them to get a grip on what is really going on. If people respond with accusations or aggression, I teach them communication and argumentation skills and encourage them to read some basic books on communication, such as Sven Wahlroos' (1995) book, *Family Communication*, or Quilliam's book, *Stop Arguing and Start Talking* (1998).

Of course a picture of the life and worldview of each partner soon begins to emerge. I use the mental map arrived at by a quick structural existential analysis of the stories they tell, to orientate myself in their worlds. I listen carefully to what they are preoccupied with and how they experience themselves. My responses to their narrative are initially facilitative, and I use Socratic dialogue to gently challenge and unravel each partner's assumptions and help them figure out how they configure their lives and perceive their own reality. I take Socratic dialogue to be about an untangling of meanings and challenging of contradictions, rather than as an attribution of meaning and a prescription of thinking as it so often wrongly defined. I leave partners the initiative to choose how they present themselves to me and aim for an even and balanced attention to all aspects they bring to the fore, but if one area of their experience is being left out completely I may enquire into this missing part of their narrative towards the end of the session, pointing out that they have not covered it at all.

The structural existential analysis I conduct is based loosely upon the framework of four worlds, with its physical, social, personal and spiritual dimensions and its virtues and evils at each level (Deurzen, 2010, 2012). There are always lots of heuristic questions in my mind:

1. *Physical dimension.* Where is the person in terms of their physical survival? How do they survive, in an environment that is not always conducive to providing the necessary safety or security? How do they take charge of the life they have and the illness, weakness or ageing process they are aware is taking them slowly towards death? How do they earn a living and what is their attitude towards working and earning their keep in the world? How do they deal with physical pain or suffering? How do they relate to nature, to their own body, to other people's bodies and to the wider reality of the earth and the cosmos? What kind of hobbies or sports do they practise? How healthily do they take care of their own body, house, belongings?
2. *Social dimension.* Where is the person in terms of the social world? Do they feel at the mercy of other people's judgements? Do they fight and compete to maintain themselves, or to win over others and dominate them? Do they crave acceptance? How does the person maintain herself amongst friends and colleagues? Where do they place themselves in the public sphere? How do they relate to the people around them? Do they have a healthy ego and sense of their own importance and right to be heard, or do they cringe and shrink from imposing themselves? Are they considerate of other people's needs? What do they contribute? What role do they play in society and what, in turn, do they expect of others?
3. *Personal dimension.* What is the person's struggle to create an inner world? How at ease are they with themselves? Do they have a strong sense of identity? Do they know themselves rather well, warts and all, both positives and negatives, or are they rather better at deceiving themselves? How

much self-knowledge is apparent? How clear and realistic are their memories? How sensitive are they and how creative and flexible in relation to
challenges that present themselves? How active is this person in becoming
more aware as time goes by?

4. *Spiritual dimension.* Where does this person place their sense of meaning?
   What are their values, their assumptions, their ideals, their beliefs, their
   hopes, their trust in the world? How do they position themselves in relation
   to eternity and infinity? Do they have a religion? Do they have a social
   conscience? Do they have a commitment to a spiritual practice of any kind?
   Are they good at telling right from wrong? Do they have a philosophical
   sense of humour? Do they have strong motivations and a clear sense of
   purpose about how they want to put their life to use? How do they decide
   what is significant or unimportant in their life? What do they think it is
   all for?

I observe how each partner deals with each of these levels of human existence
and how they confront the inevitable tensions, dilemmas and conflicts on each
dimension on their own and with each other.

Partners will often experience each of these challenges in a very different way, sometimes even seeing the same thing variously as an obstacle or
an opportunity, depending on their previous experience, their current outlook and bias, and their aspirations (which will inevitably clash sometimes).
There is a continuous onus on each member of a partnership to keep paying
attention to the difference between them, listening to the other's concerns
and expressing their own concerns in such a way that they can be heard and
understood.

Table 1.1 gives an overview of sixteen areas of human existence that we all
have to deal with, though we may not be aware of each of these all the time.

Such a framework helps me to keep a clear head and an overview of what
each partner's main concerns are. They will tend to get caught up in some of
these tasks and challenges and forget about others. For instance, some people
encounter the world from a strong sense of embodiment, others are better at
being in role and encountering others with a strong ego, whereas some may

Table 1.1 Four worlds model

	Umwelt Around world	Mitwelt With world	Eigenwelt Own world	Uberwelt Over world
Physical survival	Natural world Materiality	Things	Body	Cosmos
Social affiliation	Public world Spatiality	Others	Ego	Culture
Personal identity	Private world Temporality	Me	Self	Consciousness
Spiritual meaning	Ideal world Connectivity	Ideas	Spirit	Conscience

find it hard to be in the world at all and turn towards a secret and hidden self or towards an idealized God instead. In relationships there may be many tensions about each of these modes of being and tasks of life. As a relationship involves sharing physical, social, emotional and ideological territory, it is important for partners to become aware of how each of them is doing on each score. Of course it can be an advantage as well as a disadvantage to share your life with someone who brings different abilities and interests to the table. If you are very at ease in the natural world and your partner is more at ease in the public world, this may become a cause for disagreement and conflict or it may become an asset as you support each other in the area that is harder for you. If you have a strong sense of ego and your partner has a strong sense of self, this may be controversial, but it may work fine if you both are committed to developing the body, or you are both deeply immersed in the life of the spirit as well. On the whole there has to be a recognition of differences as well as of commonalities if a relationship is going to thrive. Much of this is often ignored or denied.

It is frequently the specific issues of sharing space and time that initially generate conflicts, though feelings and values also have a way of causing disagreement and discord. If such differences are not accommodated in some constructive way, they may create a long-term rift with a fault line that is just waiting to break the partnership apart as soon as pressure is applied by circumstances or by fate. It is vital to find areas where partners completely see eye to eye and to find a joint project before negotiations over time and space and use of shared resources, such as possessions or money, are even entered into and resolved.

Initially I just listen to each partner and work out what each of them values, feels sure about and unsure about and how the tension lines lie. In dialogue we work out whether my observations are correct or not and so each partner comes to formulate their worldview while the other listens attentively. So my structural analysis of the partners' issues with each other might include working out the following:

- *Physical*: How do the partners divide the resources available to them? How do they situate themselves in the world of their home and how do they manage practical life together? What are their own physical needs, likes and dislikes and what are their partner's? What is the response of their partner to their quirks and what is their own response to their partner's idiosyncrasies? What makes them feel most safe? What makes them feel insecure? How do they feel about their own body? How about their partner's body? Do they feel attraction, revulsion or neutrality? How do they physically relate to each other, in terms of tenderness, physical safety, joint activities, acquisition of new skills, sex, cuddles, sport, sleep, food, hobbies, household activities pro-creation?
- *Social*: How do these people engage with each other over shared public territory? How do they divide their social space between them? How do they relate to other people when they are alone and how does this change when

they are together? Do they have joint projects and do they cooperate or do they live alongside each other, or worse do they undermine each other, competing for superiority in the outside world? How do they know to trust other people? When do they mistrust others? Are they trustworthy for their partner? Is their partner trustworthy? What are the major causes of conflict? Are these familiar or new? Have they committed to each other? Do they want to? Are they loyal? Are they faithful? What do all these concepts mean to them concretely, in practice? What causes the most conflict?

- *Personal*: How do they define themselves as individuals and how would they describe their own character? What is their own timeline and sense of progress in their lives? What issues from the past do they carry with them and can they share these with the other? How do they feel that being with each other has shaped and changed their personality and identity? How do they define and confine or expand each other's character? Do they feel the other is a valuable asset or a hindrance to them? In what ways is the partner's character beneficial to them and in what way is it damaging? Can they include their partner in their innermost sense of intimacy? Does the partner feel like kin or like an enemy? When?

- *Spiritual*: What are the values they adhere to as individuals: what is it that moves them and feels important to them? How have they modified their values, beliefs and principles in order to be part of this relationship? Is this something that stifles them and creates resentment or are they able to challenge and stimulate each other to move forwards? Do they share a dream and a project or did they in the past and has this been lost? Do their principles and assumptions about the world cohere or clash? What do they value about the other's views or their presence that adds depth and value to their life? Is getting on with each other and challenging each other an important part of their life's meaning? What is more important? What might they agree to make the purpose of their joint lives? What is their vision of life and death? Are they religious, spiritual or pragmatic? Do they respect each other's beliefs and are these up for discussion?

And when identifying how the partners in the relationship specifically attend to the issue of time, I might look for the following in sequence:

- *Past*: What is the story of the couple coming together and staying together as a unit? What are their most precious memories and their deepest regrets? What are the obstacles they have had to deal with and how do they remember the good times and the bad? Do they tell stories about their first encounter and about memorable moments? If so, are these positive, negative or realistic stories? What burdens do they carry from the past? With burdens they brought into the relationship, has the partner been helpful in resolving such issues? Could they be? In terms of burdens created by the relationship, how do they tackle the past history to turn it around or build on it?

- *Present*: How are they currently experiencing their relationship in terms of the most poignant conflicts and dilemmas they are struggling with? What are the main challenges at the moment? Are these presented as stemming from the past or from current conflicts? Are these presented as insurmountable or solvable? What are the good things they have obtained over their history and can count on as joint assets? How are things now better than they were before? How are things worse now and how do they want to improve them? Do they want to work at this or are they already giving up on themselves and each other?

- *Future*: What does each of them want to achieve personally and with each other and how do they plan to reach these goals and live up to these intentions? Are their goals mainly their own, or have they been discussed, and are there shared dreams they want to realize together or help each other realize? Do they expect the relationship to be smooth in future or are they prepared to keep working at it? What are their personal plans, aspirations, expectations and hopes? Are these secret, shared or owned mainly by the other?

- *Eternity*: What, in the grand scheme of things does this relationship mean to them and how does it enable them or might it enable them to feel their life is worthwhile? How do they think of life and its purpose? What are the values they hold dear and what do they believe in? What about their ultimate values is most precious to them and feels as though it cannot be compromised? Are they able to discuss their inner deep sense of value and meaning or do they feel the other holds principles that may damage their own principles and values? Might their longings and yearnings be a threat to the other in some way? How might they find a way to bring their meanings more in harmony with each other so they can jointly benefit in the long run, passing something on to the world from the love between them?

This investigation is fairly relaxed and open ended and the different categories are usually not mentioned as a theme or a structure in the therapy. The therapist holds the framework in the back of her mind in order to feel on safe ground and to know where the exploration is going and has gone.

As sessions unfold and each partner discovers what they are really interested in and concerned about, differences and similarities slowly but surely emerge, but the therapist makes sure each partner has an opportunity to freely speak their mind and see to it that they have been heard. Of course this alone will often change the conflict as partners become aware that they misperceived the other person's experience of the situation. They also learn to know their own minds in safety. Out of this project of getting to know themselves and the other better, a process of working together gradually emerges. That project of living in a loving dialogue with trust and openness to self and other is never ending and has to be remembered and practised actively and attended to both inside and outside and after the therapy. Often relationship therapy is only the start of that process. When couples take charge of the process for themselves the therapy can end, even though the conflicts may not yet have been resolved.

Case illustration

Tom and Julie were in deep trouble. They had been together for fifteen years and had no children. They had lived alongside each other, almost as friends, each going their separate ways with work and leisure activities, but both greatly valuing the home, which they had bought and decorated together. They were not married, but had committed to their relationship and were well inserted into each other's families of origin. They were quite proud of their unusual and open arrangement and dismayed when it suddenly fell apart. They came for help after Tom had unwittingly impregnated a female friend of his, who he had occasional sex with, with Julie's knowledge and implicit permission. Julie said she had not minded the sex, because it meant that Tom didn't bother her for it. Sex was something she loathed and wanted nothing more to do with now that she was in her forties and had gone through an early menopause. Tom was also in his forties, but Tracy, the future mother of his baby, was in her mid thirties. Now that Tom was expecting a child with Tracy, Julie was suddenly extremely upset. Tom could not understand this and felt she was being quite unreasonable about a situation she had helped create. Tracy had also changed and had suddenly become very demanding of him and had asked him to come and live with her and the baby after the birth. Tom did not want this and he felt cheated by Tracy for breaking the rules of their 'no strings attached' sexual arrangement. He told Tracy that he loved Julie and wanted to stay with her, rather than moving in with Tracy and her baby. Julie did not believe him and suspected that he was fed up with her and rather fancied this new little family he had created for himself.

The therapy involved Tom and Julie exploring their different experiences of the situation, by talking about their individual views and lives and also reviewing the past, present and future of their relationship, whilst initially bracketing out the complexity of the presence of Tracy and the new baby in their lives. They worked well together as long as they talked about the past. They were kind and generous to each other and were able to listen and accept the other's preoccupations and worries with some generosity and quite a lot of understanding. They seemed to really respect each other and they agreed that they had initially had very similar ideas about how to live and had been able to create a joint life style that suited them both. They were extremely fond of each other and neither could imagine living without the other. They also agreed that their ideas about life had changed gradually as they got older and that this had happened without them realizing it. They had not really kept up with themselves and each other and were surprised to find that they had entered middle age without clear ideas of their changed expectations. Tom denied having deliberately gone along with Tracy in her becoming pregnant, but he admitted to desperately wanting to have the child, now that the situation had evolved in this way. Julie became very upset as soon as the baby was mentioned. She could hardly listen to Tom's eagerness to be involved with the baby, who was born within the second week of the start of the therapy. Julie was adamant that they had always agreed that children were trouble and she felt that Tom had lied to her about this, as he had always claimed he did not want any offspring. Tom from the outset of the therapy reported feeling beleaguered by the two women both claiming him. He did not know any longer who he was or what he really wanted or how he should act. He felt that if Julie could have allowed herself to want a child, she too would enjoy this new feeling. Julie exploded at this, reproaching him for never having brought this up while she was still fertile. Not only was it too late for her now, he was abandoning her just as they were getting to a middle age where children should no longer have been an issue. She felt betrayed by him and hated his hypocrisy in covering his tracks. She felt he had never understood her and that he had no idea about her reasons for hating sex and mistrusting children. Julie became very upset when I asked her to tell Tom about this now. Tom agreed that this was important and said that he had never dared ask her too much about it, since he knew enough to con-clude she would rather not go there. With some encouragement, Julie began to tell the story of her childhood. She had been placed in a children's home after social services took her from parents who neglected and abused both her and her siblings. She had eventually been placed in a foster home, without her siblings, but had been physically, emotionally and sexually abused by her foster father. She had willingly gone along with this as she felt she had to pay for the relative safety the foster family provided. But she had cut herself off from any feeling and she had closed her heart against men and sex and she had only been able to live with Tom because he had been such a gentleman and such a good friend and had never made many demands on her. It emerged that she and Tom had rarely had sex in fifteen years, as Tom realized she did not like it and did not want to trouble her. It became obvious that Tom's respect for her had stopped him asking too many questions and so she had never really told him about her past in the children's home and with the foster family, the regular rapes she had endured and the babies she feared. She had had several abortions by the time she was eighteen and had sworn never to allow another man inside any part of her body. She felt she had been overly generous with Tom when, in spite of her misgivings, she had allowed him to have sex with her a few times, when she was drunk. Julie's tearful story deeply moved Tom and he became very weepy in turn, as he spoke of his lack of confidence as a man and of the gratification he got from realizing he could look after Julie and make her feel safe with him. Tom had looked after his own sick mother for several years after his dad died when he was a teenager and he had felt like a lonely orphan when mum eventually died. Julie had been his best mate and he felt extremely relieved at feeling she needed him and wanted to belong with him. They had been, he said, and Julie nodded in agreement, like babes in the wood, clinging to each other. But now, said Tom, he wanted to look after the little baby that needed him. Julie said that perhaps the time had come for her to grow up too, but she wasn't convinced and felt she was being eclipsed by the baby.

It was only with some prompting that Tom started speaking of his frustra-tion in not being able to have a sexual relationship with the woman he loved. He always knew that 'Julie wasn't really up for it' and he considered that the times when she had given in to him were very special gifts. Even though Julie had tightly kept her secret fears to herself, Tom had known enough about her past not to want to hurt her. When I remarked that he had ended up hurting her all the worse for not having faced up to the issues earlier, he acknowledged this straight away, but said he had never meant to do so. His regret causing her pain and his genuine concern for her was tangible and moved Julie. She said she knew he did not want to harm her, nor leave her, but she also knew that he would not want to give up his newfound fatherhood. In fact she did not want to rob him of it and she thought he would make a terrific dad. But all of this was at the same time a terrible threat to her. She felt she had lost him. It reminded her of seeing her own parents in the street with a new baby some time after she had been placed with her foster family. She felt envy for the baby then as she did now for Tracy's baby. She was afraid of losing Tom altogether. She was also afraid of hating the baby. Tom felt dreadfully torn about what he should do. He felt great loyalty to Julie but he also felt a strong urge to claim his fatherhood, and talked about what it meant to him in great detail, making clear just how badly he wanted to care for a child, as he had done for Julie. Finally, he no longer felt as if he was just a lost orphan. He felt he was finally becoming the man he never thought he could be. Julie bitterly agreed with this and concluded that her envy of the baby was thus very logical and right. By this time baby Kim had become a real presence in their lives and Tom had already been to see her twice. Julie was certain that she did not want Tom to cut himself off from Kim, who she in some ways terribly identified with and felt much more protective than hateful towards. She was greatly relieved when I reminded her of her own response, which was the opposite of what she had feared she would feel. She felt very supported by this intervention. What had driven her to distraction was the idea that she was becoming a mean-minded person instead of the kind person she always had been. She was afraid of being like her own parents. Tom could really understand that. He also understood, after I explained to him that it seemed to me that Julie felt she had been placed in an impossible position, that Julie felt trapped. As soon as they began to allow for the other's fears and worries they became much more able to loosen their feelings and express them more clearly. Julie now started to talk about her fear that baby Kim would be mistreated by Tracy, her mom, who had many boyfriends and went out a lot. She was even able to mention her fear that her own controlling behaviour with Tom would deprive baby Kim of her much-needed father. Tom had indeed begun to act as if he was going to visit Tracy and Kim only occasionally. It now became clear this was not what Julie wanted at all. Saved from their own catastrophic expectations and fear of rejection they began to find a way to discuss the situation that did not lead to reproach, frustration and terror of abandonment all around.

   All these changes took many assiduous sessions of joint therapy, where each partner could explore their own experience freely with the other listening in and only commenting at the end. After nearly a year of hard work, the situation had changed considerably. Julie was now assured that Tom had not left her. It had become obvious that Tracy did not mean to raise her child single-handedly and that she wanted Tom to be involved. Tom was beginning to realize that he did not want to be stuck holding baby Kim all on his own, while Tracy went out twice a week, painting the town red. There were quite a few hitches and frustrations before the partners could agree that Julie, who by now was impatiently waiting for Tom each time he babysat Kim, should be allowed to be part of this complex extended family. Julie was ready to be a step-mom to baby Kim, she thought and Tom was ready to bring Kim home with him, rather than babysitting at Tracy's house. Tracy did not like the idea at first but Tom became more definite and confident as he remembered that he had never promised Tracy to be a father or a partner and that she could not really expect him to leave Julie if he did not want to do so. Tom was worried that Tracy would punish him and cut him out of Kim's life. He had no legal rights at all as Tracy had not put his name on the birth certificate. There was a time of terrible tension during which all three partners became upset and Tom stopped visiting for a couple of weeks, becoming deeply depressed at the thought he would never see his baby again. But then Tracy got in touch, wildly accusing, but also admitting that she was not coping. Tom had been generous in financially supporting her, something he and Julie had slowly negotiated and agreed together during therapy. Now he had said to Tracy that if he was going to carry on financing and looking after Kim, he wanted some recognition that he was the father.

Julie had mixed feelings about it and plunged back into despair, as Tracy tried to seduce Tom into marrying her, but eventually she accepted that Tom did not want this. They all agreed that a better solution should be found. The next phase started when Tom and Julie came in one day with a sudden new excitement between them. Julie had found out through mutual friends that Tracy was going out almost every evening, leaving Kim at home, or taking her to the pub with her, and leaving her in a buggy outside in the street, unattended. This resonated very strongly with her as she had herself been taken into care at the age of four after she had been found scavenging for food on the streets when her parents had left her home alone for several days as they were out boozing. Julie was excited to find that she cared so much for Kim, even though she had never yet met her. She gained a new inner confidence because she knew she was not going to let Tom's baby be mistreated. Tom was delighted, because he realized they were both suddenly on the same side again.

Now the important thing became to treat Tracy as best as they could. They decided to invite Tracy to come to the next session of therapy to discuss the relationships between the four of them. Tracy, who had felt very alone with her new baby, accepted gladly and stated very clearly that she wanted Tom to take his responsibilities seriously. It was a complicated emotional situation, as Tom boldly stated that he did want to take his responsibility seriously and would do so, with his wife, Julie, who was willing to acknowledge Kim as her stepchild. Tracy took much time to talk about her wanting to keep her daughter to herself and not share her with another woman. She also expressed envy at the way in which Tom acted in a loving way towards Julie. Julie's attitude changed very much in this process and she told Tracy she did not want to steal her baby away from her, just help Tom and Tracy to raise it. This led to a new situation where baby Kim started coming over to Tom and Julie's for the odd evening when Tracy wanted to go out. This soon turned into a situation where Kim was not only coming over for several evenings a week, but also for the odd weekend when Tracy wanted to go away with her new boyfriend. It ended, less than a year later, with Tom and Julie taking over the lion's share of raising Kim, as Tracy married her boyfriend and had another child with him. Now it was Tracy who acted as the occasional parent to Kim while Julie and Tom took over the legal parental responsibility.

Throughout this time the three of them used therapy sessions to find a balance in the way they dealt with these transformations. Julie and Tom continued in therapy together for a bit longer after they completely took over the care of Kim, and stopped when they realized that they had found a new way of life that suited them both and that helped them to develop and evolve whilst making sure Kim got a good start in life as well. The only big problem that remained was that their sexual relationship was still non-existent, but this was something they did not want to tackle.

Conclusion

Relationship therapy with an existential emphasis, allows partners to explore how they want to live, what they believe in and what creative changes might be possible. It enables them to find a safe place to explore the way in which they are together and for learning to become more loving towards themselves and each other. This will often extend to them becoming clearer in their relationships to others outside of their dyad as well. The work consists of inviting each partner to explore, quite intimately and safely, in front of the other, what it is that they want from and understand about life. This always involves exploring tensions, misunderstandings, dilemmas, conflicts, contradictions and resentments. The process is one of expressing, recognizing and then challenging old assumptions and prejudices and thinking through the consequences of different possible ways to act. Ultimately it is always about finding a new and creative way forward that provides dignity, meaning, purpose and maximum satisfaction to all involved. It is also about partners becoming more able to tune into themselves and learn to express who they are for the other and with the other so that they can feel free enough to be true partners to each other. Out of this comes a new way of relating and loving. It is this capacity for living together in a loving manner that is always the goal. To achieve it one is often required to explore many different paths, but the journey always involves mutual respect, reciprocity, mutuality and a fierce commitment to the other's as well as to one's personal well-being.

References

Deurzen, E. van (1998) *Paradox and Passion in Psychotherapy*, Chichester: Wiley.
Deurzen, E. van (2010) *Everyday Mysteries: Handbook of Existential Therapy*, 2nd edn, London: Routledge.

Deurzen, E. van (2012) *Existential Counselling and Psychotherapy in Practice*, revised 3rd edn, London: Sage.

Fromm, E. (1995) *The Art of Loving*, London: HarperCollins.

May, R. (1969) *Love and Will*, New York: Norton.

Quilliam, S. (1998) *Stop Arguing, Start Talking*, London: Vermilion.

Solomon, R and Higgins, K. M. (1991) *The Philosophy of (Erotic) Love*, Lawrence, KS: University Press of Kansas.

Wahlroos, S. (1995) *Family Communication: The Essential Rules for Improving Communication and Making your Relationships More Loving, Supportive and Enriching*, Chicago, IL: Contemporary Books.

CHAPTER 2

The Challenge of Otherness: Relationships, Meaning and Dialogue

DMITRY LEONTIEV

In a recent study of the long-term dynamics of family life, researchers found an explanation as to why couples often get divorced after twenty or more years of living together. Their research showed that in the early stages of marriage young couples have to face multiple challenges in the world around them, struggle with those challenges and build their family life supporting each other. Many – though not all – couples overcome these ordeals. When it is all over, financial troubles are in the past, the house is furnished and clean and the children are on their way to maturity, the spouses can relax and focus on themselves — and often they discover a lack of mutual understanding and psychological support that was of secondary importance before. As the emphasis in their relationship changes, they are not always capable of being as successful in their journey into each other's inner world as they had been in their common journey against the trials and tribulations of the world out there.

Human relationships have long been recognized as the core of what it means to be human. This chapter focuses on one aspect of them, the one that accounts for the special reality of dialogical space that emerges between two human beings. Ludwig Binswanger (1960 [1946]) described this communication space as *Mitwelt* (with-world, or social world), one of the three aspects of the *Lebenswelt* (Life-world). In this chapter I shall try to show how this space can be accessed and how it cannot.

We encounter other beings in the Mitwelt, and we do not know these beings. I am aware of myself, I have a conception of myself, and I constantly experience much that refers to myself. The Other is a mystery across the border from me. I can never obtain a visa to cross this border. I can build my view of the other person based on my perceptions of, and my inner responses to, this person, as well as on messages from this person and relevant information from other sources. Sometimes this generates a huge amount of information, and we believe that if we know so much about this person, we know the person. The challenge is whether I prefer to deceive myself and believe that I know my fellow traveller and how to treat him or her; or whether I humbly acknowledge the absolute nature of the border. In the latter case I face a second challenge: either to fall into depressive self-isolation and hopelessness or to take the risk of adopting an existential position and behaving 'sensibly', like George Bernard Shaw's tailor in this famous quote:

> ... he took my measure anew every time he saw me, whilst all the rest went on with their old measurements and expected them to fit me. (Shaw, 2008: 56)

It requires a special attitude and special efforts (results not guaranteed) to get to a space of dialogue where there is a chance to meet person to person.

Person to person: the uniqueness of human dialogue

The unique role of authentic person-to-person relationships in the human condition was clearly articulated in the 1920s by two prominent thinkers, German-Jewish philosopher and theologian Martin Buber and Russian philosopher and philologist Mikhail Bakhtin.

Buber stated in his works *The Knowledge of Man* (1998), *I and Thou* (1996), and *Dialogue* (see Buber, 2002: 1–45) that human essence can be found only in relating to another human being as Thou; that is, in a radically different way from the 'I-It' relations we have with all the other things in the world. Human being emerges from the 'I-Thou' relationship. Only in mutual relationships of this kind can I become myself. Being engaged in an 'I-Thou' relationship, I will not know anything special *about* Thou (this is possible only in 'I-It' relationships), but I will know Thou at large. Authentic life is encounter. Dialogue is the basic relationship that needs no words, no actual communication. The core of the dialogue is orientation toward each other and openness to the interaction (Buber 1996, 1998, 2002; Friedman, 1985).

Bakhtin stated that dialogical relationships are almost universal for all domains of human living. 'When dialogue ends, everything ends' (1984: 252). Personal being is always a co-being; a person cannot exist outside a strained encounter with another person. A person therefore cannot be investigated in an objectifying fashion, as a thing among other things, from the unbiased viewpoint of an impassionate observer equipped with research instruments.

> The genuine life of the personality is made available only through a dialogic penetration of that personality, during which it freely and reciprocally reveals itself. (Bakhtin, 1984: 59)

This kind of encounter does not come about automatically; it is a special challenge to reach this level of communication and not every adult will experience it. A characteristic of human dialogical relationships, unlike monological ones, is the assumed equality of both partners, mutual recognition of each other as sovereign self-sufficient selves, each possessing his/her own inner world, their own personal position in their co-being, equal claims for truth, and equal authorship rights for their actions. This mutual dialogical stance affirms the autonomy, inner freedom, incompleteness and indeterminacy of the communication partners. This is of course particularly relevant to two partners in a relationship and thus the foundation of existential relationship therapy.

Both Buber and Bakhtin, in very similar words, described dialogue as the supreme mode of human communication, as a kind of ideal relationship. Most of our actual communication with our fellow human beings (and quite often with the closest and most significant ones) proceeds in ways far removed from this. James F. T. Bugental, a prominent existential psychotherapist, proposed a sophisticated but very clear classification of levels of human communication by the depth of personal presence (Bugental, 1987: 27–48), distinguished by the intentions of the partners. The most superficial levels are the formal ones, the level of contact maintenance, and the level of standard conversation; then follow deeper levels involving critical occasions and intimacy where one cannot do without personal involvement, and then more obscure levels of personal and collective unconsciousness. Is the kind of relationship we call intimate truly intimate? Not always – it depends. Standard conversation, for instance, often occupies a huge place in the actual relationships of closely tied partners; their closeness is thus a potentiality that is not actualized automatically at every moment, it always requires some self-investment. At periods of discord partners often 'close the borders' and revert to formal levels. On the other hand, sometimes we feel ourselves diving deeper into the contact with a person we have just met, finding some profound commonality that unites us at a fundamental level.

Most of our everyday communication proceeds on the three surface levels, but this is not what the existential worldview considers to be a genuine life. Eastern tradition calls it *maya* – a dreamlike existence, in which the person is not consciously present in what he or she is doing; in the West it is labelled inauthentic, or alienated, existence, being 'on tape' to use Bugental's brilliant metaphor (Bugental, 1991: 3). Dialogue, by comparison, is an authentic, wakeful relationship, in which both partners are consciously present and personally involved.

Meaning in human dialogue

Are the attitudes of equality, mutual recognition and self-disclosure enough to bridge the gap of otherness? Maurice Friedman, Buber's adherent and the main promoter of his ideas in North America, once organized a public meeting at the University of Michigan between the two scholars whose names were most closely associated with the deepest understanding of interpersonal relationships – Martin Buber and Carl Rogers (whose ideas about person-centred counselling and psychotherapy created a revolution in this field). The dialogue between them, however, failed.

What happened? Rogers, who had described the optimal conditions for every helping relationship, including unconditional positive regard, presence, etc., was concerned with providing these conditions during the meeting, but Buber was not happy with it. He was trying to find the subject for the discussion, its meaning or topic, and felt uncomfortable in a comforting inter-personal climate that lacked an intentional object of dialogue. They failed to find a common meaning to communicate about (Anderson and Cissna, 1997). This situation (without specific reference to it) has been explored theoretically by Viktor Frankl in his paper *Critique of Pure Encounter*. He states that true encounter is always more than just interpersonal relationship; it necessarily transcends itself toward the logos, the common meaning. Communication without such logos, containing only mutual self-expression, is 'pseudo-encounter' (Frankl, 1978: 72). The logos is just what Buber desperately tried to find in his strange encounter with Rogers. It should be noted, however, that this common meaning that makes the object the intentional focus of the encounter, may coincide with one of the partners, as in the case of asymmetrical parent–child or therapist–client relationships, or even with both partners, as in profound intimate communication: the intimate partners are in an authentic, mutually open dialogue, and the meaning, the intentional focus or logos of this dialogue, is themselves in the context of their joint lives (Leontiev, 1992). They are at the same time the co-subjects and the meaningful focus of the encounter.

Meaning in psychology has always been an intriguing and at the same time a very fuzzy concept, having a Protean nature, turning to us with its different sides. First, in the English word *meaning,* two somewhat different things are melded: common cultural meaning (German *Bedeutung*), unambiguously decoded by those who share a cultural code (e.g. language meanings or traffic signs), and personal meaning (German *Sinn*), private and idiosyncratic, shared with no-one. Second, theories of personal meaning in psychology define it in quite different ways (see Leontiev, 1996). Meaning is conceived either as the integrating instance of personality (the Meaning), or as an element of the all-encompassing mechanism of activity regulation (meanings); either as something objectively existing out there in the world (cf. Umwelt), as something existing only in our mind (cf. Innenwelt), or as something emerging in the communication, in the conversational space between individuals (cf. Mitwelt).

The common denominator for all these conceptions of meaning seems to be the following: meaning is a link, a tie, a connection, a reference linking a person to something or someone beyond him/herself (Leontiev, 2006a, 2007). Cultural meanings make horizontal ties, the possibility of common languages that provide mutual understanding and coordination between fellow humans; personal meanings make vertical ties, linking the acting person to broader contexts. Meaningful action, a meaningful life, a meaningful person, unlike meaningless ones, are, first, internally coherent rather than fragmented (see Korotkov, 1998) and, second, are tied to superordinate contexts rather than being self-sufficient. Personal meaning is thus the answer to the question 'What for?'.

Relationships are based on both kinds of meanings. Cultural meanings account for the possibility of understanding each other. Nossrat Peseschkian, who emigrated from Iran to Germany in the 1950s to study at university, recalled that at the beginning of his professional career he worked as a family therapist, mostly with migrant families in which both spouses were often of different ethnic origins. There were many communication problems with such couples, because they understood many details of their joint living differently, in line with the cultural meanings learnt from their parents and their environment. What was self-evident for one, the other could not understand, and what was normal for the latter was absolutely inconceivable for the former. Peseschkian learned to turn these differences from points of mutual disagreement and irritation into points of mutual knowledge and curiosity, a resource for building a harmonious relationship. He named his approach Positive Family Therapy (Peseschkian, 1986). As his practice developed, he started working with mono-ethnic families, and was surprised to find the same problems there. Differences of cultural meanings were not due to ethnic background only; all kinds of differences in social class, religious traditions, family history, educational and professional background, regional specificity, etc., could account for variations in understanding the same obstacles and details of habitual living when two persons are trying to transform two different systems of habits into a single shared one. Cultural meanings are thus due to many overlapping cultural contexts, each of which is a source of special meanings and special instances of discordance that can be turned into positive resources for growing relationships.

In terms of Bugental's (1987) scheme, communication regulated only by cultural codes is represented by the three surface communication levels: the most surface levels are the formal level (saying what is appropriate in the given culture in the presence of another person), the level of contact maintenance (giving signals of continuing conversation), and the level of standard conversation (everyday talk when no one says anything unexpected). These levels can be expressed not only through words but also through bodily postures or movements, clothing styles, hairstyles, etc. And again, cultural and subcultural contexts define the meaning. Both partners may refer to traditions that they learnt from their parents and consider normal and natural and each may easily come to blame the other for a lack of sincerity, consideration and love.

When we move to the next levels of communication, critical occasions and intimacy, we enter the dialogue between personal meanings: events, words, actions and persons are not only impartially understood, but also experienced – they touch us, and sometimes make us change. They challenge not only our worldviews, the mental pictures we have of what the world (including the world of human relationships) looks like, but also our lively experienced feelings. This cannot be rationally justified; these personal meanings are rooted in individual history, individual goals and values and in the unique points in one's own life when one is finding oneself. The history of previous romantic relationships and early 'imprintings' may influence the attractiveness of one, rather than the other, partner and the reproduction of the same, sometimes countereffective, behavioural patterns. Becoming aware of these images, stereotypes and imprints through therapy is not in itself sufficient, but is a necessary step to becoming capable of making a truly personal choice.

When two human beings are facing each other with the intention of communicating at a deeper level than everyday talk or 'business only', be they a therapist and a client, two lovers, or whatever else, they are in a journey from the surface levels of communication toward the core essence of each other, their inner world. It cannot be cognized from outside unless individuals decide to disclose themselves in a dialogical encounter.

The dialogical encounter is a challenge because it requires that the person leave the comfortable cradle of their worldview and beliefs and step onto the path where these beliefs may be questioned or shattered.

Beyond oneself

Our being-in-the-world is always being-together-in-the-world. Every human being enters the world not as an individual, but as a non-autonomous part of a baby–mother unit, initially tied to the mother's organism by the umbilical cord. After the cord is cut, the baby is still tied to the mother by multiple psychological dependencies described by Erich Fromm (1941, 1956) in terms of psychological symbiosis. The whole of childhood and adolescence is the history of the person's progressive emancipation from these ties (Leontiev 2006b), 'continuing birth', as Fromm called it, adding that many are finally born only in their old age, while many more die before they are fully born. Becoming an autonomous individual, that is, being fully born, presumes establishing controllable borders between 'me' and 'not me' not only in space, but also in emotions, wishes, choices, worldviews and values. Before a person has grown into such an autonomous individual, he or she cannot relate to fellow human beings as to the Other Person, but rather treats them either as a part of an enlarged Me, or as part of the environment; the emotional ties may take the form of the strongest attachment, but never of genuine love, trust, care, etc. (Erikson, 1980).

When I encounter my fellow human being, I am already *a priori* tied to him/her by some objective ties rooted in our personal histories and in common contexts that unite us both, including the language of our communication, the unconscious motives, conscious goals and impersonal occasions that made us meet. But these ties are not yet relationships, they are just prerequisites for relationships. The same is true for transferential ties. The common cultural meaning, providing similar understanding of the situation, and the joint personal meaning as the object of the communication, also refer to these prerequisites.

This is true not only for communication with a stranger or a moderately known person. Even in our everyday encounters with those closest to us – a spouse, a child, a parent – we find ourselves anew each time in a situation in which relationships may happen or not happen. In the latter case the communication follows the stereotypes rooted in objective ties and recorded on 'tapes', and takes place at the surface levels of communication.

From the existential viewpoint, relationships start when the person acknowledges that in his/her encounter with the Other nothing can be guaranteed and little predicted, still less controlled. The Other is across the border of Me. I possess my inner world. I know everything about my inner world, and no one can know anything about it. I have some access to the surrounding world, I am more or less adjusted to it, I can predict it to some practically satisfactory degree. I can also have some idea of the Other as a part of the surrounding world. I can observe and interpret his/her outlook, movements and 'verbal behavior', can try to predict and control it (sometimes quite successfully) and, in my turn, respond to it. This is what usually happens on the surface levels of encounters. 'Surface' refers to the psychological gradations; full-range sexual contacts often also fall into this category, when the partner is treated as a stimulus to respond to and/or an object to control and use.

However, the Other also possesses an inner world of his/her own, the one to which we have no access. We may try to guess or interpret its content, but it is up to our imagination. There is no way to verify the guesses, except for one: by dialogue. Dialogue is an undetermined process of co-construction of common meaningful content, and the relationships focused on this content. It takes two to tango; neither of the partners can define the result of this interplay, and no pre-established factors rooted in the past can help, though they sometimes interfere. Dialogue always unfolds itself in the present; therapeutic relationships as examples of such a dialogue, cannot be reduced to transferential mechanisms without losing their essence (Maddi, 1987).

The challenge of disclosing oneself, rather than hiding behind conventional modes of behaviour, has been addressed a great deal in philosophy and psychology in the last century. The existential concept of ultimate openness to Being as a prerequisite of authentic being-in-the-world takes a central place in existential thought (e.g. Boss, 1979). Sidney Jourard, an existential psychotherapist in the USA, introduced the more specific concept of self-disclosure (Jourard, 1968, 1971) as the central one for understanding authentic human relationships: no intimate relationships can happen without such self-disclosure. Authentic behaviour based on self-disclosure engenders psychological health, and inauthentic behaviour engenders sickness. The central role of self-disclosure is especially important in psychotherapy where it is defined as an invitation to dialogue – provided that the therapist is ready to, and capable of, disclosing him or herself in the therapeutic encounter (Jourard, 1968: 52–69).

Escape from dialogue

To make the dialogue happen, both partners should be ready to disclose their inner world (though not necessarily all of it) and, most importantly, be ready to allow changes to it. In addition, two things need to be excluded: one should not attempt to predict their partner's responses and should not attempt to control them. If the partners are truly looking forward to what the Other will say or do, rather than trying to anticipate it, a new world is being created; each partner at every moment is responding to the Other and the Other is at the same moment responding to him/her, both 'taking each other's measurements'. A living tissue of pulsating relationships and common meaningful content arises from this openness to the unpredictability of the Other. There is always a substantial risk in disclosing oneself, because deliberately opening one's inner world in a dialogue can be dangerous and may be used against the self-disclosing person; this is why one more necessary prerequisite of a dialogue is mutual trust. Feelings of love bring about self-disclosure but can make a person vulnerable; lack of mutuality, pertaining to an I-It attitude and dominant motivation of self-affirmation and power, rather than of relatedness and love on the partner's side, may provoke him/her to abuse the vulnerability of a sincere lover by 'conquering', 'possessing', and 'managing' her/him. All of these behaviours are characteristic of the extrinsic success values of a self-alienated person (Fromm, 1947). This is shocking and suppresses further self-disclosure. That is why genuine dialogue is quite rare; many people prefer to exclude any risk and never disclose their inner world, even to themselves.

However, escaping from dialogue, we also prevent personality change, escape from ourselves, and lose sight of meaning and perspective. Without a dialogue there is no way to find the value base for one's orientation in the world. Postmodernism has destroyed all value hierarchies based on taken-for-granted, historical traditions because it proved that there are no objective justifications behind any of them, except for occasional historical obstacles. The strongest challenge arising from postmodernism is the lack of objective values to support our being-in-the-world, and at the same time the impossibility of living without them. An existential approach provides an answer: you are to construe and affirm your own, subjective values. But this is not enough, for this may lead to Nietzsche's ideal of 'superman', disregarding the others and affirming one's own values against those of others and at their expense. There is another bifurcation on this road: while construing and affirming values at your own risk, are you sure you are right; that is, your values are the truth, or not? If yes – you are Superman or Superwoman; you don't need other people and have no chance for an authentic dialogue. If no – you are capable of a dialogue in which your values are checked against those of other people. In this process you change in the direction that brings you closer to other people.

Entering a dialogue is risky, because there is no way to foresee what will happen in its course; that is why dialogue requires a special form of courage (see Jourard, 1971: 6–7) and trust; however, only in dialogue can one get feedback on what one truly is, become aware of the limitations and shortcomings of one's worldview and transcend the isolation of one's subjectivity, testing one's subjectivity against that of the partner and thus extending its limits. This is the way new meanings are found.

This seems to be the principal mechanism of the development of personality in its most profound and intricate aspects, and it can hardly be substituted with anything else. However, it is very often blocked by the lack of courage to disclose oneself and a lack of trust in oneself and in the Other, so that two embodied meanings are prevented from making vital contact. The point is that the dangers and risks of self-disclosure are rather evident, while the benefits are not easily visible for those who never before experienced them. Encouraging the person to gain these yet unknown benefits can be a relevant strategy for therapeutic work, as this case illustration demonstrates.

Case illustration

Tamara has been visiting me from time to time to consult on various issues in her life. On a few occasions she declared that she wanted to discuss her relationships with men, but other more urgent problems left no time for this. One day she decided to make this problem the focus of our meeting.

Divorced after her second marriage, good-looking, in her late thirties, she lived with an adolescent son and was engaged in studying psychology. During our meetings she was sensitive to what was going on and seemed to catch the emerging insights that could be a key to her problems somewhat too quickly – she seemed sometimes to be hurrying, but generally she was a 'good' client, having enough capacity for self-reflection and showing a readiness for change. I had the feeling that the rather simple interventions I proposed really did work.

That day she labelled her problem 'the fear of entering relationships'. Both her marriages (the second one was relatively long) started positively, but gradually lost their value and were no longer satisfying. Nevertheless, she had no prejudices against men or overtly traumatic experiences with them and was looking for new, satisfying relationships, though not too persistently. What she was complaining about was the recurrent pattern (twice in the last year) of her developing then ending close relationships with successful and interesting men she truly respected (and was attracted to) and who seemed truly involved with the relationship. She blamed only herself. When the relationships started, she felt very good, she 'was herself', self-confident, capable of arousing the man's feelings, matching him. But at some point she suddenly felt that she was not 'up to him', she did not deserve him – then her behaviour changed, and this change could be described in psychoanalytic terms as regression. She became more primitive, fussy, losing self-confidence and feeling herself not up to the level of her partner and not up to herself. After this she finished the relationships despite the value they maintained – she just felt she had no perspective on what was happening.

The first step of our work was making clear what essentially happened with her in these relationships. Using a form of 'Socratic dialogue' (Frankl, 1967), I helped her to become aware that she was making some choice of her own that could be different. Before this critical point in her relationships she behaved in one way and felt quite authentic; after this point she unconsciously 'decided' to be inauthentic in situations where authenticity was a supreme value.

It was not difficult to bring her to this awareness. The next stage was to understand the reason for such a choice.

I had the impression (and she readily acknowledged this) that she construed the situation in strictly dichotomous terms. Her sudden feeling of 'being not worthy of him' pointed at some 'mark' that she could either reach or miss. Win or lose, everything or nothing – there were no intermediate gradations. And, consequently, if she felt she was not likely to get 'everything', 'nothing' was the only alternative left. Her behaviour had reasons, from the viewpoint of this dichotomy.

This worldview, however, seemed to pervert the psychological nature of close relationships. As argued above, the value of relationships is not in their being a means to some goal, for instance to set up a family, to procreate or to get sexual satisfaction, though all these extrinsic goals certainly contribute to the overall motivation behind entering relationships, and to their appraisal. But the existential view suggests that close relationships, the intimate connectedness of two human beings, have great potential intrinsic value independent of any practical consequences the relationships may entail – orgasm, pastime, family life, children, etc. And if success in respect of all these intrinsic goals and consequences can be appraised dichotomously – either we had a good orgasm or not, either we have married and started living together or not – what we gain from genuine close relationships, inasmuch as we are authentic, disclosing ourselves to the *Mitwelt*, to the inter-subjective reality, refers to the process rather than to the outcomes. The true existential encounter might last a few hours, without sexual contact or practical outcomes, and still can change a person for the rest of her or his life. The paradox of otherness is, however, that the deeper the relationships are – the more intimate and authentic and hence the more satisfying – the less we can predict their further development. And, vice versa, if we try to reach maximum safety and guarantees in the relationship, we are likely to see a fall in their value.

Tamara seemed not to be aware of the mighty vital potential of authentic relationships, or at least she did not allow herself to be aware of it and was not ready to let the relationships develop on their own. My next task was helping her to let it be, to let herself not be perfect, and to give up striving for a goal. Soon she came to understand that her escaping the challenge was the result of her dichotomous construction of the nature of close relationships. She became aware of the self-restricting character of this construction. When we tried to get some idea of the reasons for such a rigid construction, she recalled her late father, a military man, who warned Tamara against easy relationships with boys – in his worldview, only relationships aimed at a 'serious' outcome were justified, there was no intrinsic meaning in the relationships as such. Tamara did not consciously agree with her father's view, especially after a few years studying psychology, but her father's script influenced her actual behaviour in her relationships with men. Having found Tamara's father's values hidden behind the screen and emerging at critical points in her developing relationships with men, I encouraged her next time to 'invite him out' in her imagination and to say: 'look, I am an adult now, I am free to decide for myself and I want to do what has meaning and value for me independently of what can follow, and you'd better accept it'.

After this talk she disappeared. Six weeks later I received an SMS from her: 'Sorry, I am far away, enjoying a new relationship. Will call you some day later'.

Conclusion

The deeper we penetrate the realm of relationships, the less predictable, controllable and comprehensible they are; and the less predictable, controllable and comprehensible they are, the more critical is their importance for our living and development. When we encase our meanings into culturally appropriate forms, we protect ourselves from the risk of trauma but also prevent ourselves experiencing the benefits of development, for these risks and benefits go hand in hand. We avoid self-disclosure for the fear of unpredictability. We don't want to know others better than we do because this would require a change in our worldview. Thus we deny both our own self-disclosure and others' self-disclosure to us. Preventing dialogue, we prevent personality change. The only alternative is regression, simplifying one's life world in all its aspects, one's personality and one's relationships to the most standardized and formal levels. The circle (or, more exactly, the descending spiral) of fear, stagnation and regression is completed.

Another spiral, the ascending one, starts from accepting the risk and enjoying the unpredictability of authentic relationships and acknowledging that the psychological truth, including the truth about oneself, is negotiable. The Other person and relationships with him/her contain a potentially infinite multitude of possibilities. Mutual openness encourages contact and interaction between inner worlds of personal meanings, and both worlds are changed in this process. Personality change engenders the growth of complexity, and the latter engenders more courage to face and enjoy unpredictable encounters and life challenges. An existential view on relationships does not promise an easy way of relating to fellow humans; what it does promise is the potential for the richer and more satisfying forms of relationship.

References

Anderson, R. and Cissna, K. N. (1997) *The Martin Buber-Carl Rogers Dialogue: A New Transcript with Commentary.* Albany, NY: State University of New York Press.

Bakhtin, M. M. (1984) *Problems of Dostoevsky's Poetics*, ed. and trans. C. Emerson, Minneapolis: University of Minnesota Press.

Binswanger, L. (1960 [1946]) 'The existential analysis school of thought', in R. May, E. Angel and H. F. Ellenberger (eds/trans.), *Existence: A New Dimension in Psychiatry and Psychology*, New York: Basic Books.

Boss, M. (1979) *Existential Foundations of Medicine and Psychology*, trans. S. Conway and A. Cleaves, New York: Jason Aronson.

Buber, M. (1996) *I and Thou*, trans. W. Kaufmann, New York: Simon and Schuster.

Buber, M. (1998) *The Knowledge of Man: Selected Essays*, trans. M. Friedman and R. Gregor-Smith, Amherst, NY: Prometheus Books.

Buber, M. (2002) *Between Man and Man*, trans. R. Gregor-Smith, New York: Routledge.

Bugental, J. F. T. (1987) *The Art of the Psychotherapist*, New York: Norton.

Bugental, J. F. T. (1991) 'Outcomes of an existential-humanistic psychotherapy: a tribute to Rollo May', *The Humanistic Psychologist*, 19 (1), 2–9.

Erikson, E. H. (1980) *Identity and the Life Circle*, New York: W.W. Norton.

Frankl, V. Å. (1967) *Psychotherapy and Existentialism*, New York: Simon and Schuster.

Frankl, V. A. (1978) *The Unheard Cry for Meaning*, New York: Simon and Schuster.

Friedman, M. (1985) *The Healing Dialogue in Psychotherapy*, New York: Jason Aronson.

Fromm, E. (1941) *Escape from Freedom*, New York: Holt, Rinehart & Winston.

Fromm, E. (1947) *Man for Himself: An Inquiry into the Psychology of Ethics*, New York: Rinehart.

Fromm, E. (1956) *The Art of Loving*, New York: Harper & Row.

Jourard, S. (1968) *Disclosing Man to Himself*, New York: Van Nostrand.

Jourard, S. (1971) *The Transparent Self*, rev. edn, New York: Van Nostrand Reinhold.

Korotkov, D. (1998) 'The Sense of Coherence: Making Sense Out of Chaos', in P. T. P. Wong and P. S. Fry (eds), *The Human Quest for Meaning: A Handbook of Psychological Research and Clinical Applications*, Mahwah, NJ: Lawrence Erlbaum Associates.

Leontiev, D. (1992) 'Joint activity, communication, and interaction', *Journal of Russian and East European Psychology*, 30 (2), 43–58.

Leontiev, D. (1996) 'Dimensions of the meaning/sense concept in the psychological context', in C. Tolman, F. Cherry, R. van Hezewijk and I. Lubek (eds), *Problems of Theoretical Psychology*, York: Captus University Publications.

Leontiev, D. (2006a) 'Meaningful living and the worlds of art', in A. Delle Fave (ed.), *Dimensions of Well-being: Research and Intervention*, Milano: Franco Angeli.

Leontiev, D. (2006b) 'Positive personality development: approaching personal autonomy', in M. Csikzentmihalyi and I. S. Csikzentmihalyi (eds), *A Life Worth Living: Contributions to Positive Psychology*, New York: Oxford University Press.

Leontiev, D. (2007) 'The phenomenon of meaning: how psychology can make sense of it?' in P. T. P. Wong, L. Wong, M. J. McDonald and D. K. Klaassen (eds), *The Positive Psychology of Meaning and Spirituality*, Abbotsford, BC: INPM Press.

Maddi, S. R. (1987) 'On the importance of the present: Reactions to John Shlien's article', *Person-Centered Review*, 2, 171–181.

Peseschkian, N. (1986) *Positive Family Therapy: The Family as Therapist*, Berlin: Springer.

Shaw, J. B. (2008) *Man and Superman*, Rockville, MD: Wildside Press.

CHAPTER 3

The Challenge of Intimacy: Fear of the Other

NAOMI STADLEN

The first moments of two-person intimacy are usually life-affirming. Each person feels deeply open and softened in love for the other. How could they ever oppose one another in a quarrel? So then, when quarrels do arise, couples often say: 'Our arguments seem to come out of the blue'.

The couples I see for therapy usually have a baby or small child. Once a baby is born, the couple find themselves rethinking what is fair in their couple relationship. They may also have different ideas about how to parent. Both may feel too exhausted to argue, yet are often exasperated with one another. 'If it weren't for the baby', each thinks, 'I'd be out of here'.

There seem to be two basic reasons why couples quarrel, including those who have not had a baby. First, it does not seem possible for a couple to maintain the total openness that seemed so natural at the start of their love. Both close up a little, which means that both return to their earlier often sedimented values and prejudices. Typically, these are the values they were brought up with. In this kind of quarrel, for example, Ann may argue with Andy because he never gives her any sympathy when she feels unwell. In her family, that was exactly when she could count on being comforted. Andy protests that Ann is always complaining. He was brought up in a stoical family where it was a matter of pride to ignore minor ailments. Each feels irritated by the alien values of the other. Their objections can be summarized as: 'Why can't s/he be more like me?'

However, it is not easy to change one isolated value. Each one is held 'in place' by more general concepts, such as: 'A loving partner should be kind to me', or 'In an intimate relationship, I need to be honest'. These general concepts are deeply held, so, even when they are challenged by the partner, are difficult to review and modify.

There is a second basic reason why couples quarrel. This kind of quarrel seems to occur not when the couple feel more distant from one another but, strangely, when they are close. It suddenly fell into place for me when a quarrelsome couple told me they had had the worst weekend ever. They explained that they had had a good Saturday outing together with their baby and felt warm and tender to one another. In the evening, Tim ran a hot bath for Tara, added some essence to it, lit a scented candle for her, and then felt he had 'done my bit' and went to take 'a business phone-call'. Tara was just sinking into the hot bath when she heard his voice and felt convinced that he was telephoning his ex-girlfriend. A moment later, she was out of the bath, holding a knife and screaming that she wanted to kill him.

Tara and Tim were both in their mid-thirties, and both had built up independent careers. Both had experienced relationships though not long-term ones. They had only known one another for three months before conceiving their baby. In retrospect, it was not surprising that both had panicked at the prospect of intimacy. Tim seemed to have switched off his feelings for Tara by deciding he had 'done my bit'. He chose to take a phone call, which he said was a business one, on a Saturday night, rather than allow himself to continue in intimate mode with her. Tara said she was terrified of letting herself believe that he loved her, only to find that he had deceived her. Just as she was starting to relax in the bath, she allowed her fears to overwhelm her loving feelings for him.

Why do so many couples ruin what could have been intimate moments with violent quarrels? Sometimes, one member of the couple is in 'bad faith' and is overtly striving for intimacy, despite serious doubts about whether the partner is trustworthy. In a therapeutic session, the person will usually voice these doubts, yet immediately add something to discount them, or disown them as 'only' the views of a mutual friend.

However, it is more usual for the therapist to hear a couple say that they long to be more intimate, but are devastated by their quarrels. When a quarrel of such a couple is 'unravelled' it nearly always exposes fear on both sides. Yet it is almost impossible to fear the unknown without attributing to it certain fears that we have already experienced. Although 'intimacy' is a common word, true intimacy is, for many people, unknown. What they have experienced, and fear repeating, are painful attempts to find intimacy, in which they opened themselves to another person but were hurt. Often our history of intimacy begins with our very first relationships with our parents. As babies, we need to be sensitive in order to learn. But our sensitivity can leave us without defence against being badly hurt. We then have an electric-fast reaction to the slightest suspicion that we could be hurt in exactly that way again (Firestone and Catlett, 1999: 35 and 163; Stadlen, 2011: 180–188 and 216–217).

Small children are quick to recognize – when they are so young that many parents think they will not notice – how often they are treated as a burden, how often they are mocked, or have their ignorance read as stupidity, or deliberate naughtiness. The odd moment when a parent mocked the child might not leave a strong impression, but habitual mockery can scar. Once adult, the person may develop an instant reaction to the mere possibility of mockery, leaving the partner unable to understand why a little light teasing seems to create such a barrier between them.

These areas can be so painful that even though couples desire intimacy, they are wary of it. One member may try to raise a particular anxiety, but in a way which threatens the other, such as by suggesting that the other one 'wouldn't understand', or 'causes' the anxiety. This kind of approach usually generates a furious quarrel. Afterwards, both of them withdraw, feeling bewildered by the other, and hurt. They then complain that they feel numb, no longer desire the partner, are bored by the relationship and are thinking of starting a 'better' one. Feeling numb is often a defence against a problematic feeling.

If a couple seek help from an existential psychotherapist, there is a great deal that this psychotherapist can do. Existential philosophers have written about our need to develop as individuals, to take responsibility for ourselves, to be authentic with others, and above all to acknowledge our own anxiety. All this is crucial for couples. A good existential psychotherapist is a fellow-explorer, open to discovering new ways of making sense of the phenomena that trouble clients. I have found several concepts in existential philosophy especially helpful.

A common theme is the difficulty of distinguishing our unique individuality from the seductive pull of fitting in with the majority around us. Søren Kierkegaard describes a person's lonely journey to find a moral life and how his friends tried to tempt him to enjoy an easier one (Kierkegaard, 1962: 129–130).

Martin Buber wrote that the human need to relate intimately is not a luxury but primary. 'All real living is meeting' he wrote in *I and Thou* (Buber, 1958: 11). He also coined the word 'mismeeting', by which he meant 'a failure of a real meeting'. He recalled this word when he met his mother after twenty years of separation. This meeting was an opportunity to address the painful issues between them. However, neither chose to take it (Buber, 1973: 17–19). Buber reveals, in his short account of how he was sent away from his mother without explanation, how deeply a four-year-old can be hurt. 'Mismeeting' could be a very useful term in therapy with couples.

Martin Heidegger passionately criticizes the notion of 'empathy', which he sees as implying a view of human beings as encapsulated 'subjects', each having to feel his or her way into the other and make inferences about the other's experiences (Heidegger, 1985: 237; 2001: 111). He points out that we are already in everyday relation to one another.

As outlined in Chapter 7 of this book, Jean-Paul Sartre affirms our responsibility for our own actions. We are not driven by our instincts, nor can we plead that we have been compelled by one another. We can try to deny our responsibility, but then we are in 'bad faith' (Sartre, 1956: 55–67). Couples who come to therapy do not seem to require lessons in bad faith. Typical accusations which ping-pong across the consulting room are: 'She makes me so angry, I can't control myself' followed by the *'tu-quoque'* ricochet: 'He's always complaining that I don't listen. But I'm a much better listener than *he* is.' Yet, however expertly couples provoke one another, the decision to get angry, or to refuse to consider a complaint, are choices for which the 'chooser' is responsible. The therapist then has an opportunity to encourage the couple to accept responsibility for their strong feelings, and to explore them.

R. D. Laing has achieved pioneering work in disentangling some of the 'knots' that couples create in their search for intimacy. For example, his essay on 'collusion' is informative and original (Laing, 1969: 90–106). He collaborated with Aaron Esterson who had undertaken research into families, and this resulted in the publication of *Sanity, Madness and the Family* (Laing and Esterson, 1964). Esterson also wrote a detailed study of the Danzig family in *The Leaves of Spring*, showing how the parents strove for the appearance of a 'successful' family, which made genuine intimacy problematic (Esterson, 1970).

However, this literature has left a hiatus as it mostly considers what can go wrong in a relationship. Is there any literature that can guide therapists in helping couples to find the intimacy they long for?

Ludwig Binswanger studied English and German love-poetry to gain a deeper understanding of the nature of love. A loving couple, he said, create a 'we', which transcends the individual separateness of each. He emphasizes the dynamic nature of love as an endless mutual giving and receiving (Frie, 1997: 96).

Dietrich von Hildebrand, an exact contemporary of Heidegger, and a student of Husserl, wrote *The Nature of Love* towards the end of his long and courageous life (von Hildebrand, 2009). Essentially moral and phenomenological, it is partly expressed in Roman-Catholic terminology. This has infuriated students when I used extracts to discuss in class. However, the book has much to offer, and should not be dismissed. Its 374 pages are devoted to the study of love, with frequent references to personal experience. It is rooted in existential values of personal responsibility, personal choice and questions of how to relate lovingly to a beloved.

'In love,' von Hildebrand wrote, 'we "lift the mask" which otherwise covers and protects our intimate inner life. In love and only in love does one turn to another in such a way that one gives oneself and in fact gives one's most intimate being. This element is eminently characteristic of spousal love…' (von Hildebrand, 2009: 51). It must be mutual (2009: 133) because otherwise it will be motivated by the 'will to possess' (2009: 135) for the goal of 'self-perfection' (2009: 123). Love of another is based on perceiving the value of the other, and is completely distinct from self-love (2009: 365). 'In love, I open the arms of my soul so as to surround the soul of the beloved person. The *intentio unionis* is an essential element of love, even apart from all the happiness that flows from union … love yearns for union …' (2009: 131). 'On the one hand, there is the full duality of I and Thou, the clear difference between them, the full consciousness of the Thou of the beloved person and his unique individuality …' (2009: 234).

If the language sometimes sounds high-flown, to English ears, there are sentences of wonderful simplicity too. For example, on spousal love, he wrote: '...it is a true encounter of persons in a shared "here"' (von Hildebrand, 2009: 130). Helping a couple to share their 'here' is exactly what I try to do.

Yet even von Hildebrand says very little about how couples sustain their love in daily life. He adds an interesting footnote on the special danger of a couple getting irritated with one another, which he calls 'spiritual sluggishness' (2009: 345n). This is a very rare example of how couples relate *after* they have fallen in love. I have found little about everyday intimacy in any psychological literature. Intimacy is usually mentioned as desirable, as if we all knew, and agreed on, what it is. But surely we know very little about it (Carlson and Sperry, 2010: 4). I shall summarize here some of my own observations.

True intimacy is moral. It is founded on honesty and trust between the couple. It never comes as a permanent state but in unexpected moments when both persons are warmly present to one another. They both feel softer, more melting and open to one another than usual. This enables something to happen which is difficult to describe. The couple deepen their understanding of one another, and sense their near-oneness. This seems to reaffirm not just themselves but the whole of life and the goodness of being alive. It restores them, however bruised, to new courage. In this way, couples may experience an upsurge of energy in one another's company. All kinds of creative ideas look clear and possible, while problems become simple and solvable. Separately, neither would have had such clarity and energy. Couples may express intimacy by touch, a look, or sexually, through silence, or through conversation. There's no blueprint for intimacy.

Intimacy seems essential to us (Carlson and Sperry, 2010: ix and xi). People who eschew intimacy often comment that some excitement in their lives seems to be lacking. They may seek out expensive physical excitements. Yet simple intimate couple moments can provide times of feeling intensely real and alive, without physical risk or great expense.

However, this openness also makes it easy for either person to hurt the other. There is always the risk with anything powerful – which intimacy is – that it can be abused. The problem for many couples is that both may have been hurt by earlier experiences. The beginning of the relationship usually feels wonderfully easy. Then, because intimate relationships are so truthful, old fears resurface. If the couple can identify their fears and realize that they do not necessarily apply to the current partner, they find it much easier to continue their intimacy, strengthen it and develop it. A couple's intimacy is in constant flux. Often the two seem to lose one another, only to discover that, despite very painful challenges, their love still holds.

But before a relationship can mature, the couple meet frequent situations that at least one of them finds difficult. Often the difficulty is mutual, though one person may be 'blamed'. Then both feel stuck and the relationship can seem stale. For example, after the birth of a baby, the mother may be totally absorbed in trying to understand him. The father can feel shut out in the cold, and may try to resolve the impasse by threatening to walk out, or by having a none-too-secret affair, as a coded non-verbal message of anger and despair. Each dreads to be abandoned, and believes the other has realized their worst fears.

This is when an existential couple therapist can be invaluable. It often needs a third person to help the couple to identify their sedimented ways of thinking, to explore their patterns of behaviour, and slowly to move far beyond the familiar stuck place.

As mentioned in the introductory chapter, existential literature has only, up till now, included a few case studies illustrating how therapists work with couples. The essential change is when couples make the shift from blaming each other to taking responsibility for themselves. They then discover that, instead of trying to 'improve' the other, they themselves can make real differences to how they relate. At last, they can see that what had appeared to be unforgivable behaviour in their partner was part of a coded 'message' that the partner was trying to communicate through odd behaviour rather than in words. Once these messages are decoded and admitted, both feel stronger and find they can be more receptive towards what the other has to offer. This process unsticks the whole relationship.

I have found it counter-productive to try to solve the couple's practical problems, however urgent. They are a distraction. Once couples decide to accept responsibility for their actions, and are willing to relinquish their familiar 'victim' roles, they quickly come up with intelligent practical solutions for themselves.

Case illustration

Couple therapy requires time (and also, for parents, the need for reliable child-sitters). This particular couple came to see me because they were thinking of separating. After twenty-five sessions, the husband said he could not spare time or money to continue. I thought it was much too early to end. Even so, they had made good progress as a couple, and assured me that they would be able to use our work together. However, while writing this case illustration, I contacted them again. I learned that they had separated and were considering divorce. With hindsight, I think I should have offered some follow-up sessions when they left, so that we could have continued to discuss their difficulties in communication, whether they stayed together or decided to separate.

At the start of our first session, I invited Ved and Venetia to tell me why they had come. Ved explained that they had met as students and known one another for twenty years. Now, in their forties, they had recently had a baby, but, he said, were on the brink of separating. Recently, Venetia had hit him while holding little Verna in her other arm. Ved said that he knew Venetia found him annoying. He didn't like being hit, but he was sure she was justified.

Venetia explained that she had seen her mother hitting her father, and had always resolved never to be like that. So she was shocked at herself now. She was finding it exhausting to be a mother. She was not getting enough sleep, and she thought her anger came from that.

I commented that it must be difficult to turn into parents if they had known one another as non-parents for twenty years. I said having a baby was a momentous change for anyone. There was so much to learn. It must have made a great difference to both their lives. I said this because I wanted to clarify the context of their difficulties. Both covered their eyes as I spoke and I realized they were crying. 'Have I upset you?' Venetia replied: 'Oh no, but I never thought of it like that. It's nice to feel normal.'

I then asked about her anger with Ved. She exclaimed: 'I just don't understand him. If I had his talent, I would be putting myself forward. If I had *half* his abilities, I'd be trying to sell myself. He doesn't make any effort. It drives me to despair to watch him.'

It sounded as though Venetia might have come from the kind of family with particular values and beliefs about the roles of each partner. However, the more urgent point to address seemed to be her first sentence, so I said: 'You don't understand Ved?' 'That's right, I simply don't understand him.' 'Well, why don't we ask him? You've asked a perfectly good question. You are truly puzzled. Shall we ask him why he doesn't put himself forward?' Venetia said later that this possibility was a new idea to her. Although they had been together for so long, she said they did not talk much. She would get enraged by Ved's behaviour, which she assumed was irrational. It did not occur to her that he might have reasons for what he did, which would have led to a much more intimate conversation.

At first, when she asked Ved why he did not try harder, Ved replied that he found it hard to answer. He knew he was talented but he was not working well. Venetia used to help him but now she had baby Verna and did not have time. Also, he did not want to be a pushy person. In a later session, he said he worked slowly because he was a perfectionist. His mother always liked everything to be 'perfect' and he, youngest child out of five, was the only one who always got things 'right'.

I didn't offer Venetia any strategy for controlling her anger, or Ved for trying to work more effectively. Instead I felt that their first session had allowed space for them both to think more creatively about how they communicated.

A later session revealed Ved's fears. He tended to express them by withdrawing. Venetia complained that he would leave the room in the middle of a conversation. He admitted that he sometimes 'distanced' himself. Before their thirteenth session, Ved walked off outside my front door and told Venetia he wouldn't come in. She telephoned him (they both had mobiles) and he said he was on his way back anyway. He came in, looking white and tearful. He felt attacked by Venetia and said that he always withdrew when he was trying not to annoy her even more.

Venetia described Ved's family. 'They meet for meals, and they all *yell* at each other', she explained. 'No one listens. Ved is the quiet one. No one listens to *him*.' Ved confirmed that this was a good description, so I asked if he experienced Venetia as another sibling who wouldn't listen to him. I said I wondered whether he withdrew from conversations with Venetia in anger, as a way of expressing his own expectation that she too would shout him down.

Ved clearly found it much easier to withdraw than to speak. I asked Venetia if she could understand his difficulty, and she said: 'Yes. I know his family. I guess I could be more compassionate to him.' They had already told me that they had started to enjoy talking to one another more at home.

A key misunderstanding had arisen when Venetia gave birth to Verna at home. Venetia went through a long early stage in pain and anxiety. She had begged Ved repeatedly to telephone a midwife, but he wouldn't. After this, she decided she couldn't feel safe with him and didn't trust him any more. I said this sounded like another example of her not understanding Ved, and of giving up on trying. Together, we formulated a question to Ved, asking why he hadn't called a midwife. This time, Ved had a clear answer. He reminded Venetia that the midwife had warned them that, if they asked for her too early, she would bring them into hospital. They had wanted a home birth, and Ved was trying his hardest to ensure that they had one. Both were in tears at recognizing that they were ultimately together in what they wanted.

This was one of the issues that I checked with them recently. I thought we had achieved a good understanding. However, Venetia said that she was still angry with Ved. Ved said that he was never good at making quick decisions. However, looking back now, he thought he should definitely have listened to Venetia rather than to their midwife.

There were other patterns that we identified at the time that prevented them from being intimate. For example, Venetia wanted more help from Ved, but couldn't respect herself if she asked him for it. Her parents had expected her to be independent, and she spent a great deal of time giving help to other people. Sometimes, she would indicate to Ved that she needed help without openly asking for it. Then, when Ved offered her help, she would snap at him, ridiculing his offer. He would withdraw, baffled and hurt. She experienced this as Ved 'being cold', without perceiving it as a *response* to herself, because she was giving him contradictory messages. When we decoded the implicit messages, and then linked together small sequences of their interactions, we could all see these interactions as meaningful 'replies' to one another. Eventually, Ved said he loved Venetia and that maybe he needed to speak more clearly to her. Venetia said at the time that Verna's birth was no longer an issue, and that she could trust Ved now.

Between sessions, they experimented with solutions to their practical problems. They hired a woman to help Venetia, then decided the woman should help Ved, and finally agreed that she was an expensive chatterbox and that they were better off without her. They resolved not to burst in on one another with urgent problems, but to talk and listen more calmly. They were also more affectionate to one another 'in the kitchen' and had bought their daughter, who slept with them, her own bed, so that they could aspire to more time at night together. When they left, they sounded confident that they could talk to one another. Even though their trust in one another now seems to have broken down, I hope they have both learned that they were capable of articulating complex thoughts and of listening to one another.

Conclusion

In this case illustration, it helped to have the couple together in the room. But I have found it equally possible to use the same ideas in psychotherapy with an individual client.

I should like to end with a paradox of intimate love. A common assumption is that intimacy can become suffocating and close. The opposite view is suggested by Martin Buber who retold an eighteenth-century Jewish-Chassidic story. 'Rabbi Shemuel told this about Rabbi Rafael of Bershad: "When he [Rabbi Rafael] was going on his summer trip, he called me and asked me to share his carriage with him. I said: 'I am afraid I should crowd you.' Then he said to me in the manner he always used to express affection: 'Let us love each other more and we shall have a feeling of spaciousness'"' (Buber, 1947: 130).

The paradox is that physical closeness does not necessarily mean crowdedness, nor does physical distance ensure greater individual freedom. When two people who love one another become close, they create *more* space between them. A degree of space is essential for intimacy. A couple can be so close that they can no longer see one another clearly. Instead they often make large assumptions about one another. Intimacy returns when they back off, and are able to feel curious about the essential mystery of one another. Usually we cannot find the closeness of intimacy without the contrast of some distance.

References

Buber, M. (1958 [1923]) *I and Thou*, trans. R. G. Smith, Edinburgh: Clark.

Buber, M. (1947) *Tales of the Hasidim: The Early Masters*, trans. O. Marx, New York: Schocken Books.

Buber, M. (1973) *Meetings*, ed. M. Friedman, trans. from German by several translators, La Salle, IL: Open Court Publishing.

Carlson, J. and Sperry, L. (eds) (2010) *Recovering Intimacy in Love Relationships*, New York/London: Routledge.

Esterson, A. (1970) *The Leaves of Spring*, London: Tavistock.

Firestone, R. W. and Catlett, J. (1999) *Fear of Intimacy*, Washington, DC: American Psychological Association.

Frie, R. (1997) *Subjectivity and Intersubjectivity in Modern Philosophy and Psychoanalysis*, Lanham, MD: Rowman and Littlefield.

Heidegger, M. (1985 [1979]) *History of the Concept of Time*, trans. T. Kisiel, Bloomington and Indianapolis: Indiana University Press.

Heidegger, M. (2001 [1987]) *Zollikon Seminars*, ed. M. Boss, trans. F. Mayr and R. Asley, Evanston, IL: Northwestern University Press.

Kierkegaard, S. (1962 [1847]) *Works of Love*, trans. H. Hong and E. Hong, London: Collins.

Laing, R. D. (1969) *Self and Others*. London, Tavistock.

Laing, R. D. and Esterson, A. (1964) *Sanity, Madness and the Family*, London: Tavistock.

Sartre, J. P. (1956 [1943]) *Being and Nothingness,* trans. H. E. Barnes, London: Methuen.

Stadlen, N. (2011) *How Mothers Love,* London: Piatkus.

Von Hildebrand, D. (2009) *The Nature of Love*, eds J. F. Crosby and J. H. Crosby, South Bend, IN: St Augustine's Press.

CHAPTER 4

The Challenge of Sexuality and Embodiment in Human Relationships

MEG BARKER AND DARREN LANGDRIDGE

In general what sets 'a relationship' (of the kind this book, and relationship therapy more broadly, focuses on) apart from other kinds of relationships (friendships, collegiate relationships, family relationships and so forth) is often taken to be the fact that it is 'sexual'. The phrases 'romantic relationship', 'intimate relationship' and 'sexual relationship' tend to be used interchangeably. Indeed, in popular magazines, television programmes and self-help books, the quantity and quality of sex within such a relationship is often taken to be a barometer of its success, or of the connection or love between the people involved (e.g. Gray, 2003; Star, 2004). This focus on sex in relationships has increased in recent years as part of what has been termed the 'sexualization' of culture (Attwood, 2004), and with it levels of anxiety around sex: The 2000 UK national survey of sexual attitudes and lifestyles (NATSAL) found that 35 per cent of men and 54 per cent of women reported some kind of sexual 'dysfunction' (Mercer et al., 2005).

Clearly, therefore, it is important that an existential form of relationship therapy considers issues of sex and sexuality within an existential framework. It is also important to begin to detail what an existential sex therapy would look like in practice, and how this might be similar to – and different from – current forms of psychosexual therapy. To date, there has been relatively little written on sexuality within existential therapy (see Smith-Pickard and Swynnerton, 2005; Pearce, 2011), and even less on existential forms of sex therapy (papers which touch on this include Barker, 2011a; Kleinplatz, 1998, 2004; Adams et al., 2006).

Historically, relationship therapy has been intertwined with sex therapy within organizational contexts. In the UK, for example, the main organization accrediting therapists in this area is the College of Sexual and Relationship Therapists (COSRT, 2011). In the National Health Service, the secondary care available to those with relationship difficulties takes the form of 'sexual and relationship therapy' clinics. The key international journals in this area are the *Journal of Sex and Marital Therapy* and *Sexual and Relationship Therapy*.

This chapter begins by presenting the dominant, medicalized, understandings of 'sexual problems' within psychosexual therapy. This is then contrasted with an existential understanding of sexuality and embodiment, drawing primarily on the work of Merleau-Ponty but also incorporating more recent feminist and queer scholars such as Elizabeth Grosz, who have built on and also challenged this foundation. The chapter then goes on to examine the multiple potential meanings of sexual experiences and practices, and the potential within existential therapy for sexual issues to reveal clients' wider world views as well as relational dynamics. Specific examples are given of the multiple meanings of erectile difficulties, and of the relationship between vaginismus and the existential challenge of being-for-oneself versus being-for-others.

Dominant understandings of sex in sexual and relationship therapy

Conventional psychosexual therapy is based upon the understandings of sexual function and dysfunction presented in nosologies such as the American Psychiatric Association (APA) Diagnostic and Statistical Manual (DSM V, in section 302.7) and the World Health Organization International Classification of Diseases (ICD-10, in section F52). Briefly these both include pain during sexual intercourse, and disruptions to any phase of Kaplan's (1974, 1979) adaptation of Masters and Johnson's (1966) 'normal' sexual response cycle: desire, excitement/arousal and orgasm.

In the desire phase, the DSM distinguishes between hypoactive desire (general lack of desire) and actual aversion to sexual contact. In the other phases (excitement/arousal and orgasm) it distinguishes between the genders, with 'female' and 'male' forms of both orgasm disorder and sexual arousal disorder (in men this latter is more commonly called 'erectile dysfunction', ED). Under male orgasm disorder there is also a separate category of 'premature ejaculation' (PE) whilst there is no equivalent category for women reaching orgasm too quickly. Under pain disorders there is a general disorder that applies to both men and women, and a specific category for women who experience uncomfortable vaginal muscle spasms in the outer third of the vagina during penetration (vaginismus). In addition to these categories, present in the DSM-IV-TR, the ICD-10 also lists two, gendered, forms of 'excessive sexual drive' (nymphomania and satyriasis).

Also of relevance for psychosexual therapy is the 'paraphilia' category (DSM-IV-TR section 302.8, ICD-10 section F65), which is again very similar in both nosologies and is considered to be a 'mental disorder', 'characterized by sexual fantasies, urges, or behaviors involving non-human objects (fetishism, transvestic fetishism), suffering or humiliation (sexual sadism, masochism), children (pedophilia) or other non-consenting person (voyeurism, frotteurism, exhibitionism)' (APA, 1994). There is not space, in this chapter, to deal with this in detail, but we will return to what an existential approach to such issues might look like later on.

Conventional psychosexual therapy begins with an assessment, a large part of which is undertaken to rule out possible organic reasons for sexual problems. This is important because many of the sexual 'dysfunctions' are linked to certain drugs (such as alcohol or antidepressants, notably selective seratonin reuptake inhibitors) or can be 'silent markers' for medical problems such as diabetes or coronary heart disease. Even if we take a critical stance towards the medicalization of sexual issues, as we do in this chapter, it behoves any therapist working in this area to have a broad understanding of the basic physiology of sex, in order to make appropriate referrals when a medical issue is indicated.

Once a diagnosis has been made, the likely therapy, in conventional psychosexual approaches, involves a combination of physical treatments (such as drugs or suggested sexual positions) with cognitive-behavioural therapy (CBT, such as systematic desensitization and reinforcement). The medical model has become the dominant way of understanding and treating sexual 'dysfunction' in the past two decades (Winton, 2001), particularly with the success of drug treatments like Viagra™ (a PDE5 inhibitor) for erectile dysfunction.

It is not possible to go into depth about all of the different CBT-based treatments here. To give just a few key examples, one common treatment for many sexual problems within relationships is Masters and Johnsons' (1970) 'sensate focus' 'homework': gradual progress between partners from touching with a ban on genital contact, to various kinds of genital contact, with a focus on them learning what each finds pleasurable and arousing. Vaginismus is frequently treated by encouraging the person to insert dilators of increasing size (or fingers) into the vagina. PE is often treated by encouraging the person to stop all stimulation when approaching orgasm several times before orgasm is allowed. CBT may also involve challenging common 'myths' and 'maladaptive beliefs' around sex, and some degree of sex education (Wincze and Carey, 2001).

It should be noted, here, that many private sexual and relationship therapists practise from positions other than the medical or CBT models (psychodynamic and systemic approaches being particularly common). Also, clinics may well consist of multidisciplinary teams of counsellors and clinicians who are informed by various approaches. However, the diagnosis and treatment model outlined here remains the standard approach conducted in clinics and outlined in the main texts on psychosexual therapy (e.g. Bancroft, 2009; see Barker and Richards, in press).

Before turning to specifically existential criticisms of conventional understandings of, and treatments for, sexual problems, it is worth briefly summarizing some of the other criticisms that have been made of this approach (see Barker, 2011a, for details). First, many authors have challenged the medicalization of sex broadly, and the pathologizing language of 'dysfunction' specifically (e.g. Ussher and Baker, 1993; Kaschak and Tiefer, 2001). Linked to this is the criticism that psychiatric categories and psychosexual treatments construct what 'normal' (and by implication good, proper) sex is, as part of wider dominant discourses (Rubin, 1992 [1984]). This constructed nature is revealed when we observe shifts in categories and understandings over time. For example, in the past masturbation was discouraged and homosexuality was included as a disorder (Kutchins and Kirk, 1997). Psychomedical constructions of sex are particularly problematic because they have a veneer of value-free scientific objectivity, which obscures the 'intensely political and value-laden content of the discourse' (Denman, 2004: 275).

'Normal' sex is clearly constructed as heterosexual penile-vaginal intercourse resulting in orgasm, given that penises are required to be erect (ED) and to penetrate (PE), and vaginas are required to be penetrated (vaginismus). The use of this passive 'penetrated' rather than a more active 'engulfing' is also telling (Pearce, 2011). Various authors have criticized this model for excluding other forms of sex (e.g. oral, anal, manual, solo, kinky) and relationships (e.g. 'same-sex' and multiple relationships, see Langdridge and Barker, this volume), as well as for being androcentric, given that sex is considered to end with male ejaculation. HIV/AIDS activists have also questioned the focus on penetration (Jackson, 2006). Categories and treatments are invariably bound up in economic concerns (such as those surrounding the lucrative business of psychopharmacology) and particular kinds of conservative politics. For example, Boyle (1993) suggests that concern with 'female sexual dysfunctions' emerged when women's sexual dissatisfaction began to threaten heterosexual marriage and the nuclear family.

On the level of the individual and the relationship, therefore, conventional psychosexual therapy can be seen as constraining and limiting what is possible, and being 'goal' rather than 'pleasure-directed' (Kleinplatz, 1998, 2004) in a way which dampens the erotic imagination (Denman, 2004) and prevents people from tuning in to their own unique desires and fantasies.

Existential understandings of sexuality and embodiment

These criticisms are very much in line with existential perspectives. Yalom (2001) states that therapists should avoid diagnoses because they prevent us from relating to the client as a person, and can become self-fulfilling prophecies. More fundamentally, existential therapy – following the anti-psychiatry approach of Laing (1962) and Szasz (1974) – sees such diagnosis and treatment on the basis of symptoms as missing the *meaning* of these symptoms and behaviours and therefore dehumanizing the individual. Kleinplatz's (2003) existential criticism of psychosexual therapy argues that the focus on relieving symptoms neglects the vital intrapsychic, interpersonal, systemic and sociocultural meanings of experiences and behaviours.

There is remarkably little consideration of sexuality and embodiment in philosophical literature in general, but there are some notable exceptions within the existential canon that may provide the basis for an existentially informed sex therapy. The existential philosopher who provides the most significant contribution to understandings of embodiment and sexuality is Maurice Merleau-Ponty (1962, 1968). His work offers a significant departure from other therapeutic theories on these issues.

Merleau-Ponty (1962) provides an elaborate account of sexuality that is at once radical and also fundamental. He argues that, rather than separating sexuality off as a distinct aspect of existence, we should instead recognize the way that it infuses all of our embodied being-in-the-world. It is therefore a fundamental aspect of intersubjectivity, always present in our relations with others. Sexuality in these terms moves beyond everyday notions of sex and sexuality towards recognition of the inherent sexual element in all encounters. Sex does remain an aspect of sexuality that is driven by desire, but sexuality becomes much broader than simply sexual acts.

It is desire that is central in our sexual being in the world with others. Sexuality, like all other aspects of embodied consciousness, is intentionally directed towards the world. This is not simply through conscious decisions about our sexual predilections but also through a pre-reflective desire that emerges through our bodies. Desire reveals that we are fundamentally embodied beings and cannot split off our selves from our bodies in the way we are often encouraged to do by popular culture. There is also no existence without sexuality for we are always in relation with others and this relationship is always characterized by sexual significance.

According to Merleau-Ponty's position, we need to recognize the diverse and diffuse nature of sexuality in all our relational encounters. This may not be driven by sex (though of course it sometimes is) but by a sense of embodied connection grounded in desire (e.g. to be intimate with another person, to connect with them). The meaning of sex and sexuality is therefore open to different and diverse understandings but the power and potency of our relationships speak not only to everyday concerns about intimacy and sexuality but also to broader aspects of how the world appears to us.

Through thinking of sexuality in such a way that sex is maintained but sexuality broadened *beyond* sex alone we can see the potential in counselling and psychotherapy for sexuality to alert us to important aspects of our lives and the meaning they have for us. For example, we may find in sex therapy that sexual difficulties relate to much broader aspects of a person's life. For example, someone who has trouble reaching orgasm may struggle to let go and be vulnerable in relationships more generally. Someone who is engaging in 'virtual' (online) sex in a variety of roles may find this a safe space to engage in a creativity of self that they find anxiety-provoking in everyday life. Similarly, in therapy, which is not explicitly psychosexual in nature, Merleau-Ponty's understandings would suggest that sexuality would always be relevant and should be part of what we explore with all clients.

Beyond these explicit accounts of sexuality and embodiment the developmental-psychological work of Merleau-Ponty (1964, 1993) also has relevance for bringing the body more directly into existential counselling and psychotherapy. Whilst there is not the space to discuss this in detail here, one of us has elsewhere outlined one possible way in which a 'fusion of bodily horizons' between therapist and client might be achieved (Langdridge, 2005: 96) using techniques more commonly associated with gestalt therapy. There is considerable potential for this to be extended when working with clients in relationship therapy such that they might physically enact aspects of their experience directly within the therapeutic space to better understand the emotional quality of relationship dynamics. Traditional relationship therapy already uses such methods where couples (or people in other relationship structures) are given practical communication tasks to perform both within and outside the therapeutic session. There is, therefore, scope for bringing together existential understandings and traditional ways of working in relationship therapy so that both are enriched and the importance of sexuality and embodiment foregrounded.

Whilst this existential work opens up a new way of understanding sexuality and embodiment that moves beyond a simple focus on the mechanics of sex, it has not escaped criticism. In particular, some more recent feminist philosophers, working broadly within the existential tradition, have questioned some of the assumptions underpinning this work with regard to gender difference and sexism (Grosz, 1994; Le Deouff, 1991). Grosz (1994) raises the issue of sexual difference in Merleau-Ponty's account, asking a critical question about the kind of body that forms the basis for his theory. His theory may appear general, not tied to any one type of body, but for Grosz this is the problem. There is no recognition of how differently sexed and sexualized bodies might experience sexuality and desire in different ways. Merleau-Ponty's model is cisgender[1] heterosexual male sexuality and this is taken as the foundation for his theorizing. Cisgender heterosexual female sexuality, whilst sharing some common features, might also demand a different phenomenological analysis, as might different varieties of transsexuality, genderqueer,[2] genderneutral,[3] lesbian, gay and bisexual sexuality.

Beyond her belief that Merleau-Ponty has failed to take sexual difference seriously, Grosz also raises the issue of how sexuality and desire in Merleau-Ponty's terms are almost de-sexualized, in contrast to those of Freud for instance. There is no recognition of the potentially disturbing and disruptive power of sex and sexuality in Merleau-Ponty's theories. Grosz concludes that:

> Where Freud perhaps too strongly emphasizes desire (enabling it to be readily equated with instincts), Merleau-Ponty does not provide it with a central enough role . . . (1994: 110)

There is clearly more work needed that builds on the insights of the work of writers like Merleau-Ponty and others but which also takes seriously the impact of the phenomenology and socio-political aspects of sex and sexual difference.

So what does this mean for an existential form of sex therapy? In the rest of this chapter we focus on two key aspects, acknowledging that there is much more that could be taken from this work. We consider the multiplicity of meanings of sexual experiences and the potential for sexual issues to reveal wider patterns of relating to others.

Multiple meanings of sexual experiences and practices

One key way in which existential sex therapy would differ from more main-stream approaches would be in its openness to a multiplicity of possible meanings of sexual experiences and practices. Conventional approaches tend to assume universal causes for sexual problems, and focus on addressing these causes. For example, it is commonly assumed that 'erectile dysfunction' results from the possessor of the penis failing to 'perform' on one occasion and then becoming anxious in subsequent sexual encounters. This is treated with medical treatments or sexual positions which increase the likelihood of erections, and by increasing confident thoughts and decreasing anxious ones, perhaps with the application of 'sensate focus' (see above).

An existential-phenomenological approach would begin with a rich description of the client's lived experience of their sex life, as well as with horizontalizing (see Adams, 2001 and Langdridge, 2007, for more on these methods) such that the focus would not purely be on sexual encounters, but this would be considered within the wider experience, and worldview, of the client. Through such exploration, the meanings that certain experiences and practices have for *this client* could be revealed (which would require the bracketing of therapist – and wider dominant – understandings of the meanings of sex) and then verified with the client (Adams, 2001; Langdridge, 2007).

For example, when Yalom (1991) worked with a client, Marvin, who under the medical model would be diagnosed with 'erectile dysfunction', they discovered that Marvin's difficulties related to his dread of impending death. Sex was the way in which Marvin attempted to soothe himself in relation to his anxiety about all the things that he had not done in his life (such as having children and a meaningful career). As he approached retirement, it became increasingly difficult for Marvin to hide from these issues, and sex stopped working as a means of self-soothing. In another example, Kleinplatz (2004) worked with a man who would also have been diagnosed with 'erectile dysfunction'. She suggested tuning in to the embodied experience of his penis. They found that – in contrast to the client's desire to be accommodating to his partner's requests for penetration – the feelings in that part of the body were of anger at the expectation of performance. Existential sex therapy was able to address wider issues of masculinity and performance, as well as of embodied experiences of emotions and what it meant to deny these.

Therapy which does not fully examine the meaning for the client may be harmful: Kleinplatz (2004) gives the example that PDE5 inhibitors might restore performance to a man whose wife has died, or who is sensing a rift between his own desires and those of his partner, or who does not feel comfortable with his new girlfriend. This might well leave him feeling alone and empty because his loss, tension or anxiety has not been addressed. It can be 'against the rules' for men to say that they do not want sex (because they are often expected to be always sexually interested and to prove their partner's desirability through their erections and orgasms). Under these circumstances, being unable to 'perform' may be the only way to get out of sex.

Here we can see that the lack of an erection can mean very different things to different people, and at different times. It could mean, for example, the loss of an important self-soothing strategy, an escape from the pressure to perform, an expression of anger, or grief, or lack of desire, a wider difficulty in 'performing' and making choices and decisions out in the world, a sense of not feeling able to voice sexual desires and attempting to have a kind of sex that one does not find enjoyable, and many other meanings, and combinations of meanings, beyond these. Similarly, it is important to explore the meanings of penetration/engulfment, and its lack, for clients with vaginismus (Kleinplatz, 1998) or of orgasm, and its lack, for those who struggle to achieve orgasm (Barker, 2011a).

Given the existential view that sexuality is always part of human existence and relations with others, it is vital for all therapists – not just sex therapists – to be well informed about the dominant cultural meanings, which are currently present about sex and sexuality and which are highly likely to impact on clients' own meanings (Barker, 2011b). Given taboos around sex, which will likely impact on therapists and clients alike, it is important that all therapy courses include training on the diversity of sexualities and practices. It also behoves therapists to supplement such formal education with additional work (for instance, through reading and/or viewing appropriate television programmes) such that they are able to talk in a matter-of-fact way about sex and sexuality with all clients. It is also worth undertaking some training in issues of race and culture so that there is an awareness about the different common cultural meanings that exist around such issues (Butler et al., 2010) without, of course, expecting that all clients will necessarily understand sex in these ways due to their cultural background, or the communities that they belong to. Rather than adhering to a model of what 'normal', 'proper' sex looks like, this would involve broadening our understanding to encompass all forms of sexual practice, and areas where the boundaries are blurred between sex and other activities such as leisure, art and spirituality. It would also involve recognizing that sexuality is not a fixed thing but that it varies from person to person and across the life of a person, so periods of asexuality or celibacy (Scherrer, 2008), or of heightened sexual desire and activity (Irvine, 2005; Keane, 2002), should not be pathologized.

In addition to challenging the notion of 'dysfunctional' sex inherent in more conventional approaches, the consideration of meanings also offers an alternative way of working with what the DSM and ICD term 'paraphilias' (see above). Instead of pathologizing certain forms of sexual practice and identity, the existential therapist would attempt to bracket personal and political preferences, and to horizontalize (Adams, 2001), regarding all forms of consensual sexual activity equally. They would then, as above, examine the meanings of each practice or fantasy for the client within their wider context and worldview, if indeed it is an issue the client feels is relevant to therapy. In the case of BDSM,[4] for example, for most BDSM practitioners attending therapy, their BDSM practices are not pertinent to their presenting issue (Kolmes et al., 2006) and there is no evidence of a link between BDSM and psychological difficulties (Moser and Levit, 1987). For those where it is relevant, perhaps more commonly the case in sexual therapy than in therapy more broadly, even a single practice – such as the common practice of spanking – could have a multiplicity of meanings. For example, it may mean humiliation, a pleasurable physical sensation, a test of endurance, a form of giving up control, a feeling of childishness, the breaking of a taboo, or an act of great intimacy with a partner, amongst many other possible meanings and combinations of meanings (see Langdridge and Barker, 2007 for more on BDSM and Langdridge, 2009, for an example of non pathologizing therapeutic work with a BDSM client).

Sexual issues and relationship dynamics

In addition to recognition of the need to work with multiple meanings of sex and sexuality, sexual issues can be particularly revealing of the ways in which clients relate to others and to themselves. For example, when working with women around issues such as sexual desire and what would be diagnosed as vaginismus, we have been struck by how frequently the tension of being-for-others versus being-for-oneself (Sartre, 2005 [1943]) emerges. As de Beauvoir (1949) describes it, most women have no sense of agency, and do not embrace their freedom or the responsibility of that freedom (being-for-oneself). Rather they continue to see themselves through the eyes of others (being-for-others). This includes a focus on appearance: longing to be gazed upon as an object of desire. It also involves a certain infantalization, as rejecting one's freedom requires remaining in a child-like state. And it includes aiming for a romantic relationship with a (male) partner who will continue to reflect their image positively, and – more broadly – gaining pleasure from providing pleasure to others.

Of course much has changed in relation to gender since de Beauvoir's time, particularly in the increases in gender equality, and changed expectations of female autonomy, following second wave feminism. However, these shifts have only gone so far, and even the most recent writing on the topic (e.g. Gill, 2006; McRobbie, 2009) reports that monitoring of physical appearance, infantalization, requirements of heterosexual relatedness, and location of pleasure in the pleasures of others, are bound up in current notions of femininity.

Understanding such existential tensions in relationships can be extremely useful in informing sex therapy work. For example, the first author (Barker, 2011b) worked with a woman with vaginismus in a way that was informed by these theories. Whilst work with this client, Helen, began by exploring her embodied experience of sex, it quickly became apparent that this was largely driven by her assumptions about how she was appearing to her (male) partner during sex, and her fears that her body was unattractive and unruly. Exploring this relationship in greater depth, it became clear that these concerns were related to a wider fear of being rejected and left alone by her partner. The emphasis was entirely on her partner to make decisions about whether the relationship would continue or not; Helen's own role in this seemed only to be to make herself as attractive as possible to him in order that he would not leave her.

While exploring these ideas of being-for-others, the focus of therapy shifted from sex and romantic relationships to relationships with others more generally. Towards the middle of therapy, the following exchange took place:

H: Is it okay to have a rant? [laughs quite joyfully at the thought of it]
M: Absolutely. This is your space to be wherever you are today. And I'm keen to hear what's got you so stirred up.
H: [raised but amused voice] It's this doctor at work. He's always leaving extra work for us and yesterday, right at the end of my shift, he dumped down a load of files for me to go through.
M: You're fuming about this aren't you? [smiles]
H: Yes I am. Because I just went ahead and did it. Again. It's just like everywhere.
M: Everywhere?
H: At home as well.
M: At home?
H: Yes because my mum's had a tough time and I always have to be there for her.
M: So everywhere you have to do things for other people?
H: And I'm sick of it. I always have to be the good friend, the good nurse, the good daughter, the good girlfriend. [counts them off on her fingers]
M: And what's that like?
H: [sighs] Knackering.

Over the course of the rest of the therapy there was an oscillation between Helen's anger at other people for making demands upon her, and concern for how they saw her and a desire to keep that gaze positive. Helen gradually shifted away from a worldview where she had to be seen in a positive light by everyone all of the time, towards one where she could make her own choices and bear the fact that she might not be viewed approvingly. Interestingly, as this unfolded, Helen became more aware of aspects of her partner that were problematic for her, such as his drinking, and was able to communicate this to him, and to see that she was choosing to remain in the relationship and might choose otherwise depending on how it progressed. With sex, she determined only to engage when she was 'in the mood' for it, and the pain went away (see Barker, 2011b, for a fuller description of this case illustration).

Of course this example involved working with an individual client, rather than with both (or more) people in a relationship. Under such circumstances issues, including sexual ones, are conceptualized as co-constructed and it is useful to explore the dynamic between partners and what each brings to the situation. For example, one might have one-to-one sessions with both clients to explore the meanings they have around sex and how these fit in their wider worldviews (given that these are often taboo topics), as well as joint sessions in which they communicate these to one another and assess how these colour their interactions. In addition, it would be useful to explore sexual and other interactions between them in detail, to understand how each response becomes a stimulus for the other as it is filtered through their meanings.

Conclusions

All therapists need to engage in broader dialogues with colleagues in the areas of sex and sexuality in an attempt to move beyond the narrow understandings of these that are often in play in sex therapy settings and wider culture, and which may well hinder, rather than help, clients who are struggling with such issues. An existential perspective on such matters offers up a way that may enable all therapists to better address issues of sex, sexuality and embodiment within their work, with the focus on understanding the experience of the client in its totality rather than the imposition of pre-existing categories of meaning of diagnostic labels upon them.

Notes

1. Being content to remain in the gender that one was assigned at birth.
2. Beyond the binary of male and female.
3. Not identified by gender.
4. This stands for bondage and discipline, dominance and submission, and sadomasochism, and is the encompassing term most frequently used by the communities themselves.

References

Adams, L. G., Harper, A. L., Johnson, E. P. and Cobia, D. C. (2006) 'New mothers and sexual intimacy: an existential framework for counselling', *The Family Journal: Counselling and Therapy for Couples and Families*, 14 (4), 424–429.

Adams, M. (2001) 'Practising phenomenology: some reflection and considerations', *Existential Analysis*, 12 (1), 65–84.

American Psychiatric Association (2013) *Diagnostic and Statistical Manual of Mental Disorders*, 5th edn, Washington, DC: American Psychiatric Association.

Attwood, F. (ed.) (2004) *Mainstreaming Sex: The Sexualization of Western Culture*, London: I. B. Tauris.

Bancroft, J. (2009) *Human Sexuality and its Problems*, 3rd edn, London: Churchill Livingstone Elsevier.

Barker, M. (2011a) 'Existential sex therapy', *Sexual and Relationship Therapy*, 26 (1): 33–47.

Barker, M. (2011b) 'De Beauvoir, Bridget Jones' pants and vaginismus', *Existential Analysis*, 22 (2), 203–216.

Barker, M. and Richards, C. (in press) 'Review of *Human Sexuality and its Problems* by John Bancroft', reviewed in *Feminism and Psychology*.

Boyle, M. (1993) 'Sexual dysfunction or heterosexual dysfunction?' *Feminism and Psychology*, 3 (1), 73–88.

Butler, C., O'Donovan, A. and Shaw, E. (eds) (2010) *Sex, Sexuality and Therapeutic Practice*, London: Routledge.

COSRT (2011) The College of Sexual and Relationship Therapists website, http://www.cosrt.org.uk (accessed 22 August 2011).

de Beauvoir, S. (1997 [1949]) *The Second Sex*, trans. T. M. Parshley, New York: Vintage.

Denman, C. (2004) *Sexuality: A Biopsychosocial Approach*, London: Palgrave Macmillan.

Gill, R. (2006) *Gender and the Media*, London: Polity Press.

Gray, J. (2003) *Mars and Venus in the Bedroom*, London: Vermilion.

Grosz, E. (1994) *Volatile Bodies: Toward a Corporeal Feminism*, Bloomington, IN: Indiana University Press.

Irvine, J. M. (2005) *Disorders of Desire*, Philadelphia: Temple University Press.

Jackson, S. (2006) 'Feminist perspectives on female sexuality', presentation at the 2nd European Female Sexual Dysfunction Conference 'The Picture in 2006', London, 21 September.

Kaplan, H. S. (1974) *The New Sex Therapy: Active Treatment of Sexual Dysfunction*, New York: Brunner/Mazel.

Kaplan, H. S. (1979) *Disorders of Sexual Desire*, New York: Brunner/Mazel.

Kaschak, E. and Tiefer, L. (2001) *A New View of Women's Sexual Problems*, New York: Haworth.

Keane, H. (2002) *What's Wrong with Addiction?* Melbourne: Melbourne University Press.

Kleinplatz, P. J. (1998) 'Sex therapy for vaginismus: A review, critique and humanistic alternative', *Journal of Humanistic Psychology*, 38 (2): 51–81.

Kleinplatz, P. J. (ed.) (2001) *New Directions in Sex Therapy: Innovations and Alternatives*, Philadelphia: Brunner-Routledge.

Kleinplatz, P. J. (2003) 'What's new in sex therapy: from stagnation to fragmentation', *Sex and Relationship Therapy*, 18, 95–106.

Kleinplatz, P. J. (2004) 'Beyond sexual mechanics and hydraulics: humanising the discourse surrounding erectile dysfunction', *Journal of Humanistic Psychology*, 44 (2), 215–242.

Kolmes, K., Stock, W. and Moser, C. (2006) 'Investigating bias in psychotherapy with BDSM clients', in P. Kleinplatz and C. Moser (eds), *SM: Powerful Pleasures*, Binghamton, NY: Haworth Press.

Kutchins, H. and Kirk, S. A. (1997) *Making Us Crazy: DSM: The Psychiatric Bible and the Creation of Mental Disorders*, London: Constable.

Laing, R. D. (1962) *The Divided Self*, London: Penguin.

Langdridge, D. (2005) ' "The child's relations with others": Merleau-Ponty, embodiment and psychotherapy', *Existential Analysis*, 16 (1), 87–99.

Langdridge, D. (2007) *Phenomenological Psychology: Theory, Research and Method*, Harlow: Pearson Education.

Langdridge, D. (2009) 'Relating through difference: a critical narrative analysis', in L. Finlay and K. Evans (eds), *Relational Centred Research for Psychotherapists: Exploring Meanings and Experience*, Chichester: Wiley-Blackwell.

Langdridge, D. and Barker, M. (eds) (2007) *Safe, Sane and Consensual: Contemporary Perspectives on Sadomasochism*, Basingstoke: Palgrave Macmillan.

Le Deouff, M. (1991) *Hipparchia's Choice: An Essay Concerning Women, Philosophy etc.*, trans. T. Selous, Oxford: Blackwell.

McRobbie, A. (2009) *The Aftermath of Feminism: Gender, Culture and Social Change*, London: Sage.

Masters, W. H. and Johnson, V. E. (1966) *Human Sexual Response*, Boston, MA: Little Brown.

Mercer, C. H., Fenton, K. A., Johnson, A. M., Copas, A. J., Macdowall, W., Erens, B. and Welling, K. (2005) 'Who reports sexual function problems? Empirical evidence from Britain's 2000 National Survey of Sexual Attitudes and Lifestyles', *Sexually Transmitted Infection*, 81, 394–399.

Merleau-Ponty, M. (1962) *The Phenomenology of Perception*, trans. C. Smith, London: Routledge & Kegan Paul.

Merleau-Ponty, M. (1964) 'The child's relations with others', trans. W. Cobb, in J. Edie (ed.), *The Primacy of Perception*, Evanston, IL: Northwestern University Press.

Merleau-Ponty, M. (1968) *The Visible and Invisible*, trans. A. Lingis, Evanston, IL: Northwestern University Press.

Merleau-Ponty, M. (1993) 'The experience of others', trans. F. Evans and H. J. Silverman, in K. Hoeller (ed.), *Merleau-Ponty and Psychology*, Atlantic Highlands, NJ: Humanities Press.

Moser, C. and Levit, E. E. (1987) 'An explanatory-descriptive study of a sadomasochistically oriented sample', *The Journal of Sex Research*, 23, 322–337.

Pearce, R. (2011) 'Escaping into the Other: an existential view of sex and sexuality', *Existential Analysis*, 22 (2), 229–243.

Rubin, G. (1992 [1984]) 'Thinking sex: notes for a radical theory of the politics of sexuality', in C. S. Vance, *Pleasure and Danger: Exploring Female Sexuality*, London: HarperCollins.

Sartre, J.-P. (2005 [1943]) *Being and Nothingness: An Essay on Phenomenological Ontology*, trans. H. E. Barnes, London: Verso.

Scherrer, K. S. (2008) 'Coming to an asexual identity: negotiating identity, negotiating desire', *Sexualities*, 11 (5), 621–641.

Smith-Pickard, P. and Swynnerton, R. (2005) 'The body and sexuality', in E. van Deurzen and C. Arnold-Baker (eds), *Existential Perspectives on Human Issues: A Handbook for Therapeutic Practice*, New York: Palgrave Macmillan.

Star, D. (2004) *Sex and the City*, Home Box Office.

Szasz, T. (1974) *The Myth of Mental Illness*, New York: Harper and Row.

Ussher, J. M. and Baker, C. D. (1993) *Psychological Perspectives on Sexual Problems: New Directions in Theory and Practice*, New York: Routledge.

Wincze, J. P. and Carey, M. P. (2001) *Sexual Dysfunction: A Guide for Assessment and Treatment*, London: Guilford Press.

Winton, M. A. (2001) 'The medicalization of male sexual dysfunctions: an analysis of sex therapy journals', *Journal of Sex Education and Therapy*, 25, 231–239.

World Health Organization (2007) *International Classification of Diseases*, 10th edn, World Health Organization. Available at: http://apps.who.int/classifications/apps/icd/icd10online (accessed 22 August 2011).

Yalom, I. D. (1991) *Love's Executioner and other Tales of Psychotherapy*, London: Penguin.

Yalom, I. D. (2001) *The Gift of Therapy*, London: Piatkus.

CHAPTER 5

The Challenge of Being Yourself while Being Part of a Couple: Bad Faith and the Couple's Dilemma

BETTY CANNON AND REED LINDBERG

The dilemma of being our self and allowing our partner to be himself or herself while being part of a couple is an important issue in existential philosophy and couples' therapy. In working with couples, we find that existential philosopher Jean-Paul Sartre's ideas on bad faith, or lying to oneself about the nature of reality, are particularly useful in allowing us to understand and work with couples' dilemmas. Sartre's insights provide the theoretical basis for Applied Existential Psychotherapy (AEP), the modality we have developed and taught over the past twenty-three years. Students tell us that a Sartrean perspective gives them a fresh way of working both with couples and individuals on relationship issues.

Sartre and Simone de Beauvoir were companions for more than fifty years in a highly creative and mutually enhancing relationship. De Beauvoir and Sartre had an unusual relationship by conventional standards in that they were open to other lovers. They considered their own relationship 'essential' while referring to their secondary partners as 'contingent'. In this they perhaps presage some of the arrangements of contemporary polyamorous couples or communities as well as many male gay couples – drawing the attention of couples' therapists to the fact that not all successful relationships look alike. The point, of course, is not the choice of a relationship modality such as monogamy or polyamory. Rather it is to encounter each other and our free development in ways that still cherish and support relationship.

The impact of Sartre's and de Beauvoir's relationship on their contingent lovers has sometimes been called into question. Nelson Algren, for example, remained bitter about his relationship with de Beauvoir. And other lovers have sometimes been appalled by the posthumous release of Sartre and de

Beauvoir's correspondence. Nonetheless, Sartre and de Beauvoir frequently regarded these people as part of their 'family' and were often amazingly loyal to them. In their primary relationship, they seem to have largely kept the pledge of transparency and respect for each other's freedom that they made early in the relationship. There can also be little doubt about the literary and philosophical fruits of their commitment.

Like de Beauvoir and Sartre, we believe it is possible to develop a more rather than less authentic relationship style – one that can be lived with commitment and freedom. We also believe that living in such a relationship can be deeply enjoyable and enriching. No doubt, since bad faith is a universal human temptation, we will often fail at this. When we do so, it is important to remember that Sartre does not define bad faith as a moral failing but as an ontological propensity born of the human condition. Hence we will be able to hold our failures lightly rather than to make them a source of unhelpful self-castigation. At the same time, Sartre does make it clear that bad faith does not work as well as authentic engagement because it does not acknowledge the fundamental conditions of being human.

Bad faith and interpersonal misery

Sartre's concept of bad faith (1972: 86–116) provides a lens for looking at what may go wrong in relationships. Bad faith comes in two forms. The first is overemphasis on facticity – or pretending to be a fact in a world without freedom. This is the form that Sartre himself tends to emphasize. When we engage in this form of bad faith, we attempt to use our partner to create a solid sense of self as object. Our relationship manoeuvres are designed to circumscribe our own and our partner's freedom. If we succeed in doing this, we may find to our surprise that we have traded excitement for security. The juice has gone out of the relationship.

The second form of bad faith is overemphasis on freedom – or pretending to be free in a world without facts. Pretending to be absolutely free without regard for circumstances or the needs of our partner leads to failure to be in a relationship at all, failure to explore the depths of being with another, or failure to show concern or care for our partner. As Sartre's play *The Flies* (1989 [1943]) illustrates, only committed freedom has meaning. Ungrounded freedom is manic in the sense of ignoring the constraints of the real world or the web of human interconnections. The dilemma is how to have an authentic relationship that respects the freedom of each partner while allowing for the possibility of commitment.

Both forms of bad faith in interpersonal relationships derive from our ontological position as human beings. What happens is that we discover the *look* of the other (Sartre, 1972: 340–400) – the look that lets us know that we have an outside in the world that is not in our own possession or control. It is instead in the possession of another consciousness. It is the other person, and not myself, who is able to view me 'objectively' as a person with certain characteristics and qualities. This discovery leads me to attempt to reclaim this outside by merging with the other in various ways, thereby attempting to take the viewpoint of the other on myself. Sartre (1963 [1952], 1981 [1971]) later expanded this concept of the *look* to include two other modes in which we become aware of ourselves as objects for the other: the *touch* and the *word*. Couples' interactions form intricate webs of looks, touches and words that impact each other and their relationship.

Inauthentic relationships lead to manoeuvres to constrict our own and each other's freedom – or to avoid commitment. These include inauthentic love, desire lived inauthentically, hate and indifference. Such manoeuvres become part of a sadomasochistic circle that precludes authentic relationship. Inauthentic love, from this perspective, is at bottom the desire to be loved. It attempts to absorb the partner's freedom in order to use it to create a certain kind of self as object. It is coercive because one's lovability and validity as a person seem to rest on it. It fails because we cannot become the 'world' to our beloved, as lovers like to say. Our beloved is a free subject like ourselves with his or her own projects and needs. Hence our beloved may turn and look at us differently than we would desire.

The failure of love may lead us to turn to inauthentic desire, which takes the opposite perspective. It involves an attempt to be the sovereign subject for whom the partner is only a desirable object. It fails because desire requires a 'double reciprocal incarnation' (Sartre, 1972: 508). What Sartre means by this is that we too must become flesh in order to enjoy our partner as consciousness made flesh. At this point, vulnerability and awareness of oneself as an object of desire re-enter the picture.

When love fails, Sartre says it may degenerate into masochism – the attempt to make oneself into a debased or humiliated object. When desire fails, Sartre says it may degenerate into sadism, the attempt to force our partner to incarnate himself or herself in pain or humiliation at our will – to ride roughshod not only over our partner's body but over his or her thoughts and feelings as well. Perhaps the appeal of sadomasochism in fantasy and practice derives in part from this universal tendency of love and desire to become combustible in this way. Both sadism and masochism fail because both we and our partner are simultaneously free subjects and objects beneath each other's gaze. I cannot escape the possibility that my partner may turn and see my sadistic cruelty for what it is. And I cannot escape the secret knowledge that it is I who masochistically play the humiliated object.

This may lead us to take one of two other positions, which also fail. The problem is that we cannot escape from the sadomasochistic circle by a retreat into hate, which Sartre says derives from despair, nor can we adopt a position of mere indifference. We will always be imprinted with the *look* of the other even if we attempt to kill or ignore it because, having once experienced this, we cannot escape knowing that we have the possibility of being pierced by the other's perspective on us. Hence in therapy we sometimes run across clients who years after a love relationship has ended are still arguing obsessively against the devaluating perspective of a lost partner on the self.

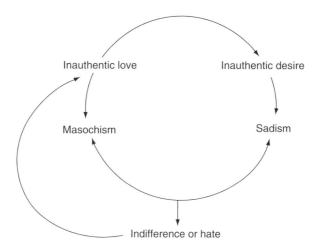

Figure 5.1   The sadomasochistic circle.

We might try diagramming the sadomasochistic circle that Sartre says leads to the 'conflict of consciousnesses' as shown in Figure 5.1.

The circle may be entered at any point on the diagram. The couple caught in an inauthentic relationship cannot escape from the circle except through a radical change in their way of being in the world and with each other – a change that Sartre refers to as a 'conversion' to respecting and valuing their own and each other's freedom.

The situation is further confounded by the fact that the couple also experiences itself as an 'us-object' in the eyes of other people (Sartre, 1972: 537–547). Sartre notes that lovers often prefer to shut out the rest of the world in the early stages of romantic involvement. Later on they will argue about how you or I make 'us' look in the eyes of others – or perhaps narcissistically attempt to impersonate the 'perfect couple' in the eyes of the community. The agonizing instability of a set of shifting dyads penetrated by the look of a 'third' is well represented in Sartre's play *No Exit*. The resulting conflicts lead his character Garcin to declare at the end of the play that 'Hell is other people' (Sartre, 1989 [1944]: 41).

Couples therapists see varieties of that 'hell' every day in their offices. Usually it is a manifestation of one or the other form of bad faith – as lived both in the dyad and in the couple's idea of their objectification in the eyes of others. Both forms of bad faith are attempts to evade the truth that relationships pose an inherent risk and an inherent paradox. We want freedom, excitement and spontaneity. But we are afraid that these will threaten the security of the relationship, or our sense of self. Or we are afraid that commitment will infringe on our freedom. Hence we engage in one or the other form of bad faith. We either embrace a freedom that is unanchored in reality or genuine care and intimacy, or we settle for a security that strangles the aliveness of the relationship. Or we alternate between the two.

Joan put this dilemma very cogently in a session with her partner Chris. She said, 'I want you in a box. I want to see you as fixed. I don't want you to move in any way, or change. You might leave, or not love me. But I don't want you to be boring!'

Exactly!

Is authentic love possible?

Many readers of *Being and Nothingness* view Sartre's perspective on human relationships as inherently conflictual and pessimistic. Only in a provocative footnote does Sartre (1972: 534) allow for the possibility for a 'radical conversion' leading to 'an ethics of deliverance and salvation' from the sadomasochistic circle described there. This footnote opens the door to a concept of authentic relationship – love and desire lived in good faith rather than as an escape from freedom and responsibility.

Sartre would later say that all of the relationships described in the section entitled 'Concrete Relations with Others' were in bad faith. He says in an interview in 1975 that beginning with his biography of Jean Genet he had changed his position a bit to allow for more positivity in love. He even goes so far as to give this as his reason for writing the book:

> I wrote Saint Genet to try to present a love that goes beyond the sadism in which Genet is steeped and the masochism that he suffered (Sartre in Schlipp, 1981: 13).

In other words, Sartre wishes to suggest the possibility for a love that transcends the bad faith version described in *Being and Nothingness*.

What does this more authentic love look like? And what is required for a couple to move in this direction? Obviously authentic love must avoid the twin pitfalls of bad faith relationships – overemphasis on facticity and overemphasis on freedom. Interestingly many approaches to couples' therapy themselves founder on one or the other of these poles of bad faith. They either emphasize differentiation over commitment and togetherness – or security over freedom and risk taking. And while they have much to teach us about one or the other of these matters, what is needed is a couples' approach that emphasizes both.

We think Sartre's philosophy provides the ground that will allow us to keep this dual emphasis in sight. It gives us the basis for understanding how couples may develop the capacity for genuine mutuality and authentic love. Sartre, in his later philosophy, says that the potential for positive reciprocity is built into the human condition. He defines reciprocity as 'a free exchange between two men who recognise each other in their freedom' (Sartre, 1982 [1960]: 110). Reciprocity, positive or negative, is there whether we like it or not. It is there because, as meaning-making beings, we comprehend (and, of course, sometimes misunderstand or twist) each other's intentions. Negative reciprocity leads to conflict and violence. Positive reciprocity leads to mutuality, care and authentic love.

In positive reciprocity, instead of attempting to manipulate or change each other, we remain open to each other, and in doing so realize that we cannot *not* affect each other. We are also able to be vulnerable and to *appeal* to each other for the *help* that we need. In his unfinished *Notebooks for an Ethics,* written shortly after *Being and Nothingness* and published posthumously, Sartre (1992 [1983]: 275–289) establishes these two concepts as the basis for ethical relationships between human beings. If we cannot allow ourselves the vulnerability of appealing, we will never be open to our partner's help. If we cannot help, we can never establish a mutually satisfying relationship.

The *appeal* is a gift to the other since it recognizes the other's freedom as well as one's own. One opens oneself up to the other with the full recognition that the other can refuse one's appeal because the other is free. The appeal differs from a *demand* in which I treat the other as an object who must (because of duty, role, coercion or some other imperative) do as I say. People tend almost naturally to respond to appeals (they can be as simple as asking directions of a stranger) because there is a kind of joy in helping each other move forward in life – unless there is an intransigent conflict that prevents this unfolding.

Many people have difficulty making appeals rather than demands. This is often the case because early in their lives they discovered that their appeals were refused or that they were shamed or humiliated for asking. Lovers must appeal to each other if love is to flower. Sartre, in his biography of Genet, has a beautiful passage in which he describes the appeal on a physical/emotional level that lovers make to each other. Contrasting Genet's solipsism with real love, Sartre (1963: 327) says that it 'is the appeal of the Other that makes the reality of love'.

Such an appeal is not merely intellectual or verbal. It takes place on the level of bodily lived experience. Sartre (1963: 327–328) says:

> We are drawn, then held, by the promise of parted lips, by the expectation that we read in the Other's eyes. In order to be able to love a voice, a face, we must feel that they are calling out for love.

He continues:

> In order to be completely true, a love must be shared; it is a joint undertaking in which the feeling of each is the substance of that of the Other. Each of the two freedoms addresses the other, captivates it, tempts it, it is the Other's love of me that is the truth of my love.

If we lack the capacity to appeal to each other, a capacity that requires vulnerability and confidence at the same time, love cannot get off the ground.

The inability to provide *help* in response to a partner's *appeal* is equally problematic in a relationship. Narcissism, the inability to even grasp one's partner's appeal unless it mirrors one's own grandiosity, is perhaps the most obvious example. So is the demand for freedom without commitment. The anxiety that provokes us to try to control our partner's attitude toward the self ultimately also manifests as lack of care. And the hostility and indifference that build up in inauthentic relationships lead to a lack of care. We must be able to appeal and to offer help in authentic partnerships.

What happens to the *look* of the other in the case of genuine mutuality? Hazel E. Barnes says it develops into the *look-as-exchange*. This is different from the conflictual looks described in *Being and Nothingness*. It also goes beyond the 'we' of the common project described there, though romantic partners often do develop a common project. Barnes (1973: 88) regards such a look not as 'a union of subjects but a mutual affirmation of respect for the Other as subject'. It resembles Sartre's enterprise of 'love' as described in *Being and Nothingness* but lacks the 'attempt to assimilate the Other's freedom'. The look-as-exchange involves the usual subject-object alternation, but with the added intention of positively understanding the Other's world and using this understanding to enhance both self and other (Barnes, 1978: 333–334). The look-as-exchange is marked not by hostility or fear but by mutual receptiveness. We can easily see it as lying at the heart of what Sartre in his later works referred to as positive reciprocity and as a fundamental component of authentic love.

From Sartre's perspective, such a look requires transparency rather than secrecy from both parties. In a late interview, he describes the importance for self-development and relationship of being seen in this loving way. Without the *look* of the other we cannot come to know ourselves. Our experience remains reflectively dark or unknown to ourselves when it is not revealed to a loving other. Sartre (1977: 12) says that:

> this dark region that we have within ourselves, . . . [which] is at once dark for us and dark for others, can only be illuminated for ourselves in trying to illuminate it for others.

Hence he thinks that 'transparency should always be substituted for secrecy'.

What then makes it possible to move from negative to positive reciprocity, demand to appeal, and secrecy to transparency? What is required is the 'radical conversion' to a position that embraces our own and the other's freedom. Only then can we abandon the materialist attitude of seriousness that denies freedom in favour of facticity. This involves a movement from what Sartre calls the *spirit of seriousness* to what we like to call (following Sartre's lead) the *spirit of play*. A playful attitude allows us to let go of the attempt to substantialize self and other. According to Sartre (1972: 740–741) play is the 'least possessive attitude' and hence 'releases subjectivity'.

The couple engaged in authentic relating begins to take a 'playful' rather than a 'serious' attitude in the sense that they no longer insist on predictability and reliability at the expense of spontaneity. They are able to let go and encounter each other anew as the relationship unfolds and develops. At the same time, they are able to engage and to care – to make a commitment to the relationship and to each other.

Working with couples: toward authentic relationship

Space does not permit a full elaboration of our approach to couples therapy. While we incorporate techniques and insights from many other therapies (including psychoanalytic, family systems, and Gestalt and other experiential approaches), Sartre's philosophy provides our conceptual framework. Sartre also helps us understand our role as therapists working with couples. The AEP couples' therapist fully recognizes that the therapist becomes the Sartrean 'third' who turns the couple into an 'us-object'. Yet similarly to the partners in an authentic love relationship, the AEP couples' therapist strives to become a new kind of other who differs radically from the alienated objectifying third of *Being and Nothingness* by offering a playful attitude and genuine openness rather than manipulation, judgement or control. The therapist in such a role, like the beneficent other in an authentic love relationship, helps the couple to bring to light and transform the 'dark region' that is unknown because unnamed in their relationship.

Case illustration

An example from the transcript of a videotaped couples' session demonstrates the importance of Sartre's concept of bad faith to our work and gives a look at some of our typical interventions. The partners in this session (Susan and Jessica) are exploring an impasse in their relationship. It is based on bad faith stances that impede the process of making an *appeal* versus a *demand* on the part of Susan, and of asking for and receiving 'help' on the part of Jessica (who had a problem with both appealing and receiving). Toward the end of the session, both partners find themselves starting to revise inauthentic ways of being in the world adopted in childhood to help them manage inherently impossible early situations.

As the session develops, we discover that Jessica is extremely anxious and that Susan's response is to judge her and give her advice about how to overcome her 'problem'. This in turn increases Jessica's anxiety, which again triggers Susan's tendency to give advice. When they hit an impasse in their dialogue, the therapist (Betty) invites each in turn to imagine the other sitting in front of them in an empty chair (a technique borrowed from Gestalt therapy). The imagined dialogues uncover family of origin issues and lead to shifts in their ways of being in the world and with each other.

Betty invites Susan to go first, both as a way to absolve Jessica of the 'identified patient' role and because it is Susan who is expressing more dissatisfaction. Susan begins a dialogue with 'Jessica' in the empty chair. It soon deepens into a dialogue with Susan's mother, whose mental illness and severe depression darkened Susan's childhood. As she continues in little girl mode, she cries out, 'Daddy, where are you?' She realizes that she was handed over by her absent father to her depressed mother. Her response was to develop an identity as 'competent fixer' rather than face distressing feelings of terror and abandonment anxiety. By doing so, she avoided facing the unpleasant reality that she really couldn't control her mother's moods, and the fear that she might be like her mother. Of course, her mother managed never to get fixed, contributing to Susan's fears that Jessica may also be 'unfixable'.

As the dialogue continues, Susan becomes aware that what she really needs is 'contact' with a mother who does not disappear into the black hole of depression and a partner who does not disappear into the black hole of anxiety. This requires a vulnerability that she has previously covered up with advice giving and a 'know it all' attitude. When she is able to acknowledge her fear and to *appeal* to Jessica for contact based on her own need, rather than to *demand* that Jessica change and see things her way, she gets a much softer, more open and satisfying response from Jessica. Jessica says, 'I can hear you better now'.

The work then turns to Jessica whose anxiety proves to be such a constant barrier between herself and Susan. The dialogue deepens from Jessica's interactions with Susan to her distress with a mother who tries to fix her rather than hold and comfort her when she is distressed. Her response is to embrace a dangerous world (provided by her father's preoccupation with the apocalypse) in which 'God is out to get me in a hostile universe'. In such a world there is no possibility of getting genuine help or comfort. Betty has her put 'God' in the empty chair. She becomes defiant, 'Go ahead and damn me then'. It was a stance she had adopted as a teen and young adult when she embraced a sexual orientation and lifestyle contrary to her family's religious principles. She also seems to be saying, 'I'll be damned if I'll give up my anxiety and distress'. In response to being shamed, Jessica, like Sartre's Genet, embraces the shameful identity that her parents imposed on her and that her partner dislikes. She wishes to be understood and comforted, but does not believe that this is possible. So instead she will live a life of defiance and misery. She will be free at all costs. She will not expect help.

There is a poignant moment toward the end of the session where all this comes to a head. Jessica notes that her mother never offered hugs or any other physical comfort. Betty invites her to ask Susan for this. When she does so, Susan has trouble with it. She says, 'I'm afraid it will be a bottomless pit'. Betty says, 'Like your mother? Take a look at Jessica. She doesn't look like a bottomless pit to me – just someone in need of a hug'. Betty says this with humour. Susan walks over to Jessica and gives her a full-bodied hug. Jessica allows herself to begin to melt into Susan's arms, although she says it is still difficult to 'trust' this new development. They hold each other for a few minutes and then continue the conversation. Both seem much softer as they look lovingly into each other's eyes. Betty asks Jessica about her anxiety, which Jessica says is much diminished. She asks Susan if for the moment she has the contact she has been wanting. She says she does.

Jessica and Susan, of course, probably have more work to do. Core issues don't usually get resolved in a single session. But if this work continues, each may find herself more and more frequently standing on the brink of radical change in her ways of being herself with her partner. Sartre (1972: 466) describes the moment of radical change as a moment of 'double nothingness'.

It is a moment in which the relationship to the past and future changes together. In undergoing such moments, couples are negating or moving away from an inauthentic past relationship style in the direction of a different future in which they are able to recognize and cherish their own and each other's freedom.

Such transformations can, of course, be unnerving. Hence they may include more than a little existential anxiety as a couple discovers that they no longer recognize themselves or their relational world as they have been up to this point. Anxiety may also be present as one or the other partner discovers the meaning of and need for commitment – recognizing that absolute ungrounded freedom is impossible and that freedom has no meaning except as it is lived in the mutuality of a co-created, committed relationship.

If all goes well, the partners have stepped into the void together, as Jessica and Susan seem to have done. They now have the opportunity to emerge with a new, more exciting, playful, satisfying and authentic way of being themselves with each other. If only one member of the couple makes the leap, this may of course lead to the dissolution or diminishment of the relationship.

We believe a couples' therapy that recognizes the dilemmas of bad faith, even more than individual therapy, offers the opportunity to make the leap together and to come together again in new, more authentic, and satisfying ways.

References

Barnes, H. E. (1978) *An Existentialist Ethics*, Chicago and London: University of Chicago Press.

Barnes, H. E. (1973) *Sartre*, Philadelphia and New York: J.B. Lippincott.

Sartre, J.-P. (1963 [1952]) *Saint Genet: Actor and Martyr*, trans. B. Frechtman, New York: George Braziller.

Sartre, J.-P. (1972 [1943]) *Being and Nothingness*, trans. H. E. Barnes, New York: Washington Square Press.

Sartre, J.-P. (1977 [1975]) *Life/Situations: Essays Written and Spoken*, trans. P. Auster and L. Davis, NewYork: Pantheon Books.

Sartre, J.-P. (1981 [1971]) *The Family Idiot*, vol. 1., trans. C. Cosman, Chicago and London: University of Chicago Press.

Sartre, J.-P. (1982 [1960]) *Critique of Dialectical Reason*, trans. A. Sheridan-Smith, ed. J. Ree, London: Verso/NLB.

Sartre, J.-P. (1989) The Flies [1943] and No Exit [1944] in *No Exit and Three Other Plays*, trans. S. Gilbert, New York: Vintage Books.

Sartre, J.-P. (1992 [1983]) *Notebooks for an Ethics*, trans. D. Pellauer, Chicago and London: University of Chicago Press.

Schlipp, P. A. (ed.) (1981) *The Philosophy of Jean-Paul Sartre*, La Salle, IL: Open Court Publishing.

CHAPTER 6

The Challenge of Death: A Confrontation with the Unknown

KAREN WEIXEL-DIXON

We do not experience our own death: not in the reflective manner in which we experience other events. It is the demise of others that often provides an opportunity to recognize the profound implications that death holds for us all.

When a couple encounters the death of a loved one, whether it is a family member, a close friend, or that of one of the partners, it can result in impoverishment, or enhancement, or a combination of these. It is likely to affect both the relationship and life in the broader context.

Many people have given little thought to the eventuality of death that touches us all; it might be said that there is no right way to prepare for this occurrence. So when couples are confronted with such a loss, they are often distressed and shocked by the emotional and behavioural upheavals that can accompany a pending, current or past bereavement.

An existential perspective on death

Death anxiety is generally recognized by existential therapists as a fundamental theme and, as such, it will also be a concern central to relationship therapy.

In Heidegger's seminal text *Being and Time* (Heidegger, 1962), the author outlines several proposals on the significance of death. Polt (1999) proposes the term 'mortality' to further clarify Heidegger's theme on death:

> Mortality is an ongoing condition of human beings, not a one-time event; it is a possibility that essentially belongs to us, not an actual happening. (Polt, 1999: 87)

We may not experience our own death, but live in constant anticipation of the event.

As both an eventuality and a possibility, death confronts us with the unknown: we do not know the how or when of our final moment; even suicide presents this contingency (it might be interrupted by chance, for example). This sense of contingency, for ourselves, our loved ones, for all circumstances, insinuates itself into the very fabric of our lives, and contributes to the persistent and vague anxiety commonly referred to as 'existential angst' (the term 'angst' is used to indicate an inherent quality of human existence, in contrast to anxiety, which is an emotional response; however, I employ the more general term in this chapter).

> In anxiety we are brought into a relationship with our own death. As death is something that cannot be confined to a particular moment or period of time, and yet can materialise at any moment, it is essentially and profoundly indefinite. The indefiniteness ... demonstrates ... the fragility and unreliability of this world. None of the meanings, the connections, the narratives given to us by our social world can protect us from death. (Bracken, 2002: 138)

As we shall see, the unexpected death of a loved one can jolt us from our complacency about the contingency of life.

Case illustration

Geri and Mark came to see me in preparation for their impending nuptials; they were in their early thirties. Until recently, Geri had been quite confident about their decision to wed: in the last few weeks, she had become nervous and volatile, and Mark felt he was being held at arm's length, as she would not talk about what was going on for her. They were hopeful that relationship counselling would provide some 'exercises' to help her control her irritability and outbursts; Mark wanted to know how he could best support Geri, as nothing he did seemed to offer her much comfort, leaving him feeling helpless and inadequate.

Geri's session

In the individual session that I offered each of them subsequent to our joint session, Geri confided that she was having recurring dreams and fantasies with reference to her first husband, Nick, who had died two years previously in an airplane crash. The content of the dreams were less significant for Geri than the fact that she was somehow preoccupied with images of her former spouse, Nick. 'Why am I having these thoughts?' and 'Is this still part of the mourning process?' were some of the questions she posed.

Geri and her former spouse had enjoyed six years of a 'loving and lasting (she thought) relationship', before it ended unexpectedly and abruptly. 'Why entertain a situation in which it could happen again?' she entreated me. This latter issue became one of her key concerns.

Geri's reluctance to discuss this with Mark was based on her feeling that she was 'pathetic' and 'immature', and possibly 'mentally unstable', for not having previously worked through some of these concerns. If she told him how she really felt, it might frighten him (as well as her), or he might change his view about who she was. She wondered if it was preferable to push him away before they made the public commitment, without a true account of her concerns, in order to preserve her image in his eyes and, more importantly, to preclude the possibility of suffering the same kind of grief her previous relationship had provoked.

Our conversation turned to Geri's views on her own death, what this might mean for her, what hopes and assumptions she had about the event, and certainly what were her fears. These were themes that had been discussed superficially previously, subsequent to her husband's demise, but only in the context of the religious beliefs held by her family, and their clergy. The exploration we now engaged in centred on what was truly significant for her, and how her beliefs converged and diverged from those of her friends and family.

Geri's family, and that of her former husband, had also expressed their opinions that it would be better for her to 'move on', and that they were certain that Nick would have wanted her to have a life that included love; Geri was somewhat suspicious of these sentiments, and imagined that the families were actually worried that they would be burdened with the responsibility of her well-being if she was alone.

When I queried what it was that she felt uncomfortable about with reference to these comments from her family, she replied with vehemence that it 'was the lack of truth' in their statement, and that she felt she was being coerced by their apparent 'good will': it came to light that Geri did appreciate that they did have good intentions, but they also had agendas of their own with reference to their obligations to her. This led to a discussion of 'truth', and the pros and cons of 'truth-telling', which had a significant bearing on her current dilemma.

Naturally, Geri also harboured some apprehensions as to what my perspective might be on her confessed fears. I made it clear that I did not hold any concern for what might have been perceived as her inability to 'move on', or her lack of 'closure' with reference to the loss of her former partner. In the first instance, I felt she needed to 'hear' herself express her deepest anxieties, and to have them heard as valid and appropriate. My respect for her experiences was demonstrated in my attempt simply to explore them, in an effort to discover, in conjunction with her, further elements of her assumptions and feelings about life, love and death.

As stated previously, I did not harbour concerns about Geri's lack of 'closure' regarding the death of her first husband: bereavement models that employ such concepts have a tendency to over-simplify the very personal process of grief. Young concurs:

> The stage models ... tend to undermine the complexity of the bereavement process and its individual nature. (Young, 2009: 164)

I preferred, in keeping with the issues as the client presented them, to share the exploration of Geri's experiences as they came to light.

Additionally, as all existential givens are inter-related, to single out grief as the only concern would be curtailing a deeper and more extensive therapeutic endeavour. Young proposes:

> all therapy involves dealing with loss of some kind…all experiences are explored in relation to each other and to the whole context of our life…(Young, 2009: 171)

Mark's session

After a cordial greeting, I opened the session with: 'Have you had any thoughts since our first session together?' (I usually start every session with an open question like this, as the client is usually in a very different place in their processes than the last time we met).

Mark was ready to talk. It had been two days since I had seen Geri for her private session, and already things were changing between the partners. In his first individual session, Mark admitted that he had previously held some suspicions regarding the nature of Geri's unusual behaviour, and Geri had spoken to Mark about some of her concerns in the last few days: it had been an emotional and tearful exchange for both of them.

Mark had been close to Geri's ex-husband, one of a trio of men who had passed from boyhood to maturity together. When Nick died suddenly, Mark had been the first to offer Geri a safe place to air her grief: they had been able to comfort each other in their mutual, if different, loss. It was a year subsequent to the accident that they had acknowledged romantic feelings for each other, and decided to marry.

Mark commented: 'I am seriously concerned about letting Geri down. I feel so fortunate to be with her, to be here for her, and lucky to be the one who has survived so many of life's difficulties. It does scare me, what happened to Nick [Geri's late husband]. It made me feel so…vulnerable, made me realize life is so short, and can be taken from anyone at anytime…[pause] I really want to protect Geri from harm and suffering, but I am not sure I am up to the job – it's not up to me anyway, is it? Life is like that…but what further assurances can I give her?' These comments were delivered with great frustration.

We explored Mark's concerns and his anger in the face of such exposure to the vagaries of existence. I pursued the naïve questions: 'What is it you fear so much, exactly?' and 'Can you say more about what it is you are angry about, and threatened by?' He seemed keen to look deeply into these matters, and he stated and then sometimes recanted his assumptions and assertions about what others expected, and what God might expect. He expressed surprise at the emotional surges that he experienced during this session.

He too, much like Geri, railed at the lack of control they had over the circumstances of life. Mark subscribed to Christian beliefs, but the inability to ascertain the will of God with any certainty sometimes added to his discomfort; it was difficult for him to decide what exactly was under his control, and what else might be ascribed to the intentions of the Supreme Being. 'How can I know what to do, with so few assurances?' he queried.

Mark's acquaintances who shared his religious beliefs had sought to persuade him that 'everything happened for a reason', and that he had a moral obligation to make this commitment to Geri with a public and religious gesture: his hesitancy was a sign of 'a lack of Faith' on his part, according to these sources. As Mark felt that his concerns were sincere and appropriate in some way, he was confused by these evaluations from his colleagues in faith; in a similar manner as Geri, he had allowed the values of others to obscure his own.

An opportunity

Geri and Mark shared common ground in that they were both gripped with the realization that the events of recent years, and the impending commitment to a future together, had provoked a great deal of anxiety. As is so often the case, this appreciation was related to an encounter with a specific death, that of a loved one: it is important, however, to understand that this anxiety about the uncertainty of life was not caused by the factual event of a death, but, rather, revealed in the situation.

It is also perhaps noteworthy, from an existential perspective, that their concerns were informed by a projected future, as well as the meaning attached to past events.

The death of Geri's husband brought her and Mark face to face with their own; such an encounter with our own mortality and finitude engages us in anxiety – the anxiety that is a condition of living:

> Anxiety is rooted in the realization that life is inevitably moving towards death. (Cohn, 1997: 70)

It should be noted, that even if we lived forever, we would still be finite, as we are not able to keep all our options open with respect to the world changing around us: this is, in part, what makes choice so difficult, and why some may attempt to delude themselves in supposedly refusing to make a choice at all.

In order to mitigate this anxiety, we immerse ourselves in the world of the 'they', the common everyday practicalities and occupations, in an attempt to divert ourselves from the singularity and responsibility with which life burdens us: this is what is referred to as 'inauthentic' existence. It is this position, known as 'falling' (Heidegger, 1962: 264), which allows us to function effectively in the face of what could be crippling realization; however, there is a price to pay for this diversion.

This state of inauthenticity designated by a denial of the givens of existence, notably those of death, finitude and responsibility, was demonstrated in Geri and Mark's deference to the expectations and values held by others: they relied too extensively on sources other than their own moral compasses for the bases of their decisions. Additionally, they sought (in vain) to deny the inevitability of suffering and loss by retreating from a full engagement with life and love.

The amelioration of inauthenticity is 'resolution': it is here we find the opportunity for a different kind of engagement with our existential predicament. In resolution, we are 'ready for anxiety' (Heidegger, 1962: 343):

> The German word 'Entschlossenheit' [translated as 'resolution']...means 'openness', the state of being 'unlocked.' (Cohn, 2002: 89)

What is 'unlocked' is our availability for responsibility: 'choosing to choose', without recourse to external sources to ultimately qualify the meaning or value or motivation for our choices.

We also can become open to the implications of death, and finitude:

> The only way to stop letting the anonymous one dictate to us is to reclaim our authentic being by becoming transparent to our Being-towards-Death. Our mortality is the ultimate truth of our being. The key to becoming authentic is to face our own death and with it our own limitations. (Deurzen, 1997: 39).

Our limitations include imperfect knowledge, unpredictable outcomes, and the uncertainties of life, to name a few: these were very much the issues that Geri and Mark were wrestling with.

It is from the platform of responsibility and resoluteness that we can avail ourselves of the opportunity to live more creatively, to be the authors of our own existence: this might be described as living authentically. We have the freedom to value things as others do, or to choose to do otherwise.

It is in the full realization of our death that we become aware of this singular responsibility:

> The non-relational character of death...individualizes Dasein down to itself. (Heidegger, 1962: 308)

With this statement, Heidegger assigns us the responsibility to engage as we choose with the givens of death, loss, finitude and relatedness without ultimate recourse to excuses, social pressures or external authorities.

Authentic engagement does not eliminate anxiety or suffering: rather it engenders a sense of ownership for one's life. In the face of the inevitability of change, we can become more flexible and responsive to life's vagaries, instead of being bound by the dulling demands of the 'they'.

In relationship work, it is important to explore how people meet these existential challenges, and what effect this has on the relationship(s). Most often it is those who have the courage to review their own perspectives that are able to form and maintain robust relationships, as they have less of an investment in contention. Those who appreciate the possibilities of authentic living, which is *choosing* to *choose even in the face of limited knowledge,* are those who have engaged, at least episodically, with the eventuality of their own death.

Together again

Mark and Geri sat on the sofa together; they had entered the room hand-in-hand, and chose their seating places. To my query as to where we were at this point, Geri offered that it had been a difficult week, but they had been talking more openly about their perspectives. Mark agreed, but added that their talks didn't result in any less hurt and anxiety, but it was better, at least for him, to have a clearer and truer idea of what was happening for Geri.

Geri continued on this theme, and commented that in the same way, it was better for her to know explicitly how Mark was experiencing her distress and fears, and that this enabled them to have a more honest platform on which to understand each other, and to make plans. They had discovered that they each and both had a resilience that could help them to 'work through' the possibilities and limitations of their partnership.

Their plans were to proceed with the wedding, and to continue with the counselling until that date. They felt that the counselling had allowed them to consider the effects of concealing and/or revealing themselves to each other; it was 'negotiation' that would be an ongoing process. Additionally, they stated that there seemed to be 'more room' for requesting support from each other: this request might not always be met with compliance, but stating the needs more openly eliminated fears and suspicions that too often 'acted as a corrosive' to the loving relationship in which they felt they had persevered. This hope of continuing in a loving relationship had been chosen in the face of the eventuality that it might end at any time, and indeed that it would be ended ultimately: they decided it was 'worth it'.

Mark and Geri concluded they were making the 'right choice', with reference to their worldview; however, making the 'right choice' does not preclude suffering – indeed, it is this very assumption that often comes under scrutiny in the course of a reflective enquiry.

The effect upon the therapist

It would be worrying if practitioners were inured to or unaware of their own anxieties about death: such a lapse could disrupt the very essential connection we have with every human being.

To work existentially means we are constantly exposed to the losses anticipated and experienced by our clients, the very same losses we ourselves are challenged with: the loss of loved ones, of opportunities, of health, of the future we had anticipated, to name but a few.

Relationship therapy can provoke my own anxieties: how I am challenged or satisfied in my engagements, how I contribute to the vagaries of any given relationship, how I am able to love or allow myself to be loved. Each story reminds me that I too am at risk: the risk of loss, of rupture to a significant relationship, the risk of hurting another person even unintentionally.

Our own death poses for us, as for our clients, that ultimate loss of existence as we know it: we may have beliefs of an afterlife, but it is still an unknown, and different, realm of being.

These concerns about death and loss should serve to keep us grounded as therapists, and can promote an empathic understanding of and with our clients: we are all facing the same eventuality. We can demand no less courage of ourselves than our clients in engaging with these issues.

The process of exploration

Relationship therapy can offer an opportunity to consider how we are in relation to/with the Other: how we *hope to be experienced by* the Other, and what strategies we employ *in order to achieve this* (as well as what happens when we do *or* do not effect the desired results); *how we experience the Other* and what effect this has on the engagement (whether this is explicitly communicated or not); how the Other *hopes to be experienced* by the party/parties involved in the engagement, and the strategies employed to assure this (and the consequences when these hopes are or are not realized). Additionally, these dynamics described above would also be considered with respect to wider inter-personal and cultural milieux.

These considerations can promote an appreciation for each party to the relationship in question as to how they contribute to the quality of that relationship (this is true for family and group as well). The clarification of these dynamics can reveal what assumptions (which would include values) about ourself, about the Other, about the world, and about the Cosmos that each of us holds; these values and assumptions comprise the 'worldview'. All of these perspectives are inter-related: although one of these concerns may be 'foregrounded' (of primary concern), an exploration of any one will reveal in part the aspects of the others.

A crisis point like that provoked by the death of a loved one can be an opportunity to examine and clarify our worldview: the values and assumptions harboured can become subject to reconsideration and revision. This was the case with Geri and Mark: prompted by the anxiety inherent in a critical decision, their perspectives on life, death, love and relationship were made explicit in our discussions. The effect of the exploration was that they recognized where they had the freedom to take a different stance on their values, and in how they engaged in the many relationships that were an important part of their lives. These particular concerns were, in turn, connected to other existential issues: temporality, meaning, limitations, and the events of the past.

The hoped-for possibility

It might be said that there is a similar aim in both individual and relationship therapy that is grounded in existential thought:

> Existential therapy may see it as its aim to help its clients to free themselves from the disturbing consequences of denial, evasion and distraction by enabling them to change their response to the existential givens... The existential therapist proposes that it is unaccepted aspects of existence itself which are at the core of the disturbance. (Cohn, 1997: 24)

He comments further:

> ...the certainty of death is perhaps the most unacceptable dimension of existence. (Cohn, 1997: 171)

In the situation reviewed in this chapter, both parties to the relationship were attempting to evade the inevitable separation from, and loss of, the loved partner. In order to preclude a form of suffering, they were, seemingly, willing to incur a 'controllable' or 'manageable' loss: the thinking was that if they deprived themselves of the joy of their association, they could evade the greater bereavement. This was a manifestation of an evasion of death anxiety: they might deny themselves a loving relationship in order not to lose it through the ultimate separation.

In the course of our explorations, this formula was revealed with a great deal of anguish, and some shame: it was difficult to really quantify the loss against the gain, and such a consideration seemed somehow to denigrate the significance they had attached to their relationship.

For Geri and Mark there was a loss incurred as well with respect to the assumptions they each held of themselves: after showing previously a great deal of courage in facing the death of husband and friend, their courage seemed to falter at the prospect of another such event; the fortitude that they had assumed was inherent to maturity was apparently depleted, at least temporarily.

They each felt that the former bereavement had not 'strengthened' their ability to meet life's challenges: it had depleted their resources. However, what emerged in the course of their sessions was the concept that the courage they might need again in a future situation would be generated by their care for each other: it would be a product of their bond, in fact, a consequence of it.

Reflections on these aspects contributed to a shift in some of their perspectives: to maintain their loving relationship in the full awareness of such inevitable loss made that choice all the more precious. Additionally, they recognized, although not for the first time, that relationships are both a burden and a blessing, and that love poses as many problems as it solves.

With respect to the wider contexts of family and social networks, they felt that because they respected themselves and each other for the worldviews they had adopted, and in large part created, that they could 'brave', if necessary, the disapprobation that they might encounter from their friends and family who might hold different views about any aspect of their lives. This perspective demonstrated an appreciation of responsibility for their choices.

In our sessions we also discussed more generally the implications of investing so much in the standards and values generally held to be acceptable by social, religious, or cultural sources: abdication of our own perspectives can undermine the sense of ownership for our lives. Aligning ourselves thoughtlessly with popular or prevalent standards may temporarily ameliorate the isolation we experience in assuming our responsibility: it allows us to diffuse the effects of the consequences of our choices.

Conclusion

Yalom (1980) writes extensively on the concept of death and therapy, and how awareness of these and related existential issues can impact on one's life:

> Although the physicality of death destroys man, the idea of death saves him...death is the condition that makes it possible for us to live life in an authentic fashion. (Yalom, 1980: 30, 31)

The death of Geri's husband and Mark's friend provided a profound, and uncomfortable, opportunity to live more authentically: they re-evaluated the bases of their choices, particularly those regarding how to live, and how to love.

Preparing for a future together meant they were faced with attaining something, that is, a loving relationship, that would subsequently, at some point, be lost to them. They could have refused the gift of love in order to avoid the inevitable separation. Such a strategy is reminiscent of Rank's description of the neurotic person as one '...who refused the loan (life) in order to avoid the debt (death)' (Rank, 1945: 126).

Geri and Mark chose instead to treasure the time they would have together, and to face together an uncertain future in terms of the quality and duration of their lives, and of their relationship.

Additionally, their values were reviewed and clarified; the difficult choices were made with reference to their own worldviews. This act of choosing imbued them with a sense of responsibility and creativity in how they might engage with their (existential) issues. Their anxiety might persist, but it would now be better understood, and appreciated as a marker of people who had the power to constructively and authentically engage with these concerns.

References

Bracken, P. (2002) *Trauma: Culture, Meaning, and Philosophy*, London and Philadelphia: Whurr Publications.

Cohn, H. W. (1997) *Existential Thought and Therapeutic Practice*, London: Sage.

Cohn, H. W. (2002) *Heidegger and the Roots of Existential Therapy*, London: Continuum.

Deurzen, E. van (1997) *Everyday Mysteries*, London and New York: Routledge.

Heidegger, M. (1962 [1927]) *Being and Time*, trans. J. Macquarrie and E. S. Robinson, London: Harper and Row.

Polt, R. (1999) *Heidegger, an Introduction*, London: UCL Press.

Rank, O. (1945) *Will Therapy and Truth and Reality*, New York: Alfred A. Knopf.

Yalom, I. (1980) *Existential Psychotherapy*, New York: Basic Books.

Young, S. (2009) 'Working with bereavement: in the midst of life we are in death', in L. Barnett (ed.), *When Death Enters the Therapeutic Space*, London and New York: Routledge.

CHAPTER 7

The Challenges of Meaninglessness and Absurdity Addressed through Myth and Role Play

DONNA CHRISTINA SAVERY

Couples coming into therapy often describe feeling helpless, trapped and empty. In most cases they feel this has happened over time. Through losing the meaning they once had in their relationship they have grown apart. No longer believing in the same ideals and values generates a sense of isolation and loneliness as well as frustration, boredom and fear. These key existential themes reflect the *absurdity* that constitutes the human condition.

As we have seen in other chapters of this book, existential philosophy has a vast body of theory that attempts to tease out what it means to be human and live a meaningful existence, but it is a challenge for both existential therapist and the individuals in a relationship to turn theory into lived experience. A phenomenological approach which uses description to check out what a particular idea or word means to the individual using it, is important as a basic tenet when working with a couple. However, words alone are often insufficient symbols to communicate the complexity of what it means to be human and in relation. Because myth is polysemic and therefore open to such a wide range of meanings it is a valuable tool for exploring existential issues safely. Using it effectively in relationship therapy relies upon the therapist asking insightful questions that help the individuals interpret its meaning for them. Joseph Campbell sums this up neatly in the following quotation:

> There is no final system for the interpretation of myth, and there will never be any such thing. Mythology is, like the God Proteus, 'the ancient one of the sea, whose speech is sooth.' ... But this wily God never discloses even to the skilful questioner the whole content of his wisdom. He will reply only to the question put to him, and what he discloses will be great or trivial, according to the question asked. (Campbell, 1993: 381)

It is common for individuals in relationship therapy to project shortcomings in the relationship onto the other and become focused on blame, each holding onto their own experience as a way of justifying their behaviour, so that the last thing they want to do is understand and inhabit the other's perspective. Using symbolization has the effect of depersonalizing it, and takes away the need to guard against exposure or criticism, enabling couples to explore one another's worldview in a less direct and less threatening way, creating a more open dialogue. For existential therapists, rooting this within a body of philosophical theory and creating a safe space where they can choose to explore it, is paramount. By learning to be more authentic in their choices, each is able to see their roles in the dynamic, and take more responsibility for them.

While this chapter gives examples of how I work with myth in the room and the ways I use role play with my clients, it does not advocate a particular methodology or toolkit (in fact any form of creative expression may be used). I do, however, use the case material and a role play exercise to demonstrate how the work is underpinned by philosophical thought. The existential therapist has her *self* and her mode of relating as her most valuable tools. She needs to be open to whatever the clients bring, to find authentic ways of engaging their passions and creativity through attunement and a co-creative relationship. This helps facilitate clients' exploration of the existential anxieties and issues at the heart of their relationship, and helps them find ways to reconnect meaningfully.

Absurdity and language

Existential philosopher, playwright and novelist, Jean-Paul Sartre defines *absurd* in his seminal work *Being and Nothingness* (2003 [1943]: 649) as 'that which is meaningless'. Albert Camus, one of his contemporaries, expounds upon this notion in his essays, plays and novels, addressing the paradox between 'the human need [for meaning] and the unreasonable silence of the world' (Wood in Camus, 2000: x).

The Theatre of the Absurd, a term coined by Martin Esslin, describes a group of playwrights (including Pinter, Ionesco and Beckett) who explore the fundamental meaninglessness of human existence. His book of the same name examines how the plays address the need for action as well as words. He exemplifies the problems of relying upon language alone to attempt to make sense of meaning in an irrational universe and exposes 'how individuals use language as much to express their thoughts as to hide the very thing they fear disclosing (Esslin, 1991).

'The Sartrean idea of *being as action* [is also] expressed more concretely in [his] novels and plays than in [his] philosophical writing' (Deurzen, 2010: 83) and Sartre's protagonists are judged as much on their words as their actions. In his short story, *The Wall* (1948), Sartre examines how in each moment words are spoken and witnessed; thoughts become actualized into something concrete that may have unforeseeable consequences. Everyone has a choice in whether to speak and what to say, yet often in relationship therapy individuals use language carelessly and find themselves unable to take responsibility for its impact and subsequent consequences. Alternatively they may hold back on what they say for fear of hurting their partner and in so doing they avoid the opportunity of addressing something that may need to be witnessed and explored, before they can engage and move forwards together. It is this withholding of engagement with the other that creates the vacuum in which absurdity arises.

Using language alone in the therapy room can result in both parties being in *bad faith* (Sartre, 2003) as much through what is withheld, as what is said. As such it is no surprise when they lose touch with one another's feelings and empathy disappears. If this fundamental ability to 'relate' disappears, simply talking logically and drawing upon a reasoned approach can reinforce feelings of isolation. Consequently they become more alienated and finding meaning in their relationship becomes more difficult.

Myth and role play

Many modes of therapy draw upon metaphor as a way of enabling clients to see blind spots in their own relationship, by providing safe distance from the pain of it. In existential relationship therapy, through phenomenological enquiry facilitated by the therapist, the individuals (not the therapist) interpret and draw their own meanings and relate this learning to their own relationships.

One of the most powerful forms of metaphor are myths; stories passed down from all cultures and periods, containing universal truths and existential dilemmas, which resonate with what it means to be a human being in relation with others and the world. Existential philosophy has a rich heritage of using myths to illustrate its ideas (i.e. the 'Myth of Sisyphus', Camus, 2000: 107; and the 'Myth of Care', Heidegger, 1962: 242). These stories and their imagery and characters are rich enough for both individuals in the relationship to interpret their own meanings, and they are encouraged to explore and share these with one another as a way of seeing how each has a different worldview and experiences and interprets meaning differently. An approach where the therapist enables the individuals to bypass linguistic defences and layers of *sedimentation* (Merleau Ponty, 1962 [1945]), can open up a whole channel to revealing meaning and provide the key to reconnecting.

The therapist does not need to be an expert in mythologies. By remaining attuned and open to what the client brings a relevant story may strike her. She can draw upon any stories, legends or fables containing characters that face existential dilemmas or struggle with what it means to be human. Therapists can also ask clients to bring in resonant stories, myths, or an archetypal character from their own cultural heritage, and go through a very similar process exploring its meaning for them individually and as a couple. The best characters are often those, like Oedipus, recommended by Aristotle (1997) whose character *traits* lead them to behave and react in certain ways. However, drawing upon the wealth of archetypal characters, who between them display the whole gamut of human traits, provides a rich source of material from many cultures and religions in which couples can identify elements of themselves, their partner and their dynamics through some of the characters' relationships with one another.

Often, the individuals in relationship undertake certain roles that they repeatedly play out. These ways of relating may have become so ingrained that they have forgotten they actually have a choice and, as a result, frequently fail to take responsibility for their part in their dynamic. Role playing characters from myths can help clients discover roles they play in their relationship and how they hide behind these as a way of avoiding facing their authentic selves. In distancing themselves from their 'presenting problems' the fear of feeling exposed is avoided, and as such both parties are likely to take more risks, and be more honest. This can enable them to begin to meaningfully reconnect and begin to see their relationship as less fixed, more fluid and in a constant state of 'becoming' (Sartre, 2003).

The exercise below demonstrates an approach to working with role play that can be used for any myth or story.

Role exercise

1. Read a myth or tell a story that strikes you as resonant or relevant to this relationship.
2. Discuss the clients' views of the defining qualities of any of the characters in the myth and their existential dilemmas. Which of these can they identify with in their own relationship?
3. Are there any characters that they don't like or can't relate to? What feelings does this bring up? Is there a time when they can remember having similar feelings?
4. The clients each choose a character from the myth or create a new character of their own (this can be based on qualities they can relate to, or some of the qualities/traits they feel their partner has). They are encouraged to improvise freely.
5. The therapist helps the clients get into role in turns, using the following prompts as an example: 'Close your eyes and think about the following: How old are you? What gender are you? What job do you do? Tell me about your partner, relatives, and friends? Think about what has happened to you since waking up this morning. What kind of mood are you in? How do you feel about coming to your first therapy session?
6. The therapist then puts the 'character' in the chair, and they role play a therapy session for an agreed amount of time, in front of the partner. (Note: time needs to be left at the end of the session for both partners to discuss how they feel about what they have experienced and seen, with the therapist present. The therapist then helps them to think about what meaning this has in terms of their relationship.)

Case illustration

Echo and Narcissus

Naz and Deepak came into therapy to address ingrained communication problems between them and what Deepak described as 'a mess' following his emotional affair. In joint sessions Naz often became emotional, blaming Deepak for the breakdown in the relationship, causing him to withdraw, often through making a joke or yawning. One of the main themes of the therapy was how Naz felt his actions constituted a betrayal that had led to a lack of meaning in the relationship. When I saw Naz alone for one session, I was struck by how much more present she was than when Deepak was with her, and commented that I had not realized she had such strong opinions. She said Deepak never listened to her so she saw little point in voicing them.

She described how she and Deepak had had an arranged marriage, after which she had gone to live with his family, complete strangers to her, and was constantly undermined by her mother-in-law. She had found this experience so debilitating, and described feeling unlovable, lonely, withdrawn and depressed and had always feared speaking out about what she wanted in case Deepak's family disapproved. This had led to Deepak doing whatever he wanted to do, and over the years he had stopped asking Naz what she wanted. She described Deepak as 'a runaway train; once he's set on a course of action you have no choice other than to go with him or be left behind. He never listens to me; it's as if I don't exist'.

I shared with her the myth of Echo and Narcissus, in which:

> Echo, a nymph, encounters Narcissus, a beautiful young man, and falls madly in love with him. Unable to initiate conversation after a curse placed upon her, she follows him around, repeating only the last words of his sentences. Her unwavering attention leads Narcissus to believing he must be entitled to hero-worship, and he gains an inflated sense of his own importance. Eventually when he no longer needs her adoration, Narcissus tells Echo to go away and as she repeats "away, away, away" she begins to fade away herself until only the echo of her voice remains and can be heard to this day. Artemis curses Narcissus for his cruelty and, unrepentant, he falls in love with his own reflection, drowning in the pool as he tries to kiss the beautiful image he sees underneath the water. Unwilling to look beneath the mask of his beauty, the beautiful narcissus flower which grew in his place is a symbol of self-obsession, entitlement and an unwillingness to look at the true self which lies behind the masks.

Naz was visibly moved but said nothing. When she returned the following session with Deepak, however, she said she had read up a lot on the myth. I asked her how she felt and she said, 'very upset. If you think I'm Echo then I'm doomed'. Deepak then said 'if she's Echo you must be saying I'm Narcissus' (I had consciously made no reference to either of them *being* a character, yet both had assumed this). I noticed that they both seemed to share these opinions in terms of their roles and said that perhaps this was a good place to explore other areas where they might find shared meaning in their dynamic through using role play. To my and Deepak's surprise Naz said she had been wondering what it must feel like to be Narcissus rather than Echo, and offered to role play him.

I asked Naz to close her eyes and imagine she was Narcissus and to think about how *he* was feeling at that moment. As I asked the questions, Naz's voice, posture, positioning and behaviour all changed as her character began to become established. After some role immersion she straddled the chair, assumed a defensive air and then after a brief prompt from me as therapist 'So Narcissus, this is your space to talk about anything you'd like to' replied in role: 'I hope you know how lucky you are to have me here as a client!'

I let 'him' carry on and he spoke about how brilliant 'he' was, how attractive, how nobody understood 'him', how 'he' deserved better, even that stupid wife of 'his' didn't appreciate 'him' and 'didn't realize how fortunate she was to have such an amazing husband'.

Naz really became Narcissus and when I prompted with a reflection or challenge, became defensive, aggressive and even angry, and eventually, sad. After de-roleing, Naz discussed how it had felt 'amazing, liberating'. She couldn't believe how much she'd enjoyed playing such a different role to the one she played in her relationship with Deepak.

Naz had been able to portray what she recognized in him, and through the experience was able to get in touch with some of the emotions and character traits which were present in her but not expressed in her relationship. Always assuming they belonged to Deepak, she became aware of how she was projecting elements of herself onto her husband and his family, as a way of avoiding responsibility for her own thoughts and opinions and always blaming Deepak for their problems, as he made all the decisions.

The myth and role work enabled her to circumvent getting stuck in a place where she had felt too angry to see her part in their dynamic, and through embodying a character that she clearly identified with her husband, she had made links and connections to how some of her own behaviours affected their relationship.

Deepak seemed quite shocked by her role play. When I asked him how it felt to observe, he showed real emotion (something usually only shown by Naz) asking her, 'Is that how you see me? Am I really that awful?'

In the act of witnessing elements of themselves and one another, both gained more awareness of what they projected onto the other, and of the sedimented roles they played out and hid behind to avoid authenticity and taking responsibility. For Naz and Deepak this session was the first breakthrough in what had become entrenched positions, and it became the catalyst for them to begin to see one another's point of view and recognize how they had become very set in their ways of relating. Naz learned to harness her more 'narcissistic' traits and little by little found her voice again. For Deepak the work was slower but whenever Naz reminded him of how she experienced him she stopped him in his tracks (a useful tool for a runaway train)! In being given the space to sit with the anguish this had uncovered, meaning was opened up for this couple.

Sisyphus

Through his fiction Sartre accomplishes the task of creating a *lived sense* of the philosophical ideas he publishes in *Being and Nothingness* (2003). Camus, too, muses on man's relationship to his environment and fate, and how to create meaning in a fundamentally meaninglessness and silent universe. In the following myth:

> Sisyphus, a trickster, is condemned by the Gods and punished with the eternal task of rolling a huge boulder to the top of a mountain, only for it to roll back down to the bottom, repeatedly. Each time on the walk back down he has the choice of whether to give in to his despair, to commit suicide and end his tormented existence or remain defiant, his spirit unbroken in his refusal to be beaten by the Gods. In this brief respite from his toil he chooses to engage again and again with it, and begin the long and exhausting task, chin against stone, face straining under the weight of his burden, to push his rock back up. (Précised version of Albert Camus' telling of the Myth of Sisyphus, 2000)

Sisyphus accepts the ontological conditions of his existence, and through recognition of his ontic choices, uses the only resources he has to create meaning out of an otherwise 'meaningless' existence. Camus argues that the very act of engagement gives Sisyphus's life meaning and helps him to confront its absurdity. He argues that Sisyphus is happy, because he constantly confronts the reality of his existence and chooses life, remaining defiant in spite o*f le quotidien* (the repetition of his day-to-day existence).

The notion of relationship therapy outlined so far in this book has been defined by at least two individuals in a relationship and the therapist. In a dysfunctional relationship, however, or where only one person comes to explore their relationships, myth can be used to explore how an individual may actually avoid relating. In the following case illustration, I demonstrate how I worked with this myth as a way of enabling my client to understanding more about himself in relationships, and as the catalyst to grieve for his dead wife.

Simon, 33, had been seeing me for nearly a year following the suicide of his much-loved wife, Jenny. He remarked early on in the process how he felt no anger towards Jenny for leaving him and the children, knowing she had problems he hadn't been able to help her to overcome. Through Jenny's death he had lost the meaning in his life and was having trouble sleeping, he had no motivation and often felt suicidal himself, saying 'my responsibility for the children is my only reason for continuing to live'.

After many months of therapy, Simon described feeling more hopeful about some areas of his life and tentatively entered a new 'relationship' with Sophia, a mother from his daughter's school. As the weeks progressed, however, he became more despondent about the relationship until one session where he arrived uncharacteristically angry. In nearly four months they had covered the whole gamut of experiences of a courting couple, from flirting, to sex, to love, then to jealousy and (more recently) arguments, silences and accusations – all through the medium of text messaging. They had never even been alone together, apart from brief contact at the school gates. Sophia had used a constant stream of excuses to avoid meeting, so in recent weeks Simon had joined a dating website where he had received interest from other women. Sophia had begun sending him abusive texts, and though he tried to pull away he got drawn back into the 'relationship' whenever a text appeared on his phone.

Simon: I just can't ignore it...I'm infuriated by her, and I must be mad, but I have to respond.
Me: What does this 'relationship' give you?
Simon: I don't know – my head tells me to get out but I just can't. I keep hoping that if we give it a try I could make her happy.
Me: What is it about you that fuels the need to make Sophia happy?
Simon: I don't know. I suspect she'd be a burden around my neck, but I won't know unless we actually give it a try.

I tried to explore what was at the bottom of this, but Simon was confounded as to why he would continue to pursue a relationship with Sophia when there were other women who were available, and who 'wouldn't be such hard work'. I was struck by his allusion to hard work, which was so reminiscent for me of the Myth of Sisyphus, so I introduced the myth. Afterwards Simon was reflective for a while...

Simon: I can see some similarities between him and me, but he has no choice, he has to either push the rock and be miserable, or push it and be positive. I don't even have to pick up the rock, and yet I'm choosing to.

Using a phenomenological approach I helped him to explore why that might be:

Simon: I think Sophia is damaged when it comes to relationships, and I want to make it ok for her...[Long silence]...I guess I felt like this with my wife too.
Me: You wanted to make it ok for your wife?
Simon: [tearfully] I didn't succeed with Jenny, I didn't do everything I could, or if I did it wasn't enough.

I commented that I had noticed he was wearing a Superman T-shirt today. He looked down and said: 'I couldn't save her'.

He became very sad and reflective for some time and I sat with him, touched by his pain, resonating with it. Eventually he spoke.

Simon: I've come in and spent the whole session bitching about Sophia, and I'm leaving with some real insight into myself. I am not just choosing the rock, it is giving me purpose, another reason to keep living, and helping me to get over my guilt about not being able to save Jenny. I guess I'm more like that guy than I thought.

As he left I asked, 'What are you going to do when you leave?'

Simon: [laughing] Check to see if she's sent me a text!

If I had shared my insights that Simon's anger was displaced guilt, and that he was using the safety of a 'simulated relationship' to work through his feelings of guilt and anger about his wife's suicide because he was still too vulnerable to have a 'real' or 'lived' relationship from the start, this would have robbed him of the discovery himself and would have had far less power. Rather than interpreting the function of his anger for him, or questioning him about it by *leaping in* (Heidegger, 1962), I worked metaphorically with the Myth of Sisyphus and the Superman symbol, using phenomenological enquiry to enable him to interpret his own meanings. He was therefore open and able to use this learning to understand more about himself in his relationships.

While this session didn't solve Simon's problems with Sophia, it gave him an awareness of why he was in this 'relationship', and therefore what choices he had in how to move forwards.

If the therapist, or indeed a partner, had read meaning into Simon's behaviour and relayed it to him, he may have been resistant to hearing this, or have felt the need to defend it. This is why it is so valuable to allow the individuals in the relationship to come to their own discovery through a journey facilitated by the therapist. Indeed, rather than providing the answers, the therapist's skill encourages them to ask themselves what mythologist, Joseph Campbell, might call the 'great' questions. As Ionesco's character Mme Martin asks in his famous play *La Cantatrice Chauve:*

Quelle est la morale?

Le Pompier's reply demonstrates that the meaning is in the individual's discovery.

C'est à vous de la trouver. (Ionesco, 1964)

This myth revealed the existential significance of Simon's personal discoveries. He was trapped in a Sisyphean cycle of repetition, wanting to protect and save damaged women, as a way of trying to heal the primal wound. This had been compounded by his wife's death, and despite it being a task he could never succeed in, the Superman T-shirt symbolized his belief that he somehow could, and he had given himself the absurd task of repeatedly trying to 'save women'. Having a relationship with Sophia, despite the pain this caused him, enabled Simon, like Sisyphus, to create some meaning and purpose as a way of avoiding suicide himself. Unlike Sisyphus, Simon had the choice not to pick up the rock, but felt compelled to until he could find another significant rock (a symbol which here signifies purpose as much as it does burden). 'Sartre reminds us, that as we are Nothingness, we need something – a bulwark – to push or work against in order to animate our being' (R. King, private correspondence, 2011).

Trying to remain authentic in one's own search for meaning while attempting to stay 'in' and committed to the relationship is a challenge in all human relationships. Much has been written about living authentically and in *good faith* (Sartre, 2003), but addressing how to do so with another person who is engaging with the same struggles, has been largely uncharted territory (though Chapter 5 of this book explores this area). When clients hit a block in therapy, the problem, about which they cannot see eye to eye or the area where they have found themselves in entrenched positions, often leads to an impasse. Using myth and role as another form of language in the room can help them to move through or around this block to open up whole new ways of relating, and can lead to re-engaging with meaning through encounter with a significant other, to counteract the absurdity of the human condition.

References

Aristotle (1997) *The Poetics*, trans. S. Butcher, ed. R. Koss, New York: Courier Dover Publications.

Campbell, J. (1993) *The Hero with a Thousand Faces*, London: Fontana.

Camus, A. (2000) *The Myth of Sisyphus*, trans. J. O'Brien, intro. J. Wood, London: Penguin Classics.

Deurzen, E. van (2010) *Everyday Mysteries*, 2nd edn, London: Routledge.

Esslin, M. (1991) *The Theatre of the Absurd*, Harmondsworth: Penguin Books.

Heidegger, M. (1962) *Being and Time*, Oxford: Blackwell Publishing.

Ionesco, E. (1964) *La Cantatrice Chauve*, Paris: Gallimard.

Merleau-Ponty, M. (1962 [1945]) *Phenomenology of Perception*, trans. C. Smith, New York: Humanities Press.

Sartre, J.-P. (1948) *The Wall and Other Short Stories*, New York: New Directions.

Sartre, J.-P. (2003 [1943]) *Being and Nothingness*, London: Routledge.

CHAPTER 8

The Challenge of Change, Choice and Loss in Relationship Mediation

JACKY LEWIS

This chapter examines how existentially informed therapist-mediators might work with couples seeking mediation in the separation and divorce process. It covers the difficulties the therapeutically trained mediator faces when trying to engage in a relationship with *two* clients in a way that is meaningful to them both. It considers the change, choice and loss that are inherent in ending a relationship from an existential perspective, drawing on the writings of Heidegger, Sartre, Becker and other existential thinkers to add depth and meaning to the topic. The chapter also considers some of the presenting difficulties within a conflictual separation, where cooperation and continuing care of children are central to the picture. Finally, the author identifies some of the client emotions that therapist-mediators can expect to encounter including disappointment, shame, despair, pride, loss of face and the desire for revenge.

Sensitive and attuned working in this field can lead people in the separation and divorce process towards the understanding that *change, choice* and *loss* are existential 'givens', inevitable in the context of any ending, and to the realization that endings can also be embraced as beginnings. This chapter looks at how mediators can adapt many of existential therapy's central tenets in order to provide effective relationship mediation. As mediation has become more central in the legal world and an increasing number of therapists may start working in this field, existential ideas will provide a rewarding source upon which to draw.

The purpose of mediation when a relationship is ending is to try to help the couple achieve an agreement that will be 'good enough' for them both to live with in order to avoid the difficulties, damage and residual bitterness that can be the result of litigating in court. The couple may have tried 'couples' counselling' to effect a reconciliation without success and have come to realize their intimate relationship is truly unsaveable.

Mediation is the arena that can give both parties a voice without the unpleasantness of litigation; if their dispute ends in court they will not be able to tell their story, or speak about their hurt or despair. The legal parameters in divorce are fairly narrow and litigation is destructive to already fractured relationships; better results regarding agreements for co-parenting and finances can often be achieved in therapeutically informed mediation. Through the medium of phenomenological enquiry, mediators work with the parties to uncover entrenched existential worldviews that are blocking movement towards resolution. Research shows (Law Commission Survey, 1994 in Strasser and Randolph, 2004: 60) that 'between 60% and 75% of *successful* litigants . . . remained dissatisfied with the outcome'; because in court proceedings litigants are *not* in control. The purpose of this chapter is not to show 'how to do' mediation, but rather to show how existential ideas can be useful in helping people to say 'goodbye' to their relationship as a couple, whether same-sex or cross-gender, married or co-habiting, and move on to a truer, more authentic way of living. Most existential thinkers believe we only have one chance at life and that it is important to make the most of this, no matter what the circumstances. An implicit question for the two people in the dynamic of a painful break-up is: 'how do you want to live the time that remains to you?'

Relationship mediation is a large topic; this chapter looks at the importance of building a strong engagement from the outset with the two clients and helping them to move through the change, choice and loss of their togetherness; it will also offer two vignettes to illuminate the concepts; these are composite examples of some general issues encountered in such mediation.

Mediators may meet the clients for one mediation meeting or may have up to six sessions or more, the number of sessions is not relevant for the purposes of this chapter, but it is rather the quality of relating that is of primary focus.

Whilst this chapter explores change, choice and loss, and mediation attempts to help separating couples to negotiate their ending, nevertheless if they have children together they will never truly 'end'. The quality of their connectedness and style of 'post-divorce' relating will resonate throughout their children's lives. Sensitive therapeutic mediation can help a couple to devise co-parenting plans that are mutually accepted and enduring.

Engaging with clients in mediation: existential perspectives on setting the tone

The journey into mediation for a separating couple is a journey into the unknown. Frankl (1988) held that humans are meaning-seeking beings and the mediator must find the skills to help them towards finding meaning within the chaotic situation they initially present. She must set the tone and explain the process to them (confidentiality, impartiality on her part, a goodwill procedure that will give both parties a voice, finding their own solution) so that a trusting relationship can be established that feels meaningful from the start.

Therapeutically trained mediators are skilled in managing emotional polarities. Separation and divorce for *one* party (and any children) may be about

change, choice and loss, the existential tenets inherent in being alive, bringing with them 'the anxiety of meaninglessness' (Tillich, 1974: 49). Anxiety
is a human 'given' of existence and humans seek certainty and security to
assuage it. We are driven by anxiety to drown ourselves in the trivial, the
social, in 'all the ingredients of inauthentic existence' (Warnock [Heidegger],
1992: 57). Human reality perpetually tries to refuse to recognize its freedom
(Sartre, 1966). For the *other* party, ending the marriage can be about attaining
liberation and gaining the independence to live a more 'real' life, sometimes
with a new partner. For this party there may be immeasurable feelings of
Kierkegaard's 'reality of freedom' (Perkins, 1969: 21). Starting to move his
life from possibility to actuality '... everything that comes into existence does
so by an act of freedom' (ibid.).

To instil trust from the outset of the process in this disparate situation, the
therapeutically informed mediator must establish a connectedness with both
mediating parties, calling for an insightful level of authenticity and grounded-
ness on her part; she must then contain the process and 'stay with' it, managing
the strong emotions raised by the conflict whilst giving both parties a creative
voice. Mediation calls for personal courageousness in the mediator and she
sets out to model courage. Speaking to both parties in advance of the session to explain something about the process helps them to enter mediation
with a stronger knowledge of the procedure, more trust in the integrity of the
mediator and reassurance that both will have a voice. Mediators accept that
conflict is an inescapable facet of human existence; conflict, reconciliation and
cooperation are part of being alive (Strasser and Randolph, 2004). Existential
practitioners believe in the relational nature of being; we are always in relation
with others. Buber holds that seeing the other as a 'thou' means that we connect with the other and with our humanity. If this can be achieved the mediator
will have created a precious 'I-Thou' encounter. A combative couple may have
spent years in an 'I-It' dynamic; mediation is an arena where they may find
the courage to move towards an 'I-Thou' mode of relating, each showing the
other that he or she is not 'a thing amongst things' (Buber, 1958: 8). Even if
they are unable to do this together, they may be drawn into entering into an
'I-Thou' relationship with a therapeutically trained mediator; the experience
of this shift may serve to positively transform their thinking and engagement
together.

The mediator strives to foster an enduring working relationship; cementing
empathic attunement between herself and the parties; they must feel that she
will be impartial in order that they can feel safe with her. If this is achieved it
is more likely that they will *want* to return to mediation after the first session.
Clients often seek out partiality, trying to get the mediator on side. It is important in the early part of the process to persuade them that the mediator's role
is not one of arbitrator or judge. Parties will only shift from entrenchment if
they feel there is a *gain*, rather than a *loss* in doing so. The mediator has to
find a way to uncover this *gain* in order to get the parties to work with her.
It is useful if the mediator can encourage a couple, who may think they don't
agree on *anything*, to find the common ground. There is always *something* that
they can agree on; it might be they agree on the fact that they both love their

children and want the best for them, or it might be an agreement that it would be good to get through their separation without spending large amounts of money on legal fees, which will often mean a depleted financial 'pot' out of which to rehouse themselves.

Sometimes one party may refuse to continue with mediation after the first session, feeling a depth of injustice in her situation from which she is unable to move away. In her despair she demands to litigate the matter. Both parties may now have to spend many thousands of pounds of joint finances in legal fees only to find themselves in a bitter and ever-escalating dispute with many anxiety-provoking trips to court, finally to have the judge directing them towards a solution much of which could have been achieved in six mediated sessions. Meanwhile the family is now alienated and the children subject to court reports. The parents stop speaking to each other and will not be celebrating the children's birthdays or special achievements together. They will no longer mark family milestones or honour their children's triumphs and attainments together. The depth of animosity can become such that a third party is used at contact changeover-time to deliver the children from one parent to another. The parents cannot bear to see each other or grant each other any kindness or goodwill. This couple's children end up in a battlefield of bewildering emotions, obliged psychologically to survive by reading parental subtext as they watch their mother and father fight out their issues unendingly, ungenerously, each refusing to give ground to the other.

Embracing change

Strasser in his book *Emotions* talks about the potential 'rigidity of the client's value system' (1999: 20) and in mediation one or both parties are frequently rigid; one party may want *everything* to change and the other want *nothing* to change. Mediators can find it helpful to uncover what change would mean to the client. To the wife whose husband has found a younger girlfriend or the man whose civil-partner has found a richer boyfriend, the enforced changes that separation will bring may give rise to issues of revenge, or of feeling left or abandoned. The couple may have been living in an empty or impoverished relationship for some years, avoiding making decisions in life; Kierkegaard would view each as 'never becoming truly a self' (Perkins, 1969: 33). If the couple has children, the changes in *their* lives will need to be managed sensitively and with consideration. Children will usually need to move between two homes, perhaps to live in a new area, make new friends, through no choice of their own. The separating couple may feel conflicted, guilty; perhaps they have been telling themselves that they *should* stay in their marriage for the 'sake of the children'. This excuse for parental inaction seems to say more about avoidance of personal responsibility for change, staying with the 'known' with its thin veneer of safety and security rather than embracing the dizzying light of freedom.

In the separation process children may be used as punishing weapons; couples can fight each other over thirty minutes of contact time or the length of the Christmas visit. This displaced activity is obviously destructive to the family group and, through gentle challenge and creative questions the mediator can start to explore the underpinning of this harsh rigidity. By challenging the *paradox* of the couple agreeing they both 'want the best for the children' yet fighting over them, she can work to unstick the conflict; moving forward, encouraging the two parties to work together towards a 'win-win' agreement and an enduring, mutually agreed co-parenting plan.

Existentially, discussing issues of temporality with the parties can be helpful; 'this is your life; how do you want to live it? How will your life be different/changed, if you could get through this separation and start to live more freely?' Heidegger talks about Dasein's authentic temporality as the resolute mode of temporal existence. Authentic temporality is realized when Dasein becomes aware of its own finite existence (Heidegger, 1996). Understanding this temporality has to do with our grasp of our own life.

Acknowledging choice

Existentially we choose every moment of the day; if we choose one thing we cannot have the other. Because the choice to end the relationship that brings couples into this type of mediation is often driven by one party, the situation could be conceptualized as the *leaver* and the *left*. One party has made the choice to end and the other has to 'run to catch up'. A husband may be choosing to push for a speedy separation, wanting to mediate an agreement as quickly as possible whilst his wife's response may be one of feeling inferior, bullied or rejected and so she may put many obstacles in the way of reaching a resolution in order to redress the embarrassment and power-imbalance she perceives. This wife may want her day in court feeling the judge will listen to her story, her pain and feelings of injustice; she may be convinced of the rightness of her case. Perhaps she fears the feelings of nothingness that her divorce will bring. 'Nothingness lies coiled in the heart of being like a worm' (Sartre, 1995: 107).

Attuned work with this party in private session can challenge this assumption of nothingness, helping her to come to terms (even be at peace) with the ending-choice of the other by embracing a more authentic way of living and the freedom to self-direct.

A man may delude himself that 'everything was fine' until a new boyfriend comes into his civil partner's life; the mediator can gently point him back to the historical difficulties that the couple had had between them. Perhaps the couple has been living a version of Sartre's bad faith for years, the fractures in their relationship left unacknowledged. Hans Cohn's view of this choice suggests that the concept of bad faith is often seen as characteristic of living inauthentically.

It is a denial of our freedom to respond to what we meet … expressing itself in phrases like: …. 'circumstances don't leave me any choice' (Cohn, 1997: 124)

Falling into 'bad faith' the party in mediation takes a dishonest position about his reality and possibilities. Mediation can encourage a party in mediation towards a more authentic, honest way of being-in-the-world.

Reframing loss

Together with the necessity of change and choice is the certainty of death and loss: these are existential givens in our lives. The ending of a relationship can be like a death for one of the parties whilst it may almost be like rebirth for the other. Heidegger views the existential angst when we are faced with our own being-towards-death in the possible annihilation of our existence. Then fear becomes a mode of attunement for us (Heidegger, 1996). Can the mediator help this party to reframe the future as the 'not-yet', and encourage her towards an unfolding of what Sartre terms the sum of her possibilities? (Sartre, 1966).

Existential dissonance reveals itself in the way we play out in ontic behaviour, the denial of the ontological reality of the ending of death. We live a whole lifetime with the fate of death haunting our dreams, even on the most sun-filled days. So how to move an entrenched and bitter party on to embrace his future? Ernest Becker believes that we literally drive ourselves into blind obliviousness with 'social games, psychological tricks, personal preoccupations' as our response to the terrible fearfulness of the 'existential dualism' that is the knowledge that we are born to die. We position ourselves outside nature and yet are 'hopelessly in it' (Becker, 1973: 26, 27). We throw ourselves into action uncritically and unthinkingly; Henry James felt that we have the strange power of 'living in the moment and ignoring and forgetting' (Becker, 1973: 23). Entrenchment now can be seen as a holding-tight to the security blanket of what *was* in order to avoid the inevitability of ending and loss.

What follows are two brief case studies to illustrate some of the issues raised in this chapter and will show elements of existential thought that inform the author's approach; giving some examples of engaging with change, choice and loss. They are composites of many different situations encountered in mediation.

Case illustration 1: Charlie and Glenys

Charlie and Glenys have been married for twelve years. Glenys's solicitor has suggested she contact a mediator to help them in their separation. The following vignettes are extracts from private sessions with each of the parties:

Charlie's private session

Charlie: 'I've done everything for Glenys, worked 18 hour days, done night shifts, looked after the kids and now she says she's found another bloke. She says she can't bear to be with me; well I'll show her that she's not going to mess around with my head in that way. I'll fight her for the kids; I can't bear the thought of them spending time with him at his place. She thinks this will be easy, that she can end twelve years of our marriage just like that, well I'll show her and I'll show that bloke. She's going to suffer...I'll take her to court...the judge will hear my side...my lawyer says I've got a strong case...'

Charlie's worldview of change and loss leads him to vengeful feelings in order to redress his hurt and despair. He knows Glenys well and knows that the way to hurt her the most is by way of the children. His very self-construct as a father and husband is challenged when he thinks of his loss and of a new man fathering his children. Strasser (1999: 31) says:

emotions not only reveal the individual's world-view, but also disclose the diversity of each individual...[how we] respond to the givens of our existence.

In order to accept the situation Charlie will need support and encouragement to feel better about himself and thus about Glenys's decision. Glenys is not ending the relationship because of Charlie's inadequacy, but rather because she loves elsewhere. He needs encouragement to see that their relationship had become an 'I-It' encounter rather than an honest situation; it had become a habit that they avoided discussing. It would be liberating for Charlie to understand Frankl's view that human freedom is the freedom:

to choose one's attitude in any given set of circumstances, to choose one's own way. (Frankl, 1993: 65)

Glenys's private session

Glenys: He was never there, always working or having a drink with his mates; he doesn't know how to listen to me; he doesn't know how to listen at all, never did. Benny is everything I've ever wanted, he was my childhood sweetheart...I married Charlie at 17, I was pregnant, young and stupid. But I've got three kids and I thought that was it, I'd made my bed and that was my life. Now I can see a way out with Benny and I can't wait for us to move in together. Charlie will just have to come round to it; I'm not a prisoner...the kids will have to accept it as well. They quite like Benny, he'll grow on them, so will his kids.

Glenys is playing out her choices but hasn't really thought through taking responsibility for them. The children are swept up into the dynamic and in reality will find it difficult to be thrown together with Benny and his family. There are many details to be worked out. Her husband Charlie, as has been seen, is in a fighting mood and bent on vengeance. Benny's partner is not mentioned here but might well also feel abandoned and bitter. This ending will need parties to view clearly and sensitively what each course of action will elicit and to plan their separation and co-parenting from their children's perspectives. Glenys' intentionality is already one of life with Benny, Charlie's is one of hopelessness, aloneness and abandonment.

The therapeutically trained mediator will have the skills and confidence to stay with the strong, vengeful feelings in this case, respectfully exploring, perhaps challenging, what each party brings. Mediation can give them both the space to give voice to their emotions and to make more informed and insightful decisions.

> Both Heidegger and Freud define human freedom as being able to choose. One choice leads to an independent self, the other choice consists in 'denial and non-recognition'...we fall prey to the 'anonymous, inauthentic mentality of "tradition"'. In this way we miss assembling our possibilities of relating towards the world into the wholeness of 'an authentic free selfhood'. (Boss, 1963: 67, 68)

Through the safe space created in mediation and the dignity afforded to each party, the therapeutic challenges and the connectedness that can be achieved, the mediator can help Charlie and Glenys shift focus from their personal battle towards meeting their children's needs through the continuing relationship this will require.

Case illustration 2: Henry and Tom

Henry called the mediator in a state of agitation to book a first mediation session 'immediately'. He and his civil-partner, Tom, had been having couple's counselling to try to work on their partnership but it now seemed unsaveable. Henry had been having a relationship with a work colleague for a year before Tom had found out, and there had been ugly scenes in front of family and neighbours. It had now got to the point where Henry wanted his freedom to make a new life with his boyfriend; he needed Tom to leave the house 'as soon as possible'. Henry had offered Tom half the equity of the house but Tom refused to talk about it.

First session

Henry and Tom sat as far away from each other as possible in the mediation room. Henry had said that they wanted to use the first session to re-establish a dialogue. Tom took up much of the mediation session with stories of how much he had tried to save their relationship and of how unjust the situation was and how unfairly he was being treated. He frequently repeated the phrase: 'we can work this out'.

The mediator wondered at Tom's seemingly 'delusional' worldview, that things could be worked out, after having had many sessions of relationship counselling culminating in an unsuccessful outcome and also noted Henry's desire for a speedy separation. It seemed that Tom was looking at mediation as another 'fix-it' process. He couldn't bear to look at an ending.

Henry was exasperated, saying that the (expensive) attempt at 'papering over the cracks' of his relationship with Tom through counselling had more to do with Tom wanting to stay in their home which Henry had purchased and Tom had interior-designed and decorated. Henry had a high-powered job in banking and it had been agreed that Tom would be the house-husband in the relationship. Tom said he couldn't countenance 'at all' moving to a smaller home, 'all my friends live in the area and have houses like ours, I would feel like a fish out of water'.

In this early conversation the mediator started to be aware of Tom's worldview and in particular the link between the house and his feelings of self-esteem.

At the end of this emotional and difficult session, as they were getting up to go, Henry snapped angrily at Tom, reminding him that he had once wanted to study art and live in Venice for a year. Tom quickly dismissed that as a dream from the 'old days'.

Tom's private session

In response to the mediator's phenomenological exploration, Tom reflected that the house stood for 'status, power, importance' and to move out would mean loss of face, shame, exposure in front of his friends. The mediator mentioned how interested she had been to hear his younger-self's dream of study and travel and yet he tied himself to a house. She looked at how things would be for Tom if he could live more authentically, leaving their civil-partnership. His eyes filled with tears, 'my parents separated when I was 9, they argued all the time, it was truly horrible ... I think it's always inside me, I just don't think about it much ... I can't think about going through that myself; I think it would break me.'

The mediator was mindful of the polarized positions of the men. Henry wanted everything to change very quickly, to end the relationship and to establish a new life. Tom wanted nothing to change and revealed a strong fear of loss. If Tom left the relationship and moved to a smaller house he feared he would lose face in his friends' eyes, he would somehow merit less respect and feel 'diminished', less important and worthy. His self-image was tied up with their large and stylish house. Tom wanted to mend a seemingly unmendable relationship in order to keep his status and stay in their home. He knew on some level that their civil partnership was sterile, that he was an unwanted partner yet persisted in his thinking that the relationship could be *fixed* so that nothing in his ordered life would change. His thinking and arguing was unreflective and circular.

With the mediator's help, Tom could start to challenge his fears that the loss he faced in the ending of the relationship would 'break' him, and she encouraged him to describe how he thought it might do so. She went on to ask him to play with the dream of a life separate from Henry and mentioned that some couples move on to view endings as beginnings.

Henry's private session

In a final private session with Henry, the mediator looked at his desire to leave Tom and set up home with his new partner 'as soon as possible'. He mentioned casually that his parents had 'old fashioned values' and when the mediator picked up on this comment, he elaborated that they believed marriage should endure 'under any circumstances'; the concept of divorce was simply untenable to them. 'In a way I wonder if my yearning for a speedy ending with Tom and a new beginning with Jeremy might be a rebellion against their tight, judgemental values. I think I really got together with Tom because they approved of him...now I'm 40 and I realize I'm starting to make my own decisions'.

Working with an impartial third party for three mediation sessions gave Henry the space to develop stronger insight into his own motivations and consider more deeply Tom's feelings. He decided to plan their separation in a more sensitive way and shape his new life in a way that would accord Tom more respect and dignity. Heidegger writes that authentic existence is resolute, while inauthentic existence is irresolute (Heidegger, 1996).

Through sensitive mediation this couple started to engage differently. Tom privately admitted to the mediator that he had felt discouraged, even unloved, in the relationship for years but that he had pushed those feelings away. Studying had been a dream for Tom but the idea of separation had now pushed him into wanting to live differently, in a more fulfilled way. Heidegger talks about Dasein's thrown possibilities: 'the past, the present and the not-yet' (Heidegger, 1996).

Interestingly, both men had allowed themselves to be defined by their childhood experiences of their parents' behaviour; accessing this and giving voice to it helped them both towards different, more authentic, life choices.

Henry and Tom had made a journey and managed to overcome their resentment and bitterness, exchanging it instead for future hope and a freer way of living their lives. By being 'pushed' into making choices, Tom, could see that he could live his life in a more liberated way, fulfilling his possibilities for study and personal growth. Through the medium of mediation rather than litigation he could see that he no longer needed to consider himself left and abandoned, he could feel a sense of pride, freedom and rebirth. Nietzsche believed that a state of enlightenment is a state of grace (Kaufmann, 1966).

Conclusion

This chapter has set out some basic tenets of relationship mediation and demonstrated how existential ideas can provide a rich and accessible seam of useful and meaningful thinking for separating and divorcing couples. The examples show how 'attuned' working may be instrumental in moving these crises onto resolution even after they have been exposed to the rigours and 'positional thinking' of legal teams. Existentially informed mediators understand that change, choice and loss are part of being alive and that trying to resist these human givens can result in a relationship deadlock that will prove painful and destructive to the couple and their children. Whilst mediation is not therapy, nevertheless it can inform and enlighten a couple bent on looking inward at their fight, and encourage a broader, more liberated, more accepting stance to the situation in which they find themselves.

References

Becker, E. (1973) *The Denial of Death*, New York: Free Press.

Boss, M. (1963) *Psychoanalysis and Daseinanalysis*, New York: Basic Books.

Buber, M. (1958) *I and Thou*, Edinburgh: T & T Clark.

Cohn, H. (1997) *Existential Thought and Therapeutic Practice*, London: Sage.

Frankl, V. (1988) *The Will to Meaning: Foundations and Applications of Logotherapy*, New York: Meridian Books.

Frankl, V. (1993) *Man's Search for Meaning: An Introduction to Logotherapy*, London: Hodder & Stoughton.

Heidegger, M. (1996) *Being and Time*, New York: State University of New York Press.

Kaufmann, W. (1966) *The Portable Nietzsche*, New York: Viking Press.

Perkins, R. L. (1969) *Soren Kierkegaard*, London: Lutterworth Press.

Sartre, J.-P. (1966) *Being and Nothingness*, London: Methuen.

Sartre, J.-P. (1995) *Essays in Existentialism*, New York: Citadel Press.

Strasser, F. (1999) *Emotions: Experiences in Existential Psychotherapy and Life*, London: Duckworth.

Strasser, F. and Randolph, P. (2004) *Mediation: A Psychological Insight into Conflict Resolution*, London: Continuum.

Tillich, P. (1974) *The Courage to Be*, London: Collins.

Warnock, M. (1992) *Existentialism*, Oxford: Oxford University Press.

CHAPTER 9

The Challenge of Communication: A Meaning-centred Perspective

PAUL T. P. WONG AND LILIAN C. J. WONG

From the perspective of existential therapy, communication with the other involves much more than therapeutic alliance and the mechanical act of transferring information from a sender to a receiver; in fact, it is not possible to talk about existential communication without understanding the nature of authentic relationship and the presence of the therapist.

The presence of the therapist

For humanistic-existential therapy, presence means more than being psychologically attentive to the interactions taking place every minute of the session; it also means the existential presence of the total being of the therapist. Presence matters because the messenger is an important part of the message. A message is credible to the extent that the messenger is perceived as credible. By the same token, therapy is effective to the extent that the therapist is perceived as competent and caring.

More specifically, the therapist needs to possess and project certain positive personal qualities. Rogers (1951) maintains that the curative effect of relationship can only be fully understood in terms of the personal qualities of the therapist: empathy, genuineness and unconditional positive regard. Similarly, Deurzen (2009) emphasizes that good existential therapists must possess positive personal characteristics, such as emotional maturity, the capacity for self-reflection, and willingness to question the status quo.

An existential therapist is open, authentic, caring and vulnerable in order to facilitate authentic encounters. According to Buber (1970 [1923]), presence matters because it is essential for establishing an I-Thou relationship. The presence of the therapist conveys love and caring for the other as a whole being. Communicating true caring in an existential encounter enables the other person to explore, change and grow. Authentic encounters and genuine dialogue are possible only within an I-Thou relationship.

Authentic relationship

According to Deurzen and Adams (2011), human beings are relational; no one can exist separately from their relationships. The foundation of all relationships is the need to belong, to love, and to be appreciated and valued in return; the healthy relationship is characterized by mature interdependence and existential communication based on authenticity and mutuality (Deurzen, 2009).

Yalom (1980) focuses on the dynamic process of the here-and-now encounter. Each therapeutic encounter reveals the phenomenological experiences and frame of reference of the client, and opens up opportunities to connect with the client in a life-changing way. Since feelings of displacement, estrangement and alienation often contribute to clients' problems, the therapeutic relationship not only provides an antidote to loneliness, but also renews a sense of connectivity and belonging. This is of particular importance for relationship therapy, since this enables partners to reconnect to each other in a real way.

Similar to Buber's concept of the I-Thou relationship, Jaspers emphasizes that we have to be willing, open and vulnerable in order to be involved in an ever-deepening dialogue. There is a reciprocal connection between communication and relationship; a trusting and deep personal relationship facilitates existential communication, which further deepens the relationship. Karl Jaspers, more than Buber and other existential philosophers, has contributed most to our understanding of existential communication, which is possible only in a deep and authentic personal relationship (Jaspers, 1957, 1959, 1970).

According to Salamun's (2006) analysis of Karl Jaspers' ideas, a human being can realize the meaning of life in four modes of being, and each mode entails a different kind of relationship and communication. In the most basic biological mode of existence, communication is primarily dictated by physical needs, spontaneous emotion and instinctive impulses, without self-reflection. In the second 'consciousness' dimension of self-realization, communication is characterized by logical thinking and rationality. In the third dimension of Being, *Geist* (spirit or reason), communication is guided by personal ideals, moral worldviews, and the capacity to see the different parts of a meaningful whole. Finally, in the *Existenz* (existential) mode of self-realization, communication is based on authentic and intimate interpersonal relationship, which enables one to discover and realize one's meaning of life.

According to Spinelli (2007), existential-phenomenological therapy operates in the context of an interpretative world as well as a relational world. At the existential level, we move towards a deeper understanding of the truth of self and the other; at the same time, we also discover more about human existence and the meaning of life. Existential communication is liberating and empowers the communicator to search for truth and personal growth.

There is no single universally agreed upon approach to existential therapy. Meaning Therapy (MT; Wong, 2010) represents a Canadian model that is integrative in its attempts to bridge the existential tradition and mainstream psychology and positive psychotherapy (Wong, 2009, 2011). However, MT still shares the same existential concerns and skill sets of other existential approaches, such as Frankl's logotherapy and the American humanistic-existential tradition. In terms of its origin, MT is an extension of logotherapy (Wong, 2012a).

One of the key themes of existential therapy is its concern with the meaning and purpose of human existence and individual lives (Deurzen, 2009; Frankl, 1985). MT employs meaning as the central construct to integrate relevant skills from other schools of psychotherapy, such as cognitive behavioral therapy (Ellis, 2004) and narrative therapy (White, 2007). According to the motto of MT, 'Meaning is all we need; relationship is all we have'. This motto holds true for both the client and the meaning-centred existential therapist.

Meaning is all we need, because all clinical problems are in some way related to a lack of proper understanding of self and personal problems, and the difficulty in finding a fulfilling life purpose. Relationship is all we have, because we can only work through authentic therapeutic relationship and genuine dialogue to facilitate healing and positive change. In couple counselling, we also empower clients to develop congruent communication as a way to resolve conflicts (Satir et al., 1991).

MT's approach is primarily based on the PURE and ABCDE models (Wong, 2010) – the two major intervention strategies in MT. Being integrative, MT employs a wide variety of clinical skills which can be grouped into four conceptual frameworks or models: Frankl's Meaning Seeking Model (Wong, in press), PURE, ABCDE and the Dual Systems Model (Wong, 2012d). Each model contains testable hypotheses and can be a framework for both assessment and intervention.

MT includes a psychoeducational component, which entails teaching clients meaning-centred intervention skills that can help them cope with their problems and live more rewarding and fulfilling lives. In this chapter, we briefly describe how each component of the PURE and ABCDE intervention strategies can guide the therapist to use appropriate clinical skills. We will present a case to illustrate how these two intervention strategies can be applied in dealing with existential and relational issues.

The PURE framework and intervention strategy

Consistent with traditional existential themes and current research on meaning (Wong, 2012b), we define meaning in terms of PURE, which stands for purpose, understanding, responsibility and enjoyment. PURE provides not only a comprehensive definition of meaning, but also a conceptual framework for working with clients who seek to make sense of their lives and try to make responsible choices in the midst of chaos and uncertainty. In couple therapy, each component of PURE represents an essential building block in improving communication and developing a healthy relationship. Together, PURE is important for broadening clients' horizon of interpretations so that their perceived meanings will be more congruent with their spouse's perceptions and the actual problem.

Purpose

Purpose refers to intentions, directions and life goals. A major part of existential therapy is to help clients clarify their own assumptions, discover their true purpose in life and empower them to strive for achievable life goals. Therefore, within the theoretical component of purpose are a number of clinical skills, such as vocational counselling, goal setting and goal striving, which can be used by the therapist depending on the need of the client.

In meaning-centred couple therapy, the most important factor for a successful relationship is that the couple enjoys shared meaning and purpose (Deurzen, 2010; Gottman, 1998), while remaining true to their own individuality. It is difficult to plan life together when the individuals have conflicting life goals and priorities. Clients also need to bear in mind that the purpose of couple communication is not just to make their own needs known to the other, but also to understand each other's needs, feelings and frame of reference in order to grow together.

Understanding

Understanding involves making sense of self, others, situations and life as a whole. Deurzen and Adams (2011) emphasize that self-understanding cannot be fully achieved without understanding others and the larger context of the human condition. Congruent communication involves making sense of self, others and events in a way that promotes mature interdependence as well as personal growth. MT teaches clients that the personal meaning they attach to an event has greater impact on them than the event itself. While clients are entitled to believe in the verity of their own perceptions, it is necessary for them to explore alternative interpretations that are congruent with the other in order to resolve an impasse and move forward.

Responsibility

As free agents, people are responsible for their reactions to what life and situation demand of them (Frankl, 1985). Responsibility also means making choices that are rational, realistic, and ethical (Deurzen, 2009). Clients are responsible for the consequences of their decisions and actions. To decrease conflict and negative emotions, couples are reminded that they are responsible for caring for each other's well-being and understanding each other's struggles in order to create a rewarding future together through congruent communication.

Enjoyment

No relationship can survive for long if it is totally devoid of joy and positive reinforcement. The practice of Purpose, Understanding, and Responsibility in intimate relationships would naturally lead to higher satisfaction and fewer problems. However, couples also need to learn to intentionally express affection and create opportunities to have a good time together. Deurzen (2009: 173) reminds existential therapists of the human potential for enjoying life: 'Human freedom and ingenuity can enable people to live well and to the full.' MT empowers clients to look at the bright side of their relationship and remember the good times they have had together.

The ABCDE framework and intervention strategy

This is another major meaning-centred model that is based on existential themes. ABCDE stands for acceptance, belief, commitment, discovery and evaluation – the five steps to cope with problems, especially those predicaments and dilemmas that cannot be resolved by human effort. ABCDE focuses on commitment to responsible actions. The ABCDE intervention focuses on repairing what is wrong, while the PURE strategy focuses on bringing out what is right. In therapy, these two interventions are typically employed together to facilitate congruent communication and positive transformation.

Acceptance

People need to accept life as it is – the good, the bad and the ugly, as well as accept the imperfections in themselves and others in order to reduce unnecessary anger and frustration (Wong, 2012c). Acceptance is one of the main themes in existential therapy. Acceptance of reality and each other is the first step towards reparation of broken relationships. Couples need to accept each other's feelings and failings, and work towards congruent communication. If one party denies his or her culpability and completely blames the other, the conflict will escalate. Cultural barriers in mixed marriages increase the likelihood of conflict. Accepting cultural differences between East and West in expressing emotions (Hoffman and Cleare-Hoffman, 2011) can facilitate communication.

Belief

Belief in the intrinsic value of individual life and in the meaning potential in all situations gives people hope (Frankl, 1985). Tillich (2000 [1952]) also emphasized the vital role of faith and belief in a similarly meaningless world. Hope is essential for healing and growth. Couples need to believe that their marriage is worth saving and their problems are solvable in order to achieve a successful outcome in marital therapy. If one party is already dead-set on divorce, it is very unlikely that the marriage can be saved.

Commitment

Commitment is another existential theme. It is sometimes conceptualized as a leap of faith (Kierkegaard, 1980 [1844]) or the courage to create in the face of uncertainty (May, 1994 [1975]). In essence, commitment refers to a determination to pursue a life goal or a task in the absence of sufficient information and assurance of success. In meaning-centred relational therapy, it takes time and effort to rebuild trust and repair broken relationships. Couples therapy will work only when both partners are committed to making the necessary changes to save a relationship and improve congruent communication. Chinese history has shown that commitment to the family values of harmony and self-sacrifice helps keep the family together (Dias et al., 2011).

Discovery

Human beings are complex and constantly evolving. Relationships are complex and fluid. Therefore, most relationship problems are multi-faceted and often related to deep-seated issues. Couples need to constantly discover new aspects about themselves, the other and problematic situations, in order to achieve mutuality and congruency.

Evaluation

Self-reflecting and assessing the effectiveness of adjustment are necessary in order to improve relationship. Fine-tuning is needed from time to time to ensure that the elements of ABCD are working well.

Meaning-centred relational therapy

A meaning-centred approach to relational therapy is based on MT, which assumes that we are relational creatures with the basic need for belonging and attachment (Bowlby, 1988; Bugental, 1956; Deurzen, 2009; Yalom, 1980; Wong, 1998a, 1998b). In addition to addressing interpersonal deficits experienced by the clients (Weissman et al., 2000), MT also equips clients with the necessary skills to build and maintain mature interdependent relationships. Good and open communication is an essential clinical tool to bring clarity and resolution to personal predicaments. However, MT elevates communication to the level of existential communication. A great deal of therapy time is spent on making explicit the implicit meanings and hidden needs that contribute to interpersonal conflict.

Given the emotion-laden quality of couples' communication, especially in unpleasant and stressful situations, MT emphasizes the importance of self-distancing and viewing each problem within a larger context of individual struggles with existential givens. Self-detachment provides some space between the person and the problem and allows clients to normalize their predicaments in light of existential universals.

Extending Frankl's logotherapy to couples, Lantz (1996, 1998) emphasizes the importance of making use of the meaning potentials in intimate relationships. Couples need to understand the demand characteristic of each relational problem and choose to do the responsible thing. Similarly, Hendrix's (2010) Imago Relationship Therapy teaches couples to replace confrontation and criticism with a reciprocal process of healing, which primarily consists of basic communication skills such as mirroring (i.e., reflecting accurately), validating and empathizing.

To reduce miscommunication, MT emphasizes active listening. In fact, MT teaches clients five levels of listening through modelling. They need to learn not only to listen with their ears and eyes but also with a compassionate heart and an open mind. Finally, they need to listen with their spirit, to be attuned to each other's silent cry for meaning and understanding. Spirituality is the core of personhood (Deurzen and Adams, 2011). To communicate at the spiritual level is to understand each other's spiritual essence and inner space (Satir et al., 1991). By demonstrating all five levels of listening – ear, eye, heart, mind and spirit – the therapist models for the couple how to engage in congruent communication and develop new ways to relate to each other.

The following case illustration demonstrates how MT is applied with a couple facing a marital crisis. During the intake session, the therapist explained that MT emphasizes meaning and relationship and requires them to learn some evidence-based practical skills to relate to their problems and engage life in a healthy and productive manner. During the termination session, the therapist summarized how the PURE and ABCDE had been effectively applied to their marital crisis.

Case illustration

James was a 67-year-old lawyer who still maintained a small legal office. His wife, Mary, was an in-house corporate lawyer working for a large insurance company. They had a happy marriage without any crises until Brad, a young and abrasive articling student, entered the picture at a critical point in the careers of James and Mary.

James had just lost his junior partner and his receptionist/legal secretary due to maternity leave. Although James had considered retirement, he felt that his mission was not yet completed, and he still had several unfinished important legal cases. He was delighted when Brad started helping him, because he was competent, fast and able to take over the work of the legal secretary. In addition, Brad also had legal insights.

Because of the backlog and several impending court cases, James and Brad had to work overtime. As a result, James overlooked the needs of his wife and unknowingly contributed to a marriage crisis. James was totally surprised by the intensity of the crisis. The immediate trigger of Mary's unhappiness was her retirement.

On several visits to James's office, James and Brad were so engrossed in working together that they ignored her presence. Her perception of alienation and rejection infuriated her and she accused James of caring for Brad more than her. James responded with anger to her accusation because it had no factual basis. When the marital conflict escalated to an unbearable level, Mary threatened to divorce James. At this point, they both agreed to seek professional help.

During the therapy, there were many tense moments because, to James, the crisis was a storm in a tea cup created by Mary's distorted perception of his relationship with Brad. But according to Mary, it was a huge painful experience to see her husband hoodwinked by a young punk who despised her.

Because of James's sense of fairness and his hard-nosed demand for evidence, he became upset with Mary when she accused Brad of intentionally insulting her without any supporting evidence. His arguments in defence of Brad's innocence only served to support Mary's hypothesis that he valued Brad more than her and that he no longer cared about or loved her. To prove his sincerity, James reassured Mary that he would let him go after completing his internship contract, even though originally he was thinking of hiring him. To reduce the conflict, he also repeatedly reminded Brad to show his wife courtesy and respect. Unfortunately, Brad's attempt to please Mary and impress her with his contribution to the firm backfired in a big way, because she took it as his attempt to send her the message that he was indispensable and that James valued him more than her.

In the course of therapy, Mary admitted that some of the stories against Brad were made up in order to convince James that Brad was a dangerous man who would destroy their law firm and their marriage. She complained about being victimized by James and Brad and she wanted to rescue James from Brad. When her irrational belief was challenged, she insisted that her perception was true, because her pain was true. It took a great deal of time to convince her that distorted perceptions can also cause real pain and to help her realize that her distorted view was largely due to her own existential crisis.

After a couple of years of working with James in their own law firm, Mary had spent the rest of her legal career as an in-house lawyer in an insurance company. She enjoyed the security of working for a large institution as a valued professional. She got along well with the management and staff. Retirement hit her hard. She felt completely displaced, disoriented and disenfranchised without an identity and without connections. Her sense of being lost gradually turned into frustration and hopelessness. This negative frame of mind worsened when she started spending a few hours a day at the office without any well-defined meaningful work, while James and Brad happily worked and went to court together.

James could not understand Mary's catastrophic response to Brad's presence. He was so exasperated by her irrational behaviour that he said to her: 'Nothing Brad has said or done calls for this kind of non-stop, hysterical, and vicious attack on Brad and me. I think you are mentally ill and you really need professional help.' In reaction to this, she went ballistic and responded by screaming: 'I will never forgive you for calling me crazy. How could you insult me to protect a young punk?' He rebutted: 'But it has nothing to do with Brad; it has everything to do with your unreasonable and catastrophic reactions. You treat me as if I have committed an affair.'

Assessment and treatment of the case

Similar to most relationship conflicts, this couple presented drastically different perspectives of the same set of events. What made this case interesting was that James and Mary had had a strong and happy marriage, which was derailed by their seemingly irreconcilably different attitudes towards Brad. Their differences were related to how they reacted to existential issues. James was primarily concerned with generative and integrative issues, mentoring a protégé to carry on his legacy, whereas Mary was primarily concerned with her identity crisis and personal losses during retirement. James's work did not suffer any disruption; he continued to do what he loved with someone he liked. But Mary was still in transition, feeling very insecure and uncertain about her future; her acute existential crisis was largely responsible for her unhappiness and the marital crisis.

James's lack of empathy and understanding

During the course of meaning therapy, James realized he shared responsibility for their marital problem because of a breakdown in communication and trust. He had taken Mary for granted and assumed that she would manage her retirement well. His main problem was his lack of awareness of, and empathy for Mary's existential crisis in a time of major life transition. He also failed to understand the intensity of her psychic pain. His dismissal of her desperate cry for help as a 'storm in a tea cup' was a clear sign that he did not understand her emotional needs. James readily confessed his failure to meet Mary's emotional needs and took immediate steps to improve congruent communication.

In reflecting on his phenomenological experiences, James also became aware of his own vulnerability and his desperate need to leave a legacy; this personal need made him overlook some of Brad's character defects and led him to prematurely embrace him as his standard-bearer. Another lesson he learned from therapy was that he needed to restore some balance in his life. Although it was noble of him to spend time fighting for justice for the disfranchised, mentoring his protégés, and contributing to the legal literature, he realized the need to spend more quality time with Mary and pay more attention to her need for physical and emotional intimacy. During the time that they worked apart, operating in two different worlds, they had already drifted apart imperceptibly.

Mary's existential crisis

Mary was in a transition stage in her life and needed to address her existential and neurotic anxieties (May, 1950). Since she was an institutional person for almost all of her professional life, her self-identity, self-esteem and personal meaning were largely based on her good performance for the corporation.

MT helped her to shift from performance-based self-assessment to a new understanding of authentic being. She needed to discover her own path and live a purposeful and fulfilling life without an institutional affiliation.

It took many sessions before she realized that James had not changed, but that she had changed because of her very unsettling life transition. Self-reflection and perspective-taking enabled her to realize that blaming James and Brad for her existential crisis was the main cause of their marital crisis. When she was able to distance herself from her emotional pain, Mary was able to understand what had caused James's strong words and anger and see that this reaction was typical for him in response to false accusations.

The PURE intervention strategy

The PURE intervention was effective in resolving their marital problem. The therapist pointed out the paradox that Mary's excessive and aggressive attempts to protect their marital relationship had had the exact opposite effect of driving James away. She finally recognized the dilemma that, on the one hand, she really loved James and wanted him to be happy and healthy, and, on the other hand, she had caused him so much pain and suffering. A lot of time in therapy was devoted to helping her find a way to resolve the paradox and achieve her intended *purpose* of strengthening her marital relationship.

The therapist accepted her phenomenological account as very real to her, but also challenged her to understand the following chain of events: existential crisis – distorted perception of events – faulty attribution about intention – trumped up charges and unrelenting attack – making James very angry with her irrational behaviour – confirming her hypothesis that he no longer loves her – heightened anxiety and anger.

Once she *understood* this vicious cycle, she was willing to explore more positive frames of reference. For example, when she was challenged to imagine how she would react to the same sight of James and Brad working together if she had a prosperous legal practice and had her own competent assistants, she answered that from such a positive perspective, she would not be bothered at all.

The therapist further challenged her to see things from James' perspective and empathize with his emotional needs. He challenged Mary to put aside her assumptions and emotions in order to have a dialogue with James regarding their differences about Brad. The therapist also pressed the point that Mary's accusation of James treating her as garbage was totally inconsistent with her own account that he had always been a loving, caring and self-sacrificial husband.

The *responsibility* component of couple therapy was to make her fully aware of the consequence of her behaviour on herself and her husband. She needed to realize her daily fighting with James had taken a toll on both of them. She had almost destroyed his mental and physical health. Therefore, she needed to take personal responsibility to work towards repairing the damage and rebuilding the marital relationship. She agreed to apologize for not trusting him and for attacking him unfairly. She also promised to grant him the same kind of personal space he used to enjoy while she was working fulltime elsewhere. For his part, James also apologized for not spending enough time with her and for not understanding her existential crisis. He felt happy that she finally admitted that she had accused him unfairly.

The PURE intervention strategy was facilitated by the ABCDE strategy. When Mary *accepted* her existential anxiety was normal for people during life transition, her neurotic anxiety about losing James to Brad was gone. She also learned to *believe* that there was plenty of life after retirement and that James still loved her. Once she was *committed* to building a new future for herself, she *discovered* that there were indeed many new opportunities for her to use her expertise and experience. In her self-reflection and *evaluation*, she was satisfied that she had successfully resolved her dilemma.

In addition to helping Mary develop a deeper understanding of herself and her marital crisis, the therapist also emphasized the importance of mutual interdependence that allows both mutuality and individuality. When Mary played the roles of victim, accuser and rescuer, she not only failed to take responsibility for her happiness, but also robbed James of his freedom and personal space. She learned that a better way to express her needs was through frequent communication and open dialogue without accusation and anger.

Both James and Mary learned the PURE and ABCDE interventions so that they could continue to use these skills to improve their communication, coping skills and enhance their well-being. In this case, the therapy has been effective. One year after the therapy, Mary had successfully re-established her independent legal practice and was serving as a legal consultant and board member for several non-profit organizations. She was able to view this unhappy chapter in her life in a different light. According to Mary's follow-up feedback, one night she broke down weeping and apologizing to James, because she was convicted of the unnecessary injury she had inflicted on him for no other reason than her own insecurity and jealousy. Their marriage was now stronger and happier than before the episode with Brad. Meaning therapy had helped both of them gain a better understanding of themselves, each other and their marital crisis Their new ability in congruent communication gave them the freedom and courage to resolve their marital conflicts and create a better future.

Conclusion

In a time of managed-care's emphasis on evidence-based practical skills, MT is able to provide empirical research as the basis for many of its intervention skills. By taking an integrative stand, MT was flexible enough to employ relevant skills from CBT, narrative therapy and positive psychotherapy to address problems related to both existential and cognitive meaning. With its psychoeducational approach to equipping clients with the necessary skills makes it easier to transition from therapy to everyday living. With these characteristics, MT may represent one of the ways to move existential therapy forward in a therapeutic world dominated by manualized evidence-based therapies.

The case presented here illustrates how MT can be applied to relational therapy. It also demonstrates the importance of (1) addressing underlying existential issues, and (2) removing barriers of communication due to distorted perceptions and misattribution. Specifically, we show that PURE and ABCDE strategies can be effectively employed to achieve these two therapeutic objectives in the context of marital conflicts.

References

Bowlby, J. (1988) *A Secure Base: Clinical Applications of Attachment Theory*, London: Routledge.

Buber, M. (1970 [1923]) *I and Thou*, New York: Scribner's.

Bugental, J. (1956) *The Search for Authenticity*, New York: Holt, Rinehart and Winston.

Deurzen, E. van (2009) *Psychotherapy and the Quest for Happiness*, London: Sage Publications.

Deurzen, E. van (2010) *Existential Work with Couples*, available at: http://www.slideshare.net/djht2/existential-couples-work

Deurzen, E. van and Adams, M. (2011) *Skills in Existential Counselling and Psychotherapy*, London: Sage Publications.

Dias, J., Chan, A., Ungvarsky, J., Oraker, J., and Cleare-Hoffman, H. P. (2011) 'Reflections on marriage and family therapy emergent from international dialogues in China', *The Humanistic Psychologist*, 39, 268–275.

Ellis, A. (2004) *Rational Emotive Behavior Therapy: It Works for Me – It Can Work for You*, Amherst, NY: Prometheus Books.

Frankl, V. E. (1985) *Man's Search for Meaning: An Introduction to Logotherapy*, New York: Pocket Books.

Gottman, J. M. (1998) *Clinical Manual for Marital Therapy*, Seattle, WA: Seattle Marital and Family Institute.

Hendrix, H. (2010) *The Two Simple Ways to Upgrade your Marriage*, available at: http://www.oprah.com/relationships/Marital-Therapist-Harville-Hendrix-Tells-the Simple-Truth-About-Love

Hoffman, L. and Cleare-Hoffman, H. P. (2011) 'Existential therapy and emotions: lessons from cross-cultural exchange', *The Humanistic Psychologist*, 39, 261–267.

Jaspers, K. (1957 [1935]) *Reason and Existenz*, trans. W. Earle, New York: Noonday Press.

Jaspers, K. (1959). *The Idea of the University*, ed. K. W. Deutsch, preface by R. Ulich, trans. H. A. T. Reiche and H. F. Vanderschmidt, Boston, MA: Beacon Press.

Jaspers, K. (1970) *Philosophy, Vol. 2: Existential Elucidation*, trans. E. B. Ashton, Chicago, IL: University of Chicago Press.

Kierkegaard, S. (1980 [1844]) *The Concept of Anxiety: A Simple Psychologically Orienting Deliberation on the Dogmatic Issue of Hereditary Sin*, eds R. Thomte and A. B. Anderson, Princeton, NJ: Princeton University Press.

Lantz, J. (1996) 'The existential psychotherapist as a host in couples therapy', *Journal of Couples Therapy*, 5, 67–78.

Lantz, J. (1998) 'Basic concepts in existential psychotherapy with couples and families', *Contemporary Family Therapy*, 18, 535–548.

May, R. (1950) *The Meaning of Anxiety*, New York: Ronald.

May, R. (1994 [1975]) *The Courage to Create*, New York: W. W. Norton & Co.

Rogers, C. R. (1951) *Client-centered Therapy*, Boston, MA: Houghton Mifflin.

Salamun, K. (2006) 'Karl Jaspers' conceptions of the meaning of life', *Existenz, 1*. Available at: http://www.bu.edu/paideia/existenz/volumes/Vol.1Salamun.html

Satir, V., Banmen, J., Gerber, J. and Gomori, M. (1991) *The Satir Model*, Palo Alto, CA: Science and Behavior Books.

Spinelli, E. (2007) *Practising Existential Psychotherapy: The Relational World*, London: Sage Publications.

Tillich, P. (2000 [1952]) *The Courage to Be*, New Haven, CT: Yale University Press.

Weissman, M. M., Markowitz, J. C. and Klerman, G. L. (2000) *Comprehensive Guide to Interpersonal Psychotherapy*, New York: Basic Books.

White, M. (2007) *Maps of Narrative Practice*, New York: W. W. Norton & Co.

Wong, P. T. P. (1998a) 'Meaning-centered counselling', in P. T. P. Wong and P. Fry (eds), *The Human Quest for Meaning: A Handbook of Psychological Research and Clinical Applications*, 395–435, Mahwah, NJ: Lawrence Erlbaum.

Wong, P. T. P. (1998b) 'Implicit theories of meaningful life and the development of the Personal Meaning Profile (PMP)', in P. T. P. Wong and P. Fry (eds), *The Human Quest for Meaning: A Handbook of Psychological Research and Clinical Applications*, 111–140, Mahwah, NJ: Lawrence Erlbaum.

Wong, P. T. P. (2009) 'Existential positive psychology', in S. Lopez (ed.), *Encyclopedia of Positive Psychology*, Vol. 1, 361–368, Oxford: Wiley-Blackwell.

Wong, P. T. P. (2010) 'Meaning therapy: an integrative and positive existential psychotherapy', *Journal of Contemporary Psychotherapy*, 40 (2), 85–93.

Wong, P. T. P. (2011) 'Reclaiming positive psychology: a meaning-centered approach to sustainable growth and radical empiricism', *Journal of Humanistic Psychology*, 51, 408–412.

Wong, P. T. P. (2012a) 'From logotherapy to meaning-centered counseling and therapy', in P. T. P. Wong (ed.), *The Human Quest for Meaning: Theories, Research, and Applications*, 2nd edn, 619–647, New York: Routledge.

Wong, P. T. P. (ed.) (2012b) *The Human Quest for Meaning: Theories, Research, and Applications*, 2nd edn, New York: Routledge.

Wong, P. T. P. (2012c) 'Acceptance and wellbeing', speech presented at the 3rd Australian Positive Psychology and Wellbeing Conference, University of Wollongong, Sydney, Australia.

Wong, P. T. P. (2012d) 'Toward a dual-systems model of what makes life worth living', in P. T. P. Wong (ed.), *The Human Quest for Meaning: Theories, Research, and Applications*, 2nd edn, 3–22), New York: Routledge.

Wong, P. T. P. (in press) 'Viktor Frankl's meaning seeking model and positive psychology', in A. Batthyany and P. Russo-Netzer, *Meaning in Existential and Positive Psychology*.

Yalom, I. D. (1980) *Existential Psychotherapy*, New York: Basic Books.

CHAPTER 10

The Challenge of Ethics and the Call to Responsibility

ALISON STRASSER AND MARIA CLARK

Responsibility is one of the core ideas discussed in existential philosophy. It is distinct from the common perception that responsibility is about accountability or a personal duty. The existential understanding is a complex and intricately interwoven postulate that encompasses the broader themes of freedom, awareness and choice. This more expansive idea of responsibility can precipitate a journey within the relationship that involves not only the partners but also the therapist reviewing and owning their responsibilities.

In relationship work, the therapist navigates the complexity of differing expectations, assumptions, conflicts and secrets held separately by each partner. She will find herself at times torn between the partners; sometimes colluding with one and then the other, holding a secret and waiting with baited breath for it to be revealed to the other, and her own internal conflict between maintaining confidentiality and the desire for openness and transparency. Thus responsibility cannot be divorced from an ethical concern that encompasses personal values, professional codes and social norms.

This chapter will introduce some of the philosophical ideas relating to responsibility and then continue to discuss these ideas in relation to the therapist's responsibility when working with relationships. A case illustration will highlight and explore the practical application of this panoramic view of responsibility for the therapist and the partners.

All of the existential philosophers add their own distinctive shades to the concept of responsibility; each adding a richness and a particular understanding. From a big picture perspective, responsibility as connected to freedom is one of the universal existential givens in that, as humans, we are free and also responsible for our own course of actions in life, albeit within the finitude and facticity of existence. This concept is one of the common uniting features of existentialism summed up by Sartre:

> Condemned to be free. Condemned, because he didn't create himself yet, in other respects is free, because, once thrown in the world, he is responsible for everything he does. (1956: 509)

At this stage, we realize that responsibility is more than the sum of our own actions and necessarily includes our behaviours with others and towards the environment around us. Levinas (1989) adds to this perception by writing that we are called to responsibility before we are called to exercise our freedom and describes the purpose of our fundamental responsibility as a human being as existing primarily for the good of the other.

Taking up our responsibility cannot occur in a state of bad faith or 'blindness' to whom we imagine we are as individuals. Hence in therapy we are on a journey towards good faith or authenticity, requiring us to become more mindful of our actions and their consequences. In this process of recognition and understanding we are on our path to becoming, our path towards authenticity, our path towards becoming responsible and taking responsibility. Nietzsche (1974) also views responsibility and freedom as taking charge of our lives while Kierkegaard links choice and action, in that it is not just about our ability to choose but rather choosing is man's 'responsibility for the manner of his existence' (1992: 54).

Another significant component of responsibility as described by Heidegger (1962) is that of 'care' or *Sorge,* comprising of two modes: that of 'concern', which is how we relate to objects or things and that of 'solicitude', or how we relate to human beings. Within solicitude we can either relate in a 'leaping in' manner removing the other's responsibility to respond in their own way, such as in telling the client what to do, or we can 'leap ahead' allowing the other to take responsibility for their response. This occurs in existential therapy when the therapist, in listening to the clients, facilitates the opening up of possibilities, explores their resultant responsibilities, thereby allowing the client to choose their personal course of action. In parallel, the therapist also enables the partners to become more aware of the differences and consequences of these two modes of leaping in and leaping ahead communication patterns.

Any chapter about responsibility in a relationship necessitates the inclusion of the recognition that love is both the ability to 'know' and understand oneself for oneself and through the eyes of the relationship. As Derrida says,

'the radical otherness of the other . . . is the condition of my relation to the other' . . . the inability to know the other 'from the inside' is integral to human relationships and so also to love: 'I cannot reach the other . . . This is not an obstacle but the condition of love'. (Derrida, 2004: 14)

Case illustration

Dean and Susanna came to couple therapy so they could both understand why Dean had, and continued to have, extra marital affairs even though their marriage was ostensibly a good and loving relationship. The underlying message was that Dean required therapy and Susanna needed to understand his motivations – and only secondary to this were her reasons for continuing to stay in the relationship. From the outset, it appeared that both Susanna and

Dean had different notions of responsibility: from the existential perspective, Susanna held Dean responsible for the state of their marriage and was blind to her contribution; whereas Dean bore limited accountability by acknowledging his affairs while in reality wanting Susanna to take responsibility for fulfilling his desire for the loving family environment. Both Dean and Susanna were demonstrating the Sartrean belief (1943) that when we look to the other to define us, we are living in Bad Faith and in not taking up the mantle of responsibility, are denying our freedom.

They had been married for thirty-one years with two independent, adult children and four grandchildren. Married in their twenties after two years of dating they quickly established a family surrounded by their extended relatives. As offspring of Greek immigrants, Dean entered into the family import/export business creating new and successful markets. As the children reached their teenage years, Susanna took off in her own direction becoming an executive director in the corporate world.

In the first ten minutes of the first session, Susanna commanded Dean to talk about his extra marital affairs. The first, with a mutual acquaintance, began after eight years of marriage. His various infidelities were numerous and inevitably led to Susanna learning about each as and when they occurred through either his disclosure or by Dean leaving a trail of evidence. Susanna described her reaction to each as one of total devastation, humiliation and annihilation; yet she continued to believe and trust in Dean's remorse and despair, hence her reason for remaining in the relationship. Dean confirmed Susanna's perception by displaying deep shame and admitting to his feelings of confusion and lack of understanding of his own conduct. He couldn't comprehend how he could hurt Susanna, the woman he loved, valued and deeply respected.

Although Dean and Susanna were seemingly articulate, they both were stuck in their particular positions with regard to their perception of their situation. Hence in relation to responsibility, they were limited in their choices. One of the key ideas of existential therapy is that as clients become more aware, they widen their horizons, opening up their possibilities and consequently broadening their choices. However, choices are inter-relational in that:

> No choice can be mine or yours alone, no experienced impact of choice can be separated in terms of 'my responsibility' versus 'your responsibility', no sense of personal freedom can truly avoid its interpersonal dimensions. (Spinelli, 2001: 16)

The reason for coming to therapy at this point was the threat by his last lover to expose the illicit relationship to family, friends and the wider community of Dean's business world.

After two sessions it was mutually agreed that Susanna and Dean would attend separate, individual sessions before continuing with the next joint session. The therapist realized that Dean was uncomfortable, terrified, yet assertive and unable to express himself fully and freely in front of Susanna. Simultaneously, although Susanna initiated the therapy, she appeared to be waiting for Dean or the therapist to reveal some knowledge rather than admitting to her own vulnerability and her contribution to the relationship.

In the process of these individual sessions both Susanna and Dean disclosed aspects of themselves and also particular stories that had the potential to rupture perceived notions of themselves and the other in their relationship. Susanna, in her despair and confusion, hungry for knowledge and facts, had hired a private investigator to monitor Dean's movements. Dean admitted that during his last affair he had felt endlessly tormented by Susanna and that he had contemplated leaving her. Indeed, he had felt defenceless and guilty, feelings heightened by Susanna's emotional tirades and physical attacks. In both situations the therapist was asked not to disclose these facts to the other partner. It was explored and noted that Dean did not feel unsafe or physically threatened by his wife as he accepted Susanna's behaviour as an act of frustration and despair. Susanna feared that if Dean found out he would feel admonished and would leave. Dean wanted to protect Susanna from the embarrassment of such a primitive and emotional outburst. For both the main fear was the end of the relationship.

Dean and Susanna came weekly for the first six months of their therapy, progressing to fortnightly until they finished after 11 months. On commencement, Dean was already in personal therapy, Susanna refusing to consider this option as she considered the marital difficulties to be Dean's problem and therefore not her responsibility. However, after seven months she sought her own therapy as she began to recognize her role in the relationship.

Responsibility in practice

As discussed in the first section, responsibility from an existential perspective is all embracing and inclusive in that it encompasses concepts of freedom, awareness and choice.

The negotiation of the therapeutic contract and the parameters of confidentiality are intrinsic to the implicit safety of the therapy and mirror the paradoxical nature of life.

> While therapy strives to provide safety, it also aims to allow clients to become aware that the world inside and outside the therapeutic walls is not one of safety and security. It is necessary for clients to find their own potential within the realms of uncertainty. (Strasser and Strasser, 1997: 74)

Obviously, the specific criteria of the contract will vary according to the therapist's own beliefs; such as what happens when one of the couple are unable or do not turn up to the session or whether it is appropriate to see each of the couple separately or to keep them together throughout. Additionally, the therapist needs to be aware of the legal limits to confidentiality, such as the obligation to report to external authorities as in cases of potential child abuse. This is an aspect of responsibility in terms of needing to be cognizant of current legal and ethical requirements as stipulated by registration bodies and laws that will differ from country to country.

The need to clarify confidentiality is arguably the most significant and some-times hardest aspect for the therapist to maintain. For instance, the decision to see each partner separately is fraught with the possibility of risk since a 'secret' of some kind often emerges. This is a beautiful paradox in that, if you keep the couple together, this 'secret' may never arise and separating them entails the holding of this 'secret' by the therapist in the hope that, through the partner taking responsibility, he or she may reveal it to the other.

From the moment of entering the therapeutic space, Dean and Susanna demonstrated years of living in bad faith, each pretending to the other and to themselves that their marriage was sustainable. Rather than attempting to find fault or elucidate the specific problem in the relationship, the existential therapist began with attempting to discover each of the partner's worldviews and their particular biases and assumptions that both give rise to their current viewpoint of safety and simultaneously prevent them from adopting another perspective. These biases and assumptions are known as sedimented views where

> human beings become stuck or fixed in certain belief systems and behaviour patterns that deposit themselves deep down in our belief system in a similar fashion to the sediment that sinks to the bottom of a liquid. (Strasser and Strasser, 1997: 80).

By identifying and clarifying Dean and Susanna's personal sedimentations, they began to understand and challenge their own biases and assumptions as well as those that pertained to the relationship.

Clearly Dean and Susanna had been able to sustain their relationship for many years. Susanna believed and needed to believe that Dean was both strong and determined, yet caring and nurturing, which was one of her sedimented beliefs. Dean's propensity to charm and his ability to captivate her was both familiar and meaningful to Susanna in that she felt significant, cherished and adored. To be loved in this way was at the heart of her personal ideals of marriage. Hence, her exasperation and the despair that arose from the con-tradictions she experienced each time she found out about another infidelity. Throughout their marriage they continued to have a healthy sex life, Dean continued to buy her beautiful and personal presents and Susanna persisted in blaming herself each time she found out, scrutinizing his capacity for loyalty both to herself and to the family.

Dean blamed himself for Susanna's unhappiness. Each time he slept with another woman he felt the power of being a man, a sedimented belief of need-ing to see himself as strong. Yet he loved Susanna. He was in awe of his wife's capacity to be loyal and to forgive. She was strong and she gave him the secu-rity of the family life he cherished and this capacity to provide him with a safe haven was the main reason for his initial attraction to her thirty-two years ago. However, Susanna's strength also created a sense of shame and unworthiness in Dean that left him feeling silenced and inadequate.

Congruent with the existential approach, the therapist aims not to direct but to guide so that the therapist and the couple remain 'open to mystery and surprise' (Lantz, 2004: 173). This becomes more fluid when integrating the phenomenological process since it promotes an attitude on behalf of the therapist of being aware of the couple's worldview and the assumptions being made (bracketing), to assist them to describe their story and to respond at the level of description rather than explanation. This attitude is also significant in that it prompts the therapist to pay attention to the multiple levels of relationship occurring (Spinelli, 2005) in that the process reveals how both the couple and the therapist respond to each other in addition to how each perceive themselves in relation to the other. It is also the responsibility of the therapist to not only help reveal the couple's worldview but to draw attention to the contradictions and differences that become apparent for each individual and for the couple-in-relationship.

Although it is possible for these relational aspects to emerge with the couple in the room together, in the case of Dean and Susanna part of the decision to also see them separately was about the therapist feeling the necessity to experience each as an individual in their own right and to appreciate how they relate to another person without the partner in the room. Susanna's tendency was to hold court in the couple sessions while Dean appeared to be cowered into silence, stumbling to find words to express himself.

Having made the decision to separate a couple, the ensuing individual sessions are different to individual personal therapy in that the focus is on the relationship and the various realms of self in the encounter (Spinelli, 2005). Essentially we are asking each to talk *about* the other in order to facilitate the process of speaking *to* the other when they are together.

For instance, questions may converge on how the client sees herself in the relationship, how she views her partner in the relationship and indeed how she perceives the therapist in the triad. During the individual sessions the issue of confidentiality is best revisited since the change in dynamics also constitutes a variation in the safety of the initial contract with the couple. It is usual for each partner to reveal quite different information to that disclosed within the couple session and it is important to clarify what can be discussed openly with the other partner and what is deemed as private and confidential.

In his individual session Dean came alive; he had found his freedom to articulate not only his actions but also his feelings. He could talk without fear of becoming entangled in Susanna's emotions and enjoyed being heard for what he had to say, uncensored by himself or Susanna. When with Susanna he always felt like the bad boy needing to atone for his sins.

In Susanna's individual session she continued with her tirade of facts and the therapist noted that this barrage referred most often to her being consumed by her sense of responsibility towards the family. Indeed, these words created a wall, which kept the therapist at bay, not allowing for any interjections or space for reflection. The therapist felt unheard in what might be deemed as a parallel to the way Dean described his inability to express himself with his wife. Although Susanna spoke with strength and conviction, as the session continued she eventually admitted that she feared her weakness and assumed that she could not be a good wife, for otherwise Dean would have remained faithful.

At the relational perspective, Dean was more absorbed in his own world and his need to be seen as strong and good by his partner. Susanna was more concerned with others: both in terms of how she could ensure that these others would perceive her as strong and clever and more importantly in terms of how she could enable the family to continue to be seen as upstanding and respectable. Susanna felt that Dean through his indiscretions was destroying this rosy picture.

When viewed more systemically, the value of strength and the polarity of weakness emerged as a shared tension for both partners; a similarity in their worldviews. It was noticeable that after their individual sessions both Dean and Susanna were more freely able to reveal their feelings and vulnerabilities and to more easily speak about what they had discovered about themselves. They had begun to drop their façade of demanding strength in the other and instead had begun to befriend the spirit of uncertainty, the path towards accepting what they would describe as weakness.

The therapist was able to facilitate a process whereby each could explore what it meant to be strong and weak, both for themselves and in the eyes of the other. Susanna's strength and determination was what had attracted Dean in the first place but which also over the years became intimidating and a barrier to communication whenever he felt uncertain and weak. For Susanna, Dean's strength was his playfulness and his ability to make her feel unique and loveable. Yet on further exploration she realized that his gifts were often presents for himself and that his playfulness allowed him to shirk responsibility, culminating in Susanna being the caretaker for the family. These conversations illuminated the positives and negatives as well as the possibilities and limitations of their original choices in their partnership.

Through the process of becoming more aware we begin to reflect and understand about the choices we have made, and the choices that we can make to live life in a more authentic manner. As an aspect of enhancing our freedom, becoming aware of these choices is indeed an intrinsic component of living a responsible life. Yet within these parameters lie multiple dimensions of self (what I say to myself about myself, about my encounter with the other, what I say to myself about how I imagine you experience me, and what I say to myself about what we are co-creating in our encounter – Spinelli, 2005) so that self-awareness for each of the couple is not only about who they imagine they are in relationship to each other but also their recognition of the impact they have on each other.

As Dean and Susanna began to see that their choice in partner was to some extent based on an illusion of their own unmet needs of recognition, success and security, they both had to address and understand their personal sense of self. Simultaneously working within the relationship realms, Dean, Susanna and the therapist revealed their perceptions of each other, adding to their overall insight of self and how others saw them. We need to know ourselves in order to have an intimate and emotional connectedness with another. Paradoxically, we can only know ourselves by being in relation to others. In couple therapy, as highlighted with Susanna and Dean, the interconnectedness of the relationship between each other and between the couple and the therapist was a process that allowed these facets to emerge in a manner that was meaningful to them both.

Responsibility also takes courage since there are risks involved. As the therapist opens up the space for the couple to hear themselves, it essentially opens up the possibility that they each might hear things that they do not want to hear. It becomes scary because they are not only discovering themselves but also hearing what the other thinks about them. Another way of articulating this is that if you have to speak to me, you also have to listen to me. Listening is about having the courage to hear difference, to remove our own expectations around thinking and to hear something different. In our questions the therapist is not only helping to reveal both the known and how this is managed in the relationship, but more importantly the unknown, what has not been heard before. These are examples of 'leaping ahead' whereas most couples quite literally 'leap in', wanting to get their own point of view heard and unable to accept differences in the other.

As most people do, Dean and Susanna began therapy by asserting their opinions, wanting the other to change and not understanding that responsibility is about gaining wisdom beyond the stated issues. Working relationally opens up the client's world to the experience of the other in a way that is not possible when working individually. Susanna had to face that Dean experienced her as wanting to take away his freedom; that her strength was overpowering, leaving him emotionally stifled and contracted. Dean had to listen to Susanna's belief in his selfishness and his inability to share with the family. Both had to come to terms with a sense of self that was the opposite to what they had originally formulated; in that Dean had described himself as loving, dependable and caring while Susanna had depicted herself as weak, dependent and retiring.

Therapist's responsibility

It is not only the clients that are required to reveal themselves. Working within an existential-phenomenological frame requires that the therapist is aware of their own assumptions or biases that have arisen in their personal journeys, including personal, cultural and theoretical theories about couples and relationships in general. Broad assumptions might include that intimate relationships should be grounded in mutual intimacy, or that the sexual relationship is symbolic of the everyday encounter. Other assumptions might be that the therapist should give equal time to each person; that the couple should be kept together for the duration of therapy or to the contrary, that couples should have individual sessions in conjunction with the couple sessions. Each of these assumptions will have consequences, both positive and negative.

Clients usually have an expectation that their point of view will be validated and legitimized by the therapist. It is not necessary that the therapist give equal time to each partner but rather it is his or her responsibility to acknowledge both their positions and to explore further what this stance is revealing in terms of their particular and unique relationship. For instance, at the beginning

Susanna dominated the therapeutic space, demonstrating her neediness to be seen and heard both by Dean and the therapist. This harked back to seeking her voice within her large family of origin. On the other hand, Dean opted out of the therapeutic space allowing Susanna to take control. That indeed was a mirror of their relationship. It was easier for him to avoid asserting his needs with Susanna and find his voice in the arms of another woman.

The therapist too becomes involved in the triad and is required to step into her own reflections about who she is in relation to each partner and to the couple as a unit. Working with Susanna and Dean brought up the assumption vis-à-vis giving equal time to each partner, yet periodically this swung from the feeling of colluding with Susanna and truly identifying with being deceived and the feeling of being exploited and disregarded by Dean. At other times the pendulum swung the other way, by aligning with Dean and experiencing what it must be like to be dominated by Susanna and understanding his desire to find succour with another woman.

In the case of Dean and Susanna this involvement was further accentuated during the individual sessions with Dean initially creating a seemingly complex and irresolvable dilemma. As Dean revealed his secret self, the self that he was unable to show to Susanna, the therapist found herself drawn towards and perceptibly aligning more with Dean. Contrary to his reluctance to speak in the couple sessions, Dean gushed, revealing his fears and doubts and his intense desire to be free to be the man he became with his various lovers. He had become both engaging and charming with the therapist. Indeed, on reflection, the therapist had become the 'other' woman, the person that Dean could be comfortable with; willing and able to be open and vulnerable.

Rather than admonishing herself, the existential therapist allowed these feelings to emerge and to notice what this might mean with regard to the couple. As the realization of what she had become for Dean dawned, the therapist began to question Dean on the differences and similarities he experienced when he was with Susanna, his lovers and also with the therapist. These reflections allowed Dean to begin to understand what prevented him from being the 'free' person that he wanted to be with Susanna.

Conversely, by identifying with Susanna, questions and reflections around how it was to be deceived and what was so important around remaining loyal could be asked. As the work done in the individual sessions converged into the couple sessions, one of the 'elephants in the room' could be aired; namely, for Susanna to both admit and to recognize her strength and the impact, both positive and negative, this had on others, including Dean.

A similar reflective process is used when working with secrets. On a simplistic level it is usually assumed that if a secret is revealed to the therapist, as in the situation with Dean talking about his desire to leave Susanna, it is the therapist's responsibility to question the client's assumptions so that he or she can take a more reasoned and self-reflective stance. In the case of Dean, this exploration examined not only his wish for the secret to remain but also his responsibility in relation to Susanna and the rest of his and her family. In this particular instance Dean, in his individual session with the therapist, decided not to disclose to Susanna about his desire to leave the relationship because he realized that it was more important to understand his inability to reveal himself in the partnership. Dean later shared that his freedom to speak to Susanna openly and honestly began in his individual sessions with the therapist. This is where he learnt how he could be respected by another and trust that his secrets would not be spoken.

However, Susanna decided to tell Dean that she had hired a private investigator and surprisingly this triggered weeks of anguish for both of them. The revelation for Dean was a betrayal of trust and this took him back to the time his mother 'spied' on him, following him and his friends to the shopping mall. He never forgave his mother for not trusting him when he had always been such a good, responsible boy. This emergence of a common theme of betrayal and trust gave way to both Susanna and Dean's anxiety and their ontic response to the threat of uncertainty and abandonment. In the process, they both revealed to themselves, and to each other, an existential despair that took them to the depths of hopelessness and utter loneliness.

Freedom and responsibility

As Dean and Susanna progressed through therapy they essentially had to question their worldview in regard to themselves and their perspective of each other. Dean had to take on board that he was both selfish and caring, while Susanna came to terms with the concept that she was both weak and strong. Conversely, they had to begin to accept the other for who they were and to re-learn how to love each other through the lens of their perceived weaknesses.

As one partner takes ownership for their personal assumptions and their reactions to the other then, almost automatically, the other assumes their own responsibility, moving from disowning to owning their own actions. In this process of becoming more self-reflective and aware there is an emerging openness to possibility, an opening towards self and an opening towards the other. This action in itself allows the other to reciprocate.

> Selves who attend are relational selves, or selves-in-relation. Crucially, attention goes on in relation; it is something we do as selves-in-relation. What is revealed by me attending to you is revealed to us, not to me and to you individually. (Talbot, 2000: 106)

Thus, simultaneously, the therapist too is vulnerable in the relationship, taking ownership for misunderstandings and bias. There is an ebb and flow within the relationship as each person in the triad moves away from the defence of their position towards the vulnerability of being open and different.

From an existential position, freedom cannot be separated from responsibility. Throughout, Dean had seemingly desired his freedom. Yet until he was able to understand that for the duration of his marriage he had avoided expressing his fears, rather playing on the strengths that he felt Susanna desired, he was in fact unable to attain his wish in the marriage. Susanna too, as a woman brought up in the era of women's liberation, felt that her work and sexual life were examples of her freedom. She also had to take responsibility for herself in a different way, to realize she had both succumbed to Dean's wishes without expressing her own desires and, in opposition, had assumed responsibility for others, including Dean. Unable to confront, she chose the option of remaining passive and doing everything herself.

The therapist's freedom became apparent as she was able to fully appreciate the complexity of Dean and Susanna's individual needs for themselves and for each other. Her ethical challenge was in her responsibility to maintain confidentially, to keep the secrets that emerged in the individual sessions and to work phenomenologically with these confidences, while also challenging herself to understand her personal biases and assumptions. In facilitating both Dean and Susanna to understand and acknowledge their individual worldview and the impact this had on each other the therapy sessions allowed a softening of their view of themselves and each other. Their beliefs around strong and weak became more flexible as they engaged with their own and each other's vulnerability.

> The paradox is that when I realise I am weak and vulnerable and there is no external rule book, I discover that in my freedom I can develop responsibility, stamina and personal strength. As long as I act as if I am invulnerable, I cannot come to terms with the vulnerability of being a person. (Deurzen and Adams, 2011)

Susanna and Dean were able to use the phenomenological process as a means of standing back and observing at a personal and relational level. This allowed them to question their choices and responsibilities both for themselves and to the relationship as a separate entity. They had begun to accept their weaknesses as strengths, their shadows as truths and to be more responsive and responsible to selves and each other. Through exploring the multiple layers of responsibility and confronting the ethical challenges as they emerged, Susanna, Dean and the therapist embraced their limitations, enabling them to accept relationships as a mystery not to be solved.

Dean and Susanna left couple therapy after eleven months, having regained a broader understanding of the complexity of relationship; the responsibility of love and the burden of freedom in that they both knew that for Dean to remain faithful required them both to risk the sharing of their secrets.

References

Derrida, J. (2004) *Deconstruction in a Nutshell: A Conversation with Jacques Derrida*, New York: Fordham University Press.

Deurzen, E. van and Adams, M. (2011) *Skills in Existential Counselling and Psychotherapy*, London: Sage.

Heidegger, M. (1962) *Being and Time*, New York: Harper & Row.

Kierkegaard, S. (1992) *Either/Or: A Fragment of Life*, London: Penguin Classics.

Lantz, J. (2004) 'World view concepts in existential family therapy', *Contemporary Family Therapy*, 26 (2), 165–178.

Levinas, E. (1989) 'Substitution', in S. Hand (ed.), *The Levinas Reader*, trans. A. Lingis, Oxford: Blackwell.

Nietzsche, F. (1974) *The Gay Science*, trans. W. Kaufmann, New York: Vintage Books.

Sartre, J.-P. (1943) *Being and Nothingness: An Essay on Phenomenological Ontology*, London: Routledge.

Spinelli, E. (2001) *The Mirror and the Hammer: Challenges to Therapeutic Orthodoxy*, London: Continuum.

Spinelli, E. (2005) *The Interpreted World: An Introduction to Phenomenological Psychology*, London: Sage.

Strasser, F. and Strasser, A. (1997) *Time-Limited Existential Therapy – the Wheel of Existence*, Chichester: Wiley.

Talbot, S. E. (2000) *Partial Reason: Critical and Constructive Transformations of Ethics and Epistemology*, Westport, CT: Greenwood.

PART II

APPLIED EXISTENTIAL
RELATIONSHIP THERAPY

Chapter 11

Children and Relationship Therapy

CHRIS SCALZO

Introduction

When the concern of a couple in a relationship turns towards a child, something is inevitably disclosed about their way of relating to each other and ultimately to the world. This may of course present huge and often overwhelming challenges, but also rich reward and the further growth of a successful relationship involving the creation of new life. This chapter explores existential issues around children and birth that couples may bring to therapy. They are principally around notions of choice, at the start of their journey through parenthood or around the dynamics of the family. The decision to try to bring new life into the world raises many existential issues relevant to psychotherapy. It potentially places the couple in a new role as parents, shifting not only their relationship with each other, but also their perception of themselves.

The potential of existential psychotherapy with families or an exploration of the existential issues affecting families, has been developed remarkably little, with a few notable exceptions (Cooper, 1972; Hadlane and McCulskey, 1982; Stadlen and Stadlen, 2005). Typically when children have been viewed from this philosophical perspective it has been with their own emotional development and well-being in mind (Merleau-Ponty, 1992, 2002; Moustakas, 1966). Literature has focused on the benefits of existential psychotherapy being practised with children (Scalzo, 2010, 2011; Quinn, 2010) or with exploring the impact of the family as a socializing force (most significantly by Laing and Esterson, 1970). The family itself has sometimes even been understood as an extension of anti-psychiatry rhetoric, as a means of social education. The real tension, however, within an existential approach to couples therapy lies in acknowledging that our existence is a priori a being-with-others, informed by history and context, and yet the therapeutic process requires us to take personal responsibility for our own choices and actions.

Existence is fundamentally relational as we cannot exist in isolation. Resolution of the potential conflict this creates can rest in an understanding of our potential for authenticity. This challenge is almost inevitably illustrated when issues relating to children present themselves. The birth of a new child is a life changing moment and one that many parents view as defining, in how they perceive their sense of self.

The philosopher Heidegger wrote that humans are beings preoccupied with their own identity: what it means to be, and what it means to be in relation to others.

> Being-in-the-world gets its ontological understanding of itself in the first instance from those entities which it is not but which it encounters 'within' its world, and from the Being they possess. (Heidegger, 2000: 85)

In other words, it is only from being in a world with other people that we are able to perceive of and begin to understand ourselves. This is particularly pertinent when existential issues relating to children are brought to therapy. The presented issue may initially be perceived as a turning away from 'true' aspects of the individual's personal struggles or a deflection of their relationship with each other. When viewed existentially, however, there is no fleeing from reality within the therapeutic process, but instead only a picture of it.

Despite, or in many ways because of, the constraints that exist from our being-in-the-world we are curious about our choices and our limits. It is this curiosity or concern that by its very nature makes us what we are. The process of bringing new life into this world is a hugely significant event for those involved and, as such, like the death of someone close to us, it allows us to re-evaluate time. The impact of such a momentous change forces us to see our own mortality and directs us all to the choices we are making in our current day-to-day lives: am I in the right job, am I married to the person I love, am I the parent I hoped to be?

The existential challenges inherent in becoming a parent are numerous, but mainly fall under the following five categories:

- *Identity*: adjusting from being someone's child to someone's parent.
- *Awareness of choice*: defining what type of parent I will be and what will influence this.
- *Meaning*: producing a new creation, but also acknowledging the limits of our mortality.
- *Relatedness*: experiencing parenting as an inter-subjective experience.
- *Responsibility and love*: determining whether or not we are good enough parents.

Identity

The transitions involved in entering parenthood are numerous and great, and can often give rise to huge anxiety. A new parent or parent to be may, for example, feel pressure to act and behave a certain way, living their life with new maturity and purpose. This is based primarily on their own experiences of being parented, which are then used to form the basis of an image or essence of what a 'good' parent should be. This will of course be formed in the context of the world of which they are a part, and the social pressures their cultural history and worldview may bring with them. Even when a new mother wishes to parent in exactly the opposite way to which they were raised, this relationship remains their first experience of being-in-the-world. The reality of life, however, is always different to an idealized perception of parenthood, which is impossible to achieve.

From an existential point of view it is also important to remember there is no true essence of self or parenthood; as such, no quintessential good parent. As van Deurzen clearly states when discussing notions of authenticity, '…the existential view is that self is relationship and process' (1996: 174). Whether viewed as parent or child, there is no true self, more real than any other. When with their parents, a client may act one way, when with their partner or therapist, another. All ways of behaving are representative of them, and all are equally real. It is, therefore, this notion of 'process' that is the most helpful way of considering the challenges inherent in redefining a sense of being a couple in a relationship, but also being parents. If they are able to acknowledge the inescapable truth that people are not fixed commodities who are perceivable in just one role, or fixed at any one point of time, then they may begin to open themselves up to the possibilities of experience. There remains, however, a complex relationship between the identity of being a parent and understanding this is not a fixed reality or static 'self', but also acknowledging that our understanding of what a parent *is*, has arrived from somewhere.

Similarly it is, as Merleau-Ponty puts it, 'ingenuous' to believe there is 'an impregnable subjectivity, as yet untouched by being and time' (2002: xi). What we are left with is the opportunity to turn towards our experience and as Merleau-Ponty continues, 'The real has to be described, not constructed or formed.' If a couple are able to start by describing their experiences and their relationship together, then invariably the anxieties of what a parent should or should not be will become less important. From here, they may continue to realize that their identity as parents does not arrive from getting to know about this or that, but in a true sense comes from knowing we are all accountable for ourselves.

Case illustration 1

Paul and Judy arrived for therapy with the feeling that they were failing as parents. They were both highly successful in their professional lives, but also highly critical of each other as parents. The pressure they put on themselves to 'get things right' meant they generated extreme tension in their relationship, causing a paralysis in the way that they cared for their 18-month-old son. They were frustrated that he had not gained weight, or met the expected developmental milestones they felt he should have achieved and each parent blamed the other. Both Paul and Judy described coming from strong, stable family backgrounds with extremely supportive parents, and they had come to therapy with the hope of understanding why so much tension continued in *their* relationship.

It was quickly apparent their striving to become perfect parents had over-shadowed and dominated their own relationship. Paul and Judy had grown to accept that the only way the tension between them could be resolved was when they became the best parents they could be. Their measure for this would be reflected in the achievements of their son, whilst paradoxically it was this pressure and tension between them that had now begun to prevent him progressing in the way they hoped.

It is possible to see how the pressure, constructed from a background of being successful in their lives to date, and even of having apparently nurturing parents themselves, meant they carried a high expectation into being parents. Gradually through their therapy Paul and Judy were able to begin to question the reality of the quintessential, perfect parent they had originally been striving for. They still retained high expectations of their son, but after further discussion of what they were able to change themselves, they ultimately began to be more supportive of each other, and not feel the need to criticize as frequently.

Awareness of choice

As Sartre wrote, 'Man makes himself: he is not found ready made: he makes himself by the choice of his morality, and he cannot but choose a morality, such is the pressure of circumstances upon him' (1973: 50). In our lives we are always faced with choice. Sartre, along with other existential thinkers tells us that we are finite. We are born, we die and we are faced with human suffering and loss. These are existential 'givens'. We are faced with constraints which are inescapable and which are perceived as painful. And most importantly we are aware of this, in many ways making it worse. It is the combination of our finitude and self-awareness, or awareness of our finitude which gives rise to questions that simply do not arise for other creatures, such as what is the meaning of life? Why is there suffering? Indeed, what sort of parent should I be?

In understanding what type of parent a client considers themselves to be, or what they may wish to be, there exists a strong temptation for us to search elsewhere for what may influence these choices. Traditionally psychoanalysis has looked internally for the basic drives and desires which motivate human behaviour, and certainly Freud believed that the libido and all its derivations were the most powerful forces acting upon mankind. This has led to an analytic perspective of parenthood that is typically concerned with the sharing of attention and affection amongst a newly triangulated set of relationships, illustrated in the unconscious needs of the Oedipus narrative (Grier, 2004). This in turn affects the individual's capacity to see, reflect upon and manage themselves in relation to others. Existential thought, however, offers a type of meditation on the human condition, that proposes notions of 'cause and effect' represent a hopelessly naïve worldview that is in many ways the root of our suffering.

When a child is brought into a relationship, the choices each person may face will inevitably change. Caring for a child, whether as a biological parent or step-parent, brings with it huge responsibility and a new family dynamic. The couple must find a way to navigate through the consequences of these changes and also acknowledge that although the context they find themselves in is different, there are still choices present. All too often in relationships it is possible for one partner to lose sight of these choices and to fall into 'bad faith' allowing themselves to believe it is the context which has responsibility for their outcomes and not themselves. This denial of real autonomy and responsibility is reflective of Sartre's definition of the idea of bad faith. Thus if we are to look at an existential model for true responsibility in parenthood, it is not just about being responsible for the welfare of a new child whilst maintaining a relationship, but ultimately about taking responsibility for our own choices.

From an existential perspective the limits influencing the emotional experiences of parenthood are about the choices we make, and the subsequent anxiety arising from an awareness of the choices we are therefore unable to make. In relating to the world, every parent is at any point directed in one way, and has other possibilities before them, which have not been taken. This may hold some similarities to analytic notions of a sense of our own emotional stability being influenced by our relatedness, but is different in that existentially speaking, these challenges of being-with-others need not be seen as unconscious processes influencing our choices. Feelings of inadequacy that a client brings to therapy may relate to the focus and choices they are making in one direction: 'If I work too often does this make me a neglectful parent? If I attend too much to the baby, does this make me an inattentive partner or lover?' Frequently the pressure in relationships is presented by couples not just through an awareness of the actions they are not taking, but also in the end, by not acknowledging their own responsibility for the choices they do.

Case illustration 2

Sian and James were both in their second marriage and Sian had brought children with her into the new relationship. Sian had been widowed some years before and after their marriage they had decided it would provide more stability for her three sons if James then moved in to live in their house. Her sons, however, were struggling to come to terms with a new stepfather in the home and James too was struggling with the adjustment of new experiences and choices each day, as part of a blended family. Sian increasingly felt James was to blame for the unhappiness of her sons and this invariably led to problems in their relationship.

Each week they arrived for their sessions with plenty of time to spare, but looking progressively more tired. James discussed the stressful nature of his work covering different shifts for a large transport company, monitoring an entire fleet of buses in a large city. His role was to anticipate potential delays and blockages often caused by traffic accidents or road works. He felt that the difficult behaviour of Sian's sons prevented him from being able to relax at home, that he was losing sleep and was now starting to make mistakes at work too. They both felt their relationship, although in its infancy, was already at breaking point.

James often described himself as the organized, practical one in the relationship, but that this responsibility brought with it great pressure. He added that Sian, by contrast was more readily able to offer the emotional support he felt he and the children needed. His hope for parenting, however, was still to approach it much like his work, choosing to anticipate every potential conflict and resolve it prior to its occurrence. The repercussion of this, however, was that Sian's children felt smothered and suffocated, and Sian herself had come to believe that James was excessively controlling.

After many sessions of them both describing the actions and consequences of the choices James in particular was making, it became clear that he felt compelled to make these choices, in order to try and retain some control in such a new and alien environment. After time, however, it was possible to see that it was in fact James himself who ultimately had responsibility for the choices he made, and not the context in which he found himself. The sudden change from living alone to sharing a house with a new wife and three boys represented a huge change in circumstances for them all, but it was their denial of freedom to choose an alternative that had led to an inability to take responsibility for their actions. In relationship therapy it is not our place to make moral judgements on how someone may or may not choose to parent, but through dialogue there is an opportunity to bring to the awareness of our clients the choices they are making, allowing them to consider their own responsibility.

Meaning

We have already seen how the limits of existence give rise to possibility and choice. The most primordial of these limits of being are birth and death; in effect the two possibilities we are unable to avoid. Even as soon as we are born there is inevitability that at some point we will of course die. As Macquarrie succinctly states in discussing the existence of *Dasein*, 'He is always old enough to die' (1972: 197). The boundaries of birth and death, however, generally appear far away from our everyday experience, and in the words of Heidegger we are for the most part, 'lost in the they'. In producing new life, giving birth or becoming a parent there is the opportunity to be jolted in our everyday existence. This new focus draws attention not only to the process and implications of introducing new life to the world, but also brings awareness of our own limitations. In this way the potential is created for a new focus on the meaning of our choices and relationships.

Heidegger is perhaps the existential philosopher who has the most to say about the impact of the limits of birth and death on existence. The precariousness of life, however, is not his primary focus as he incorporates this awareness into the everyday, by reminding us that being is essentially a being-towards-death. In doing so he relates the start and end of life to a general understanding of temporality. Existentially, time for Heidegger is not a linear concept of unfolding moments, and although attention may be pointed only in one direction at a given moment, our experience of life is more than a series of occurrences. Our past is characterized by the givens of experience, the future by possibilities, and for the present we are essentially 'falling', absorbed into the everyday. It is important in a relationship that a balance is maintained with regard to understanding time. If an individual finds themselves too caught up in the present they may struggle to take responsibility for their choices in the relationship, and not truly engage with their partner or child. If the focus is too much on future possibilities, an individual may become preoccupied with future projections, perhaps of how their child will develop and in extreme cases the parent may become consumed by future fantasies.

Most importantly, however, in relation to couples and their children, is the prospect for new parents to be too directed towards the past. In this case the givens of the past can seem overwhelming and paralyse a parent's ability to feel in control of their future options. The impact of this preoccupation with the past may lead to acute anxiety or compulsive behaviours, seeking the reassurance of past patterns or complete disenchantment in future possibilities.

Case illustration 3

Graham and Jodie presented for therapy together following a miscarriage. This was their first pregnancy together and they had both suffered periods of low mood and a listlessness with life for some months after. They had begun to question their relationship together and Jodie in particular experienced growing feelings that she was in some way to blame for the loss of their child. She felt that Graham blamed her for the miscarriage and she had spent a great deal of time questioning her actions and examining her past, looking to find a cause or explanation to their tragic loss.

Whilst they had both considered trying to conceive again, neither of them had been able to regain their initial enthusiasm for having a child. Graham exclaimed in one session the frustration he felt with Jodie's 'constant desire to rake over the past'. He said that this just brought him closer each day to re-experiencing the loss he wished to put behind him. He felt clear that there was no reason, and no blame to be apportioned, but regardless of this Jodie seemed to carry guilt with her. It was clear that the givens of their past experiences were painful for them both. An imbalance for Jodie towards the past had begun to draw her future possibilities and choices away from her. She felt the only way to feel in control was to relive her past actions and she started to develop repetitive habits in the hope of exercising more control over her current situation.

Within the sessions together we spoke more about the choices she was taking in her everyday life and increasingly her choice to stay in a relationship with Graham. Through this discussion Graham too was able to focus on what drew him to the relationship and to develop greater autonomy over the decisions he was also making in his life. When such life-changing events take place, our experience of time often changes and life is re-evaluated. For Graham and Jodie they were able to move slowly towards understanding time in a new way, having had their lives disturbed in ways that dramatically shifted the focus of past, present and future.

Relatedness

When we are first 'thrown' into the world there is no driving force, only relatedness to the world around us and the conditions of what Fromm (1976) calls the 'human situation'. Existential philosophy takes relationship as its starting point. As Merleau-Ponty wrote, 'we are immediately in touch with the world...' (2002: xiii). We are all part of a world that we cannot step outside of and look back at. Couples who attend therapy must therefore be seen as two people in a relationship with each other, but also in relation to the world, including children they care for, as well as the therapist before them. A similar context must also be acknowledged when a couple present for therapy with issues relating to children. Both individuals may relate to each other as potential parents in a relationship, but they are also beings with experiences of having been children themselves, parented by their own families or carers. The relationships in the room are not ones which can be considered in isolation. All the many experiences each person brings must be understood as shaping the worldview and assumptions they bring with them. From here they can only transcend their history by taking responsibility for who they choose to be.

Existentially, then, the challenge of caring for any child is not something to be considered as separate from other aspects of a couples' relationship. How they care for the child and understand their relationship towards the child is revealing of who they are. Following the birth of a child and start of a new family unit there may be an illusion of leaving a previous family group behind and 'breaking free', but in fact a historical lens and understanding is always brought into the construction of a new family. Often this is realized through a choice of partner or style of parenting.

Family history and life experiences may be viewed as opportunities for defences or barriers preventing a couple from transcending their family circumstances and realizing the full potential of their relationship. One partner may, for example, see themselves as the person their father wished them to be, or identify as a passive parent within the family, or an overbearing, strict parent who is compelled to hold firm boundaries by the over-emotional reaction of the other partner. All of these positions are in response to a relationship. The process each individual has of understanding themselves may therefore initially appear forced upon them by someone else. The challenge is for each client, particularly in the process of relationship therapy, to not only consider their position in relation to their partner and their history, but also become aware of whom they wish to be themselves.

Case illustration 4

Mary described the stress and pressure she felt from Tom's lack of support when it came to bringing up their six-year-old son, Ben. She told me that

Tom had the potential to be a wonderful father as she could see the affection he showed to their younger daughter. Tom blamed Mary for Ben's poor behaviour, saying it was 'clearly her fault he acted as he did, because she spent more time with him'. By contrast he would take their daughter to play groups and to the park every day, and his face illuminated every time she came into the conversation. Mary was close to losing her job, as Ben's behaviour had become so challenging he was frequently sent home from school. Although Tom was not working, his response appeared to be one of general avoidance and blame: 'you spoil him so much . . . sometimes parents have to say no', he screamed at her one time. In their sessions together Mary and Tom always sat apart and rarely touched. Although they both agreed Ben was the problem in their relationship, Tom said he felt 'miles apart from Mary' and told me he would often fall asleep on the sofa choosing not to go to bed with her.

One session, Tom said aloud that he did not love Ben. When Mary became upset and tearful he described his guilt at his own feelings, explaining this was not how he wished to be. He regretted that he had never felt able to show any emotion to his son or give him a hug. Tom went on to describe how he had never felt affection from his father who had died when he was young. His stepfather who had been part of his life much longer, was someone Tom described as cold and Victorian. At the start of their relationship Tom had been drawn to Mary's affectionate and tactile nature, but as their son had slowly matured from being a baby, they had felt their closeness dissolve.

This exploration of their history and context opened a broader understanding of the challenges of parenthood and the perspectives both Mary and Tom brought to their relationship. They were able to acknowledge and explore the emotional needs they both experienced as a couple and the role each family member then played in meeting these needs.

Responsibility and love

To take feelings and in particular 'love' as an entity in itself for reflection is perhaps somewhat un-existential. Certainly existentialism is not solely a philosophy of emotions, but existential thinkers would perhaps attend more to the feeling of love than logical philosophers, recognizing it as part of human experience. Reflection and exploration of feelings, such as love can also lead to a philosophical truth, that may be unobtainable through emphasis on logical cause and effect. The 'to and fro' of loving and being loved is perhaps at its most powerful in relation to children. This is of course different to the sexual love between a couple but is equally a reflection of the profound totality of being-with-others.

Sartre discusses in *Being and Nothingness*, how in order to obtain an interpersonal and sexual relationship love must play a part, perhaps born from a desire to assimilate the other to self. This can only happen if one person is able to have the other love them, but at the same time they too must in some sense become an object in order to be desired. This reciprocal relationship is certainly present if we consider a young infant, who needs the practical nourishment their mother provides in order to survive, but also needs to encounter the existential experience of relatedness in order to develop a sense of being for themselves. Without love as a manifestation of being-with-others it is impossible for a child to develop a sense of being, with freethinking autonomy and responsibility.

It is possible to feel a great deal of sympathy for parents today, who often feel they do not know enough, or love enough, or are unable to do what they really want to do for their children. Parents are often confused. They increasingly worry whether they are good enough parents. In the same way that the love of an adult sexual partner may feel under question following points of conflict, parents too will often worry if their child still loves them, after an aggressive outburst. The demands of a child are, however, frequently unrealistic as they are still developing a tolerance and understanding of living in relation with others. Children are hence still defining their understanding of what it is to be a free agent with choices, responsibilities and a concept of time that encompasses a whole span of experiences.

If parents are to take responsibility for their choices, this does not depend on them choosing the best outcomes when confronted with each situation. Although this is frequently a point of conflict for couples attending relation-ship counselling, no parent could be expected to respond perfectly to meet the complete needs of their child in every situation. Instead, true responsibil-ity comes from attending to the needs of their child through recognizing them as a developing individual emerging as part of the world. For some couples, the child is viewed simply as an object, meeting their needs for emotional ful-filment, or may become a conduit for the challenges they are facing in their relationship. If a couple are able to be genuinely available to meet themselves achieving love in a selfless expression of their being-with-others, then they may also be available to offer and receive love to their child. In discussing the devel-opment of the child into adulthood, Wenkart offers sentiments from which we are all able to grow and enjoy loving relationships: 'In the very act of becom-ing aware of his individuality, the capacity for relatedness develops. Isolation and alienation are terrifying experiences; in relatedness there is peace' (1966: 204). Existential approaches to therapy aim to create a discourse. They high-light how the existence of every one of us as living beings is defined by our choices and actions, our restrictions and our freedoms, and at the same time, it is inescapably linked and co-defined by our relatedness to the world.

References

Cooper, D. (1972) *The Death of the Family*, Harmondsworth: Pelican.

Deurzen-Smith, E. van (1996) 'Existential therapy', in W. Dryden (ed.), *Handbook of Individual Therapy*, London: Sage Publications.

Fromm, E. (1976) *The Sane Society*, London: Routledge & Kegan Paul.

Grier, F. (2004) *Oedipus and the Couple*, London: Karnac Books.

Haldane, D. and McCluskey, U. (1982) 'Existentialism and family therapy: a neglected perspective', *Journal of Family Therapy*, 4 (2), 117–132.

Heidegger, M. (2000) *Being and Time*, trans. J. Macquarrie and E. S. Robinson, Oxford: Blackwell.

Laing, R. D. and Esterson, A. (1970) *Sanity, Madness and the Family*, Harmondsworth: Pelican.

Macquarrie, J. (1972) *Existentialism: An Introduction, Guide and Assessment*, Harmondsworth: Penguin Books.

Merleau-Ponty, M. (1992) *Eye and Mind: The Primacy of Perception*, Evanston, IL: Northwestern University Press.

Merleau-Ponty, M. (2002) *Phenomenology of Perception*, New York: Routledge.

Moustakas, C. (ed.) (1966) *Existential Child Therapy*, New York: Basic Books.

Quinn, F. (2010) 'The right to choose: existential-phenomenological psychotherapy with primary school aged children', *Counselling Psychology Review*, 25 (1), 41–48.

Sartre, J.-P. (1973) *Existentialism and Humanism*, trans. P. Mairet, London: Methuen.

Scalzo, C. (2010) *Therapy with Children: An Existential Perspective*, London: Karnac Books.

Stadlen, A. and Stadlen, N. (2005) 'Families', in E. van Deurzen and C. Arnold-Baker (eds), *Existential Perspectives on Human Issues*, Basingstoke: Palgrave Macmillan.

Wenkart, A. (1966) 'The child meets the world', in C. Moustakas (ed.), *Existential Child Therapy*, New York: Basic Books.

CHAPTER 12

Relationship Therapy with Lesbian, Gay, Bisexual and Trans Clients

DARREN LANGDRIDGE AND MEG BARKER

The history of the psychotherapeutic professions and lesbian, gay, bisexual and trans (LGBT) clients is a deeply troubled one (Davies and Neal, 1996). Thankfully most of the negative attitudes of the past seem to be changing with all of the major UK therapy associations (BACP, UKCP, BPS) providing guidance on working ethically with clients from sexual and gender minorities and making statements critical of conversion/reparative therapy (which is designed to change someone's sexual orientation). In spite of such changes, pathologizing stances concerning LGBT clients still exist amongst some therapists, particularly those from a psychoanalytic perspective and some religiously informed therapists. The earliest school of existential therapy – Daseinsanalysis – does not escape charges of homonegativity and heteronormativity either. Medard Boss, the founder of Daseinsanalysis wrote in his book *The Meaning and Content of Sexual Perversions* (1947/1949) about homosexuality as a sexual perversion and, even as recently as 1987, thought that the healthiest state for a woman was to have children in a loving relationship with a man (Boss and Kenny, 1987).

The British School of existential therapy, by contrast, has a history in which notions of psychopathology are rejected. Building on the work of important figures in anti-psychiatry, notably Ronnie Laing (1960, 1961), the British School has adopted a strong critical perspective on psychopathology. Instead, there is a focus on maintaining the phenomenological attitude, wherein the therapist seeks to set aside their preconceptions and stay with the client and their own meaning-making process. Serious attention to the phenomenological method, as the basis of existential therapy, offers up the potential to step aside from the normative assumptions that underpin so many therapeutic theories and instead to work with our clients to understand the world as it appears to them.

148

In brief, the phenomenological method involves the therapist engaging in a series of strategies designed to better help them stay with the experience of the client and how the world appears to them (Langdridge, 2007a, 2012). The four key elements are: bracketing, description, horizontalization and verification. Bracketing involves the therapist attempting to set aside their preconceptions, as best they can, so that they can better understand the world as it appears to their client. So, for instance, when a client speaks of feeling attracted to the same sex we would not simply draw on our knowledge (and assumptions) about homosexuality but rather hold these views to one side and focus on getting the client to describe what they mean by this. Description forms the core of all phenomenological work, as we resist reductionist explanations for experiences (such as the belief that their same-sex feelings result from an abusive relationship with someone of a different sex). Description rather than explanation, for both therapist and client, forces us to stay with experience as lived and to resist bringing in our preconceptions. Horizontalization helps this process further by reminding us of the need to see meaning against the horizon of their social, political and cultural background and resist putting aspects of a client's experience in hierarchies of meaning or importance (by engaging in the process of equalization), at least until we have been able to check in with them in detail about the meaning and importance of different aspects of their account. An LGBT client may present to us due to having difficulties in their relationship but we must not assume that their being LGB or T is particularly important here unless they tell us so and, furthermore, we equally should not ignore the broader socio-cultural context of their experience of being LGB or T. Finally, we always need to check in with our clients about the meaning of what it is that they are telling us. By continued checking and rechecking (the process of verification) we can gain a firmer sense of the world in its appearing for our client, as free as is ever possible from our own biases and preconceptions.

Through rigorous application of the phenomenological method there is the potential for all therapists working with LGB or T clients to resist imposing their own worldviews onto their clients' experiences. This takes considerable skill and consistent attention as our natural attitude is inevitably the background to our everyday way of engaging in the world. Subtle assumptions about what is healthy or unhealthy, good or bad, right or wrong, creep into our work all too frequently. A gay couple may present to us with problems in their relationship where, for instance, they have an open relationship and have frequent and regular sex with others. It would be all too easy to assume that the cause of their problem was the open relationship and that they would be better off in a 'normal' monogamous relationship. This may of course be the case, but it may also be that their difficulties relate to a failure in communication or some other aspect of their relationship. By working phenomenologically we are reminded of the need to bracket such assumptions, to stay with description rather than explanation and to continually work to verify all our understandings with our clients themselves.

LGBT affirmative therapeutic practice

It is arguable that whilst a phenomenological attitude is undoubtedly beneficial, it is not – on its own – enough for effective therapeutic practice with
LGBT clients. In recent years there has been considerable growth in LGBT
affirmative therapies in the UK, USA and elsewhere in the world. One of the
most significant developments in the UK was the publication of the Pink Therapy series of books (Davies and Neal, 1996, 2000; Neal and Davies, 2000)
and in the USA publication of the handbooks of Perez et al. (2000) and
Ritter and Terndrup (2002). What these books represented was a watershed
in understandings of working psychotherapeutically with LGBT clients, mirroring earlier work developing black and feminist affirmative psychotherapies.
Here was a clarion cry for all counsellors and psychotherapists to treat LGBT
clients equally to heterosexual and cisgender clients (people who remain the
gender that they were assigned at birth). And even more than this, a call for us
to work to affirm LGBT identities as expressed, in recognition of the impact of
a heterosexist/cissexist social world (that is, a world that assumes everyone is
heterosexual and the same gender as that which was assigned when they were
born) on the development of all sexual and gender minority clients.

Langdridge (2007b) distinguishes between two forms of affirmative therapy
in use amongst humanistic and existential counsellors and psychotherapists – a
'strong' and a 'weak' version. The weak version is a form of 'ethically affirmative' therapy where LGBT identities are valued equally with heterosexual and
cisgender identities, mindful of the particular socio-cultural needs of LGBT
clients. This should be the mainstay of practice for all therapists working with
sexual and gender minority clients, although even here there is often work
to be done on the part of the therapist to ensure that they are prepared to
meet LGBT clients in such a way. It is not appropriate, for instance, for therapists working with minority clients to expect the client to educate the therapist
about their lifestyle, even if the therapist is accepting of what they hear. With
this 'weak' form of affirmative therapy, which should be the standard for all
ethical practice with minorities, the therapist has an obligation if they are to
work with LGBT clients to educate themselves about LGBT experience and
culture. They need to work to meet the client appropriately so that the client's
experience is like that of any other client.

The 'strong' form of affirmative therapy is more radical and involves the
therapist in affirming LGBT identities directly in an attempt to ameliorate the
impact of heterosexism, heteronormativity and cissexism (see Barker, 2011a).
This approach requires that the therapist move beyond the phenomenological
attitude to work with their clients in full recognition of the power of the social
world to limit ways of being that are at odds with the norm.

Davies (1996), drawing on Clark (1987), argues that the LGBT affirmative
therapist should actively encourage and support LGBT thoughts and feelings
and attempt to reduce feelings of shame and guilt. Shame and guilt are intrin-
sically connected emotions (Strasser, 2005) that are particularly valuable for
providing insight into both a person's own value system and wider cultural

norms. An existential perspective is particularly concerned with the exploration of values and a person's worldview (Deurzen, 2001) and it is here that close scrutiny of emotions on the part of both client and therapist may be particularly valuable when working with LGBT clients. Feelings of shame and guilt on the part of an LGBT client represent an insight into what matters to them but also the possibility of a personal struggle with the values of the wider social world into which they are thrown (Heidegger, 1962). With this in mind, it is important that we see a person's emotional expression in the broader social context (of a heterosexist and cissexist world) and do not rush too readily to collude with a client in behaviours that may be enacted to ameliorate uncomfortable feelings. Instead, we may need to stand with them, acknowledge their struggle, but work with them to question the way that such emotions might be emerging as a consequence of an oppressive social context rather than through any individual culpability. So, for instance, if a client speaks of shame and guilt at the thought of being LGB or T we need to explore the broader social context of the client, as much as their internal world, for the way in which it may act to pattern their emotional life. Existential relationship work will invariably involve a dimension of awareness raising and liberation, which is clearly particularly pertinent here.

Beyond work addressing feelings of shame and guilt on the part of the client, the LGBT affirmative therapist informed by ideas from existential philosophy will also examine difficult feelings that emerge in their encounters with LGBT clients. A therapist may, for instance, experience shame or disgust when hearing a story of sexual expression beyond their own experience. This should not be dismissed as counter-transference, as we might see in psychoanalysis, but rather be understood as something emerging in the very real relationship between client and therapist (Cohn, 1997). The values of the therapist are revealed here, along with important aspects of the relationship. Attending to and then working with such emotional responses are an important aspect of an existentially oriented approach to counselling and psychotherapy. This can be difficult, however, especially when our emotional responses (e.g. disgust at the sexual life of an LGBT client) challenges our understanding of ourselves (as a liberal minded and phenomenologically informed therapist). Should these feelings be too overwhelming and not something that can be addressed through self-reflection, supervision or personal therapy, then the therapist would be wise to refer the client on to another therapist who is more comfortable with such things.

Standing back from a client who is struggling whilst adopting an ostensibly neutral phenomenological attitude is also at odds with the spirit of an LGBT perspective. Neutrality in the face of an LGBT client who has been thrown into an oppressive social world is actually conservatism and fails to recognize the power of the therapist in working with a client to act as co-critic of the social world itself. An affirmative therapist would instead work actively and directly to indicate that they value even tentative expressions of LGBT identities and behaviours, allowing space for these to be explored in full acknowledgement of the difficult feelings that may accompany them. This is not to say that a therapist should assert their worldview here, at the expense of the client, but rather gently support them through, for instance, disclosing explicitly that they value such exploratory moves, and so moving beyond a simple descriptive phenomenological stance in their explorations. These explorations may lead to the rejection of nascent LGBT feelings but even here the client will have experienced a therapist who has actively disclosed their own stance in support of such moves, even if they do not always lead to full expression.

This position is troubling for some therapists who believe that it might prematurely foreclose possible ways of being and involve them stepping outside the phenomenological attitude (du Plock, 1997; Goldenberg, 2000). We think this is mistaken and fails to recognize the subtle ways in which all therapists operate within an ideological position and communicate these to their clients within their work even when engaged phenomenologically, whether knowingly or not. What is being called for here is more explicit recognition of the ways that we can communicate acceptance and the need for the therapist to work directly with their LGBT clients to counter the heterosexism and cissexism that they face.

Moving beyond the rigorous application of the phenomenological attitude is not something that should be undertaken lightly, however, and here Ricoeur (1970) provides a useful idea for therapists seeking to engage with suspicion. He cautions against what he terms the projection of the illusions of subjectivity by the analyst turning the critique first and foremost on him or herself. This should not be a one-off event but a continual effort to challenge our 'natural attitude', or everyday way of seeing the world, so that we can better work with challenging client material. That is, whenever we move beyond the phenomenological attitude we should always ask ourselves where our interventions are coming from, linking them with our own emotional world and critically thinking through our motivations. This critique needs to operate equally regardless of the motivation for our intervention. That is, we need to be equally sceptical of whatever we bring to the encounter with our clients that is critical or affirming of their LGB or T identity or behaviours. This is not to say that such interventions will be misplaced but rather that whenever we engage beyond the phenomenological attitude we need to be mindful of the needs of each individual client first and foremost and how our own worldviews may colour our interventions.

Davies (1996) and Ritter and Terndrup (2002) also advocate the therapist fulfilling an educative role with LGBT clients, especially concerning HIV, safety and access to services. This is also unusual for many therapists but not so peculiar for the existentially informed therapist. The aim amongst existentially oriented therapists is for a real adult relationship between client and therapist (Deurzen, 2001). Discussion of safety and practical issues may therefore form an appropriate part of the therapeutic relationship. This requires sufficient professional development on the part of the therapist of course and it is here that a therapist working extensively with LGBT clients may seek out appropriate training.

A powerful case for the 'strong' version of LGBT affirmative therapy has been made by Langdridge (2007b), drawing on the work of the hermeneutic-phenomenological philosopher Paul Ricoeur. There is not the space for detailed discussion here but Langdridge uses Ricoeur's (1970) distinction between hermeneutics of empathy (the usual mode of understanding in phenomenology) and hermeneutics of suspicion (as seen in psychoanalysis) to suggest that it might be possible to bring external hermeneutics, such as those from the LGBT psychological literature and/or queer theory, into practice informed by existential ideas. The more general argument is that it is not ethical or just to expect a client alone to do all the work in countering the prejudice that they have invariably experienced growing up in a heterosexist and cissexist world. There is recognition of the way in which we are all ideologically situated and that whilst the phenomenological stance is still the mainstay of effective practice informed by existential ideas, there is room for the therapist to do more, in full acknowledgement of the power they have to help a client to find ways of opening up new possibilities.

The first author's experience of working with Barry and George provides an example of how such an affirmative stance to existential therapy might play out in practice. He describes this in the following case illustration.

Case illustration

Barry and George are a gay couple who came to me as they were having problems in their relationship. They were both middle-aged, white and relatively wealthy. They had been together for seven years and whilst their relationship was initially very good the last few years had not been going as well as they would like. I saw both of them together and could see that they still had considerable affection for each other but felt that they 'had grown apart'. They were doing more and more on their own and less and less together. They had an open relationship and had this from very early in their relationship. Barry talked much more than George and spoke of how he missed the closeness that they used to have and that they 'now feel more like flatmates than lovers'. The early part of our work involved me staying with their experience in a relatively strict phenomenological stance, only breaking this to ensure that both had space to talk of their experience.

After this early stage it became apparent that Barry and George had lost touch with each other in a variety of ways. Their sexual life had petered out due in part to what they saw as some perceived incompatibilities in their sexual preferences. Barry was into BDSM (Bondage and Discipline, Dominance and Submission, and Sadomasochism: a term frequently used by members of communities interested in these consensual activities) whilst George preferred more 'vanilla' sex (sex which is not 'kinky' like BDSM). George also expressed concerns about whether an open relationship was really for him, wondering whether this was the cause of their problems. They had also been turning to others for social stimulation, tending to spend time separately with friends to indulge their interests in art, cinema and the theatre. It would have been easy to conclude that George's explanation for their problems was the truth of the situation and that they either needed to return to a more conventional monogamous relationship or to go their separate ways. I was not convinced by this for when I explored George's concerns further it became apparent that he had actually been quite content with their open relationship for some time and that some of his disquiet stemmed from his more conservative upbringing and worry that others (particularly his family members) might disapprove of the open nature of the relationship. There was considerable shame attached to the open relationship and also to any possibility of engaging in BDSM activities with his partner.

After some time and with a strong sense of what was occurring, I broke from the phenomenological attitude and started working directly with George, supported by Barry, to clarify his concerns and explore the source of his shame. I supported all options equally but did not shy away from affirming the possibility of an open relationship being a valid option for them both. I also challenged George about his beliefs about an open relationship being inappropriate, seeking to explore where these beliefs stemmed from. It became clear that the negative views about an open relationship were not something related to his personal values, but resulted from his anxiety about the views of others (within the context of our exploration of the Mitwelt – or social realm – and the relationship between this and his Uberwelt or philosophy of life). The shame he felt was deeply contextual and linked with the social context in which he had been brought up. I was careful to check in with George at all times about his own needs (for instance, concerning his desire for safety and commitment) and whether this could be met in an open relationship. It was clear to George that he could feel safe within such a relationship.

My work with Barry was similarly directive, with me asking about his values and whether he might find a monogamous and 'vanilla' relationship satisfying. It was clear that Barry had spent considerable time examining his own views about relationships (and had experienced monogamous relationships previously) and felt that an open and kinky relationship was the best way of realizing his sexual and relational self. We questioned this in relation to the threat to this relationship and Barry was distraught at the prospect of losing George but could not reconcile himself to a different relationship form.

With this element of the therapy concluded we then moved on to look at how they might find ways of being with each other more. Their relationship had become one founded on I-It relating (Buber, 1958), with them both losing sight of their desire to care for each other and engage meaningfully beyond the day-to-day practicalities of living. We looked back at the early stage of their relationship and what they had lost, examining what had changed. We also looked at how they might find a way to come together sexually such that both felt that their desires were being met by the other and they could find a way of being together sexually that was joyful and loving. It was through puppy play (where they assumed roles of master and dog in a training situation) that they found a way to bridge their apparently different desires. Their commitment to each other was always strong and once the underlying concerns about the nature of their relationship were dealt with it was a relatively simple matter of discussing how they might enjoy each other more. They found they could re-connect with ease and realized that their problems were quite simple as they had simply forgotten the joy that they experienced with each other, explaining their problems away in a manner that meant they were unlikely to find that joy again. Once their ad hoc rationalizations were explored their experience of each other shifted also with them once again falling in love. They returned to a place where they could achieve a sense of transcendence through their relationship with each other (Buber, 1958).

Beyond LGBT affirmativity

As seen above, a critical stance towards heteronormativity, and an LGBT affirmative practice, involves awareness and interrogation of more than just therapist understandings and attitudes around the diversity of sexual and gender identities. It is also important to expand knowledge, and to question assumptions, around relationship structures and around sexual practices more broadly, as well as considering the intersections between sexuality, gender and other aspects of experience such as race, religion, class, culture, age, ability and geography.

If we consider relationships in this context, their heteronormative status invariably leads to an assumption of 'mononormativity' (Barker and Langdridge, 2010a, 2010b): that monogamous relationships are the normal way of relating, and that anything outside of monogamy constitutes 'cheating' or 'infidelity'. This 'natural attitude' fails to capture the rich variety of relationships that people experience and loses sight of the key existential concerns (of, for instance, care for another) that underpin all relationships, whatever their form. Clearly this mononormative stance is also questionable on a global scale given that only approximately 43 out of 238 societies worldwide are monogamous (Rubin, 2001). This has implications for practice within a multicultural context. Also, various forms of open non-monogamy exist within contemporary Western culture. Open relationships (where there are sexual encounters outside the main couple) are particularly prevalent amongst gay men, and polyamorous relationships (where there are multiple sexual and/or romantic relationships) are common amongst bisexual people, with estimates of around half of people in each of these groups being openly non-monogamous in these ways (Bonello, 2009; Wosick-Correa, 2010). These forms, coupled with forms of 'new monogamy' (Nelson, 2010) and swinging (McDonald, 2010), which involve some degree of openness within heterosexual relationships, mean that relationship therapists should not assume that their clients have a monogamous contract. Rather they should explore, with clients, their preferred degrees of emotional and sexual exclusivity. Considerations of such issues often relate to existential tensions between freedom and togetherness (and related tensions around privacy, solitude, independence of decision-making and extent of 'belonging' to the other) (Barker, 2011b). It would be useful for therapists to familiarize themselves with the various forms of contracts and relationship philosophies which openly non-monogamous people apply to their relationships in order to work around these areas with clients (Barker and Langdridge, 2010).

In relation to sexual practices, as we have suggested elsewhere in this volume (Barker and Langdridge, Chapter 4), it is useful to expand our understanding of sex beyond normative notions of penile-vaginal intercourse. This would include exploring the diversities and range that exist in sexual desire, from asexuality and celibacy to levels of sexual activity far exceeding our own, without pathologizing this as hypoactive, on the one hand, or hyperactive, excessive or addictive on the other. It would also require expanding our understandings of sexual identity and practice beyond gender of attraction, to encompass other areas such as the roles people enjoy playing in sex, the positions they like, the activities that most turn them on, the sensations they find pleasurable, the sounds they make, the places or times of day they want to have sex, whether they like physical and/or visual and/or narrative forms of stimulation, and so on (Barker, 2012). BDSM is an umbrella term that covers some of this diversity. As with the heterosexual questionnaire and homoworld activities (mentioned below), it can be useful to consider exercises which require us to confront our own assumptions about such practices (e.g. Barker, 2005, 2007) and for therapists to inform themselves about the diversity of practices and identities in existence and the variety of meanings these may have for those who take part in them (see Langdridge and Barker, 2007 for more detail on BDSM, and Richards and Barker, 2012, for further information for practitioners on LGBT affirmativity and beyond).

It is also important to remember that understandings of sexuality differ across culture and context. If we take the example of people who have an 'opposite sex' relationship but who also have sex with people of the 'same sex', amongst white people in the UK such behaviour is often seen as a reason to mistrust people who are viewed as 'really gay' but lying about it (Barker et al., 2012). There may be a context in black British communities of such people rejecting potential LGBT identities due to these being viewed as part of white culture (Boykin, 2005). And there may be greater allowance of sexual fluidity, without identity labels, in some South and East Asian contexts (Gosine, 2006). It should be remembered that such cultural categories are extremely broad and that there are likely multiple meanings attached to such behaviour within each group, related to class, religion, generation, geographical location, personal experience and many other factors (see Butler et al., 2010; das Nair and Butler, 2012).

Training and continuous professional development

All LGBT people live in a social world in which they are viewed as non-normative, and where attraction and relationships between one man and one woman is regarded as the normal form of sexuality. Related to this, these genders are regarded as dichotomous and opposite in many respects (women being emotional and men rational, women soft and men tough, etc.). Also, penile-vaginal intercourse is seen as the normal form of sex (see Barker and Langdridge, this volume, Chapter 4, for further implications of this). When engaged in training (whether this is initial therapeutic training or CPD) there are a number of methods that may be used to highlight the values of a therapist. These may alert people to their own 'natural attitude' concerning LGBT issues and possibly to the need to engage more fully in an existential phenomenological attitude.

For instance, we can see the implications of heteronormativity for LGBT people if we imagine a world reversed, where being LGBT was regarded as the norm, whilst heterosexuality was viewed as peculiar and requiring of explanation. Key features of an existential approach concerning the need to live according to one's own values and, most importantly, stand out from the herd (Nietzsche, 1968) are particularly salient here. Recognition of the unique nature of existence is central within existential theory and acts as a valuable corrective to the tendency to project one's own views onto others. There is an expectation within existential theory, which is particularly important for existentially informed therapists, that we must all work hard to identify our values and assumptions and recognize the historically and culturally situated nature of existence. The 'homoworld' short story (Butler, 2010) is a useful exercise for people who are heterosexual themselves to use to reflect upon what it might feel like to be outside of the sexuality norm. For example, in homoworld heterosexual people have to decide whether to come out (and deal with the stress of possible rejection or prejudice) or to hide their relationship (and deal with the stress of keeping such an important thing secret). Also they have to deal with questions from others about the ways in which they decide to commit to their relationship or to have children. On a very everyday level, they are surrounded by LGBT representations: on billboard advertisements, in pop songs, and on the street where it is generally only LGBT people who are kissing or holding hands.

The heterosexuality questionnaire (Rochlin, 2003) is similarly useful, highlighting common questions which are asked about LGBT identities, but not about heterosexuality, such as what you think caused your sexuality, whether you are *really* that sexuality, and whether it might be better just to keep quiet about it (see also Earlham College Students, 2011). Dominic Davies, the founder of Pink Therapy (Davies and Neal, 1996), suggests that heterosexual therapists should do 'homowork' to experience – albeit briefly – what it is like being LGBT. This could include reading an LGBT magazine in public, holding hands with a 'same-gender' person, wearing non-gender normative clothing, or keeping their heterosexuality in the closet for a week by ensuring that they do not give it away in conversation (for example, not mentioning a partner's gender when talking about what you did at the weekend or when talking on the phone with a tradesperson) (Butler et al., 2010).

The use of training techniques such as these provides a simple but effective route to encourage therapists to think existentially about sexual and gender minority issues and challenge their 'natural attitude'. Through the use of such training techniques the critical spirit at the heart of an existential perspective may therefore gain greater clarity and improve practice with LGBT issues in existential relationship work.

Conclusions

This chapter has made a case for the importance of paying particular attention to the needs of LGBT clients when engaged in relationship therapy. Whilst phenomenology provides an invaluable approach to therapy seeking to focus on people's experience as lived, it may well be necessary to go beyond a hermeneutics of empathy to encourage a hermeneutics of suspicion: a critical analysis of the impact of the heteronormative and cissexist culture in which clients are living. This has implications for heterosexual and cisgender clients, as much as it does for LGBT ones, as explored further in our other chapter in this volume (Chapter 4) in relation to gendered experiences of sex, but most importantly offers a route in which we can work existentially with sexual and gender minority clients to better meet their needs.

References

Barker, M. (2005) 'Experience of SM awareness training', *Lesbian and Gay Psychology Review,* 6 (3), 268–273.

Barker, M. (2007) 'Turning the world upside down: developing a tool for training about SM', in D. Langdridge and M. Barker (eds), *Safe, Sane and Consensual: Contemporary Perspectives on Sadomasochism,* 261–270, Basingstoke: Palgrave Macmillan.

Barker, M. (2011a) *What's Wrong with Heteronormativity?* Available at: http://learn. open.ac.uk/mod/oublog/viewpost.php?post=78518 (accessed 22 March 2011).

Barker, M. (2011b) 'Monogamies and non-monogamies – a response to: "The Challenge of Monogamy: Bringing it Out of the Closet and Into the Treatment Room" by Marianne Brandon', *Sexual and Relationship Therapy,* 26 (3), 281–287.

Barker, M. (2012) *Rewriting the Rules: An Integrative Guide to Love, Sex and Relationships,* London: Routledge.

Barker, M. and Langdridge, D. (eds) (2010a) *Understanding Non-monogamies,* New York: Routledge.

Barker, M. and Langdridge, D. (2010b) 'Whatever happened to non-monogamies? Critical reflections on recent research and theory', *Sexualities,* 13 (6), 748–772.

Barker, M., Richards, C., Jones, R., Bowes-Catton, H., and Plowman, T. (2012) *The Bisexuality Report: Bisexual Inclusion in LGBT Equality and Diversity,* Milton Keynes: The Open University, Centre for Citizenship, Identity and Governance.

Bonello, C. (2009) 'Gay monogamy and extra-dyadic sex: a critical review of the theoretical and empirical literature', *Counselling Psychology Review,* 24 (3 and 4), 51–65.

Boss, M. and Kenny, B. (1987) 'Phenomenological or daseinsanalytical approach', in J. L. Fusshage and C. A. Loew (eds), *Dream Interpretation,* New York: PMA.

Boykin, K. (2005) *Beyond the Down Low: Sex, Lies and Denial in Black America,* New York: Carroll & Graf.

Buber, M. (1958) *I and Thou,* Edinburgh: T & T Clark.

Butler, C. (2010) *Homoworld*, available at: http://www.bps.org.uk/downloadfile.cfm?
    file_uuid=035DD3B4-1143-DFD0-7EBA-89C49CB6637E&ext=doc   (accessed
    22 August 2011).
Butler, C., O'Donovan, A. and Shaw, E. (2010) *Sex, Sexuality and Therapeutic Practice*,
    London: Routledge.
Clark, D. (1987) *The New Loving Someone Gay*, Berkeley, CA: Celestial Arts.
Cohn, H. W. (1997) *Existential Thought and Therapeutic Practice: Introduction to
    Existential Therapy*, London: Sage.
Das Nair, R. and Butler, C. (2012) *Intersectionality, Sexuality and Psychological Thera-
    pies: Working with Lesbian, Gay and Bisexual Diversity*, London: Wiley-Blackwell.
Davies, D. (1996) 'Towards a model of gay affirmative therapy', in D. Davies and
    C. Neal (eds), *Pink Therapy: A Guide for Counsellors and Therapists Working
    with Lesbian, Gay and Bisexual Clients*, 24–40, Buckingham: Open University
    Press.
Davies, D. and Neal, C. (eds) (1996) *Pink Therapy: A Guide for Counsellors and Thera-
    pists Working with Lesbian, Gay and Bisexual Clients*, Buckingham: Open University
    Press.
Davies, D. and Neal, C. (eds) (2000) *Pink Therapy 2: Therapeutic Perspectives on Shaw,
    Working with Lesbian, Gay and Bisexual Clients*, Buckingham: Open University
    Press.
Deurzen, E. van (2001) *Existential Counselling in Practice*, 2nd edn, London: Sage.
du Plock, S. (1997) 'Sexual misconceptions: a critique of gay affirmative therapy and
    some thoughts on an existential-phenomenological theory of sexual orientation',
    Journal of the Society for Existential Analysis, 8 (2), 56–71.
Earlham College Students (2011) *Straight Privilege Checklist*, available at: http://
    www.cs.earlham.edu/~hyrax/personal/files/student_res/straightprivilege.htm
    (accessed 22 August 2011).
Goldenberg, H. (2000) 'A response to Martin Milton', *Journal of the Society for
    Existential Analysis*, 11 (1), 103–105.
Gosine, A. (2006) ' "Race", culture, power, sex, desire, love: writing in "men who have
    sex with men" ', *IDS Bulletin*, 37 (5). Available at: http://www.siyanda.org/docs/
    Race_Culture_Power_Sex_Desire-Gosine.doc (accessed 22 April 2011).
Heidegger, M. (1962) *Being and Time*, trans. J. Macquarrie, Oxford: Blackwell.
Laing, R. D. (1960) *The Divided Self: An Existential Study in Sanity and Madness*,
    Harmondsworth: Penguin.
Laing, R. D. (1961) *The Self and Others*, London: Tavistock.
Langdridge, D. (2007a) *Phenomenological Psychology: Theory, Research and Method*,
    Harlow: Pearson Education.
Langdridge, D. (2007b) 'Gay affirmative therapy: a theoretical framework and
    defence', *Journal of Gay and Lesbian Psychotherapy*, 11 (1/2), 27–43.
Langdridge, D. (2012) *Existential Counselling and Psychotherapy*, London: Sage.
Langdridge, D. and Barker, M. (eds) (2007) *Safe, Sane and Consensual: Contemporary
    Perspectives on Sadomasochism*, Basingstoke: Palgrave Macmillan.
McDonald, D. (2010) 'Swinging: pushing the boundaries of non-monogamy?' in
    M. Barker and D. Langdridge (eds), *Understanding Non-Monogamies*, New York:
    Routledge.
Neal, C. and Davies, D. (eds) (2000). *Pink Therapy 3: Issues in Therapy with Lesbian,
    Gay, Bisexual and Transgender Clients*, Buckingham: Open University Press.
Nelson, T. (2013) *The New Monogamy: Redefining your Relationship after Infidelity*,
    Oakland, CA: New Harbinger Publications.

Nietzsche, F. (1968) *The Will to Power*, trans. W. Kaufmann and R. J. Hollingdale, New York: Vintage Books.

Perez, R. M., DeBord, K. A. and Bieschke, K. J. (2000) *Handbook of Counseling and Psychotherapy with Lesbian, Gay, and Bisexual Clients*, Washington, DC: American Psychological Association.

Richards, C. and Barker, M. (2012) *Sexuality and Gender for Counsellors, Psychologists and Health Professionals: A Practical Guide,*. London: Sage.

Ricoeur, P. (1970) *Freud and Philosophy: An Essay on Interpretation*, trans. D. Savage, New Haven, CT: Yale University Press.

Ritter, K. Y. and Terndrup, A. I. (2002) *Handbook of Affirmative Psychotherapy with Lesbians and Gay Men*, New York: Guilford Press.

Rochlin, M. (2003) 'The heterosexual questionnaire', in M. S. Kimmel and A. L. Ferber (eds) *Privilege: A Reader*, Boulder, CO: Westview Press.

Rubin, R. H. (2001) 'Alternative family lifestyles revisited, or Whatever happened to swingers, group marriages and communes? *Journal of Family Issues*, 7 (6), 711.

Strasser, F. (2005) *Emotions: Experiences in Existential Psychotherapy and Life*, London: Duckworth.

Wosick-Correa, K. (2010) 'Agreements, rules, and agentic fidelity in polyamorous relationships', *Psychology and Sexuality*, 1 (1), 44–61.

CHAPTER 13

Working with Partners with Asperger Syndrome

DIGBY TANTAM AND EMMY VAN DEURZEN

Introduction

As we have seen in previous chapters, communication between partners in an intimate relationship is difficult at the best of times, as it often gets blocked by people's inability to know and express what they really feel and think, without offending the other. When partners have autistic traits this difficulty is multiplied tenfold. People in this predicament may not even know that they have emotions and will rarely recognize the other's feelings. This makes it very hard to gauge interactions. In these circumstances communication can become nearly impossible. It might even get completely blocked, leading to the couple living alongside each other, without really living together, other than in practical ways. This presents a considerable challenge to the relationship therapist as each partner becomes ensconced in their own world, unaware of each other's needs, desires and fears. The lessons that can be learnt from working with this kind of extreme disconnection are of great importance to our understanding of existential isolation and when working towards better communication in all forms of relational therapy.

Asperger Syndrome

Many people with an Autistic Spectrum Disorder (ASD) go through life without ever having a partner. Some live celibate lives, some go to prostitutes, and some have risky brief sexual encounters. The latter may be abusive in nature.

Our Sheffield study of adolescents and adults with Asperger syndrome and high functioning autism found that about a third of our respondents, half of whom had never had a diagnosis before, had a partner. Since our sample included more young adolescents than any other group, and since we were asking about a current partner and thus missed people who may have had a partner in the past, this suggests that many more able people with an ASD – perhaps the majority – do have partners at some time or another, though such relationships may not last.

Relationship problems due indirectly to ASD

Before we consider the difficulties that they and their partners may have, we need to stress that having an ASD may not in itself be the primary influence on the outcome of a relationship.

The risk of anxiety is much increased in most people with ASD, and anxiety tends to reduce the likelihood of partner conflict being resolved and, unless it can be buffered by increasing support from the other partner, may lead to a long-term increase in conflict that can destroy the relationship (Tantam, 2011).

Many people with an ASD – 90 per cent in the Sheffield survey – have been marginalized, teased or bullied – their 'otherness' emphasized and reinforced. In many people with and without ASD, this can lead to an irritable sensitivity to criticism and a tendency to withdraw from situations of conflict or challenge. In other people it may lead to a tendency to devalue intimacy with others, and replace it with an emotional investment in an inner life or in private pursuits. A few develop a patina of uncaring blithe confidence. Any of these tendencies – paranoid, schizoid or narcissistic in the jargon of the psychiatrist, or distrustful, withdrawn or shameless in more ordinary language – reduces the capacity for intimacy (something often associated with ASD anyway – Tantam, 1988) and therefore the likelihood of an enduring relationship with a partner.

So even before considering the effects of living with an ASD or with a person with an ASD, we have to consider that person's experience and the impact of that experience on their characteristic ways of being in the world. This is likely to be an experience of existential isolation.

Relationship problems due directly to ASD

Many people with ASD describe themselves as being hypersensitive to stimuli, and react as if they are. They find themselves to be more aware of flickering lights, for example the flickering of fluorescent lamps. Low-level noise such as machinery hums or the chatter of people who work together in open plan offices, or loud and unexpected noises may perturb them greatly. More specific noise intolerance may occur to children's voices, particular tunes or jingles, the noise of vacuum cleaners, or barking dogs. Many of these sounds are high-pitched which fits in with the often-proposed hyperacusis, or increased awareness of sound theory, but emotional significance may also lead to some sounds being given more attention. Loud voices, for example, usually mean a quarrel. So the common aversion to loud sounds may really be an aversion to quarrels or confrontations.

It is probably best to consider the reaction to sound as one kind of over-arousal, or 'sensory overload', which may also occur as a result of a busy day, an argument, an unexpected and unwelcome change, or a machine breaking down. Over-arousal may not be apparent until a person 'melts down' in a tantrum in which words may be said, things hit or broken, or occasionally physical aggression exhibited. Such meltdowns may cause considerable upset or hurt to a partner. The person with an ASD may not understand this and may expect that a simple apology will put the genie back in the bottle.

Expectations

One of the simplest models of relationships is exchange theory. This supposes that people stay in a relationship so long as the profit of doing so outweighs the cost. The concept of profit focuses on the importance of a partner's expectations. When a partner enters into a commitment with someone with an ASD, and when they know something about the condition, their expectations are likely to be realistic. They may, for example, not intend to have children and therefore have fewer worries about their partner's condition being hereditary, and they may be attracted by the fact that a partner with an ASD rarely has secrets or a double life. But when a diagnosis has not been made or an unrealistic expectation has been given, then the discovery that a partner has an ASD can be devastating. Some people with Asperger syndrome may be able to wine and dine a romantic partner by following a kind of script that they may even have read in a self-help book. But polite solicitude of that kind may not translate into being able to meet the needs of an intimate partner on a daily basis, or knowing intuitively how children feel about things. So, though the person with ASD may have come across as very authentic initially, their inability to fit in with the inauthentic expectations of the social world may become an increasing problem. The artificial nature of their mode of relating may soon start to grate. When a person begins to have a suspicion that their partner's apparent social ability or care is learnt rather than coming from a romantic and loving heart, it can lead to considerable distress, disappointment and anger.

Relationship difficulties in these circumstances are often attributed to the moral failings of the parties concerned. It is often all too easy to assume that the actions of people with ASD, if they cause offence or frustration to other people, are due to the originator failing in care, lacking in compassion, or being self-centred rather than being due to a disability or impairment. Moral failings evoke criticism and retaliation, even punishment. Diagnosis is often a double-edged sword. Disability evokes sympathy and understanding, but also condescension and the risk of humiliation. It may help partners to find ways of staying together, or legitimize one partner leaving the other.

Common complaints

Whether or not there is a formal diagnosis, partners in relationships where one individual has an ASD often come up with similar complaints about their loved ones.

When only one partner has an ASD, the common complaints of the affected partner include:

- I never seem to get things right
- I have high standards (for tidiness, for sameness, for time-keeping or other things) but these are not respected

- I often feel exhausted and over-stressed, but no account is taken of this
- She uses sex/ he uses money to pay me back or to control me
- I'm frightened that he/she will give up on me
- I want to be close, and yet when we are together I feel all my routines are upset

The complaints of the unaffected partner often include:

- If only s/he would know what I wanted, without me telling him/her
- She/he never remembers my birthday
- He/she has never liked my family or my friends, and can be quite rude to them
- I don't know why he can't just get a job
- There are days when he/she is just cold and I don't know why
- I do all the housework
- He starts jobs in the house but never finishes
- If we are going out, we always end up being late even if we start hours before we need to
- I am getting edged out of the house by all the things he collects
- He/she spends more time on his/her special interests than on me or the family

Key skills for working with people with an ASD

For any therapist who works with people with an ASD, careful use of language is very important. If it is used idiomatically it may be misunderstood. The therapist needs to try to put things in a black or white way and not use shades of grey. Social jokes are not appreciated and should be avoided in order not to alienate people. Puns, however, may be specially enjoyed. People with ASD should not be judged on appearance or on their facial or non-verbal expression. Remember that a person's non-verbal expressions or lack of them, if they have Asperger syndrome, may conceal deep feeling that is buried inside. Many people with ASD expect to be humiliated or criticized. Men will often deal with this with hostility or stonewalling, women with submission or apparent compliance but both may experience it as abusive. Beware of these reactions as they indicate a breakdown of trust in the therapist. You have to aim to reassure and allow expression of the unspoken fears.

One good way of engaging with people with ASD is that they enjoy answering apparently unanswerable questions and will pursue fair questions with some enthusiasm, to find that there are answers after all. The use of Socratic dialogue, where therapist and clients enter into an active dialogue and debate, can prove very effective.

Working phenomenologically, and in particular the bracketing of the therapist's own values and beliefs, is particularly important when working with this client group. It is often easy for neurotypical therapists to side with the neurotypical partner in the couple, and the partner with ASD will be half expecting this, often believing that neurotypicals are a tribe that excludes people with an

ASD. It is more crucial than normal to be fair and evenhanded and search to understand and support each of the partners. In doing so you will have to be willing to be very concrete and practical and to sometimes translate one partner's words to the other, checking all the while that you are not misinterpreting and that the other agrees.

You also have to take arousal levels into account. Some partners find that they do better maintaining two households that provide sanctuary when the relationship becomes too tense. Trying to make them conform to the usual norms and abandon this dual life is often counterproductive. Helping them to identify their own values and norms, on the other hand, often frees them to adopt a more authentic relationship style.

Remember that people with an ASD may, unlike most other clients, portray themselves in a worse light than is really justified. Sometimes the therapist needs to act as an advocate for them and sometimes, too, for the partner who may not put their own emotional needs into language that is concrete enough for the partner with ASD to grasp. People with an ASD are originals. Many partners prize just this and value having found someone so special to love. Therapists must be prepared to match this originality with originality of their own and with the flexibility to adjust to the people in front of them and preparedness to delight in being surprised by them.

Working with a married couple with ASD

Cliff and Cathy (names chosen by the partners' themselves as pseudonyms for this case illustration) had been married for thirty years, but had spent ten of these living separately. When they came for couple therapy they had resumed living together but were not sure they could carry on doing so as they were both very unhappy with the relationship once again. I (EvD) worked with them for about two and a half years, initially on a fortnightly basis, and then on a monthly basis, with each session lasting for an hour and forty minutes. Cliff and Cathy were both in their sixties and retired. They had raised three children and one of the issues they mentioned at the start of therapy was that Cathy felt pretty desperate about her relationship with the children. She felt that Cliff had regularly bad-mouthed her to the children, who now blamed her for the break up and the misery this had caused everybody. Both partners were also very tired of the constant fighting and misunderstanding between them. Cathy regularly felt suicidal and she despaired of Cliff ever understanding her. Cliff felt battered by Cathy ever since he had received a diagnosis of ASD some years previously. Cathy thought that the diagnosis explained all of their past problems and she was delighted to have found the reason for their difficulties. She could not see why Cliff objected to being reminded of his autism. The idea that his brain was wired differently allowed her to tolerate some of his idiosyncrasies, when these had previously been impossible to accept. She was apparently unaware of Cliff's hurt and anger, each time she mentioned AS. He would visibly cringe and shut himself off each time the word was mentioned. To Cathy this looked like anger, when to me it seemed like pain. Cliff immediately, and gratefully, affirmed that it felt like pain and that he was not angry. Cathy was very caught up in her own inner world and did not really see Cliff as a suffering person, but rather as her aggressor and tormentor. She suffered greatly from his gruffness, as he was sometimes quite rude, aggressive and unkind. Cliff accepted these descriptors of his conduct with a somewhat enigmatic smile, as if he was shy, apologetic and yet somewhat mischievous about his unruly behaviour. Cathy readily accepted that she was hypersensitive in general and certainly had an acute sense of being slighted or being treated as deficient. But she was also sure she didn't make it up or exaggerate and that she knew exactly when she was being treated badly. She would react strongly, though only inwardly, to any negative remark or poke that came her way from Cliff and gradually cut herself off more in order to protect herself.

Cathy herself had also been told that she had autistic traits and she found this a comfort rather than a problem. But perhaps she wasn't taking responsibility for her way of being, nor for the way it affected Cliff. She just wished Cliff would join in with her in celebrating their different way of being. To Cathy, having an ASD was like being told you were left-handed. It was just a fact and meant your chemistry was a little different. It was not something to be ashamed of, but something that explained why you could not fit in so well with other people. It was a kind of freedom, even perhaps something to claim as a special quality. For Cliff the autism label was deeply unpleasant as he had always been able to assert his way of being and had got through life well enough without a diagnosis. When challenged on this point by Cathy, he admitted that he had always been a bit of a loner and also sometimes somewhat of a bully in relation to other people at work, riding rough shod over them, if they did not fit in with him. He said he did not much care about what other people thought of him or how they responded to him. Cathy immediately reacted with upset to this statement but felt reassured when I explored it in more depth with Cliff, who was able to state that he was only talking about strangers. He cared deeply about Cathy's profound unhappiness and it mattered greatly to him what she thought of him, but felt incapable of doing anything about it. Cathy wept and said it was the first time that Cliff had said such a thing. She could not quite believe he meant it, but fervently hoped he did and felt so much better for it.

Both partners agreed that Cliff had treated Cathy badly in the past and that this was the reason she had moved out. They also agreed that it was the diagnosis that had enabled Cathy to move back in with him as it had given her hope that he did not mean to do what he had done and that he might be able to change. However, she still felt trampled on by Cliff and lately things had gone from bad to worse and she needed to find out whether they should stay together or not and if so how they could improve their relationship.

As usual I had separate sessions with each partner and continued these separate sessions in front of the other partner once we started meeting jointly. This allowed me to understand first of all where each of them was coming from, exploring their worldview and way of being, so that I could translate what they were saying to the other. Of course in doing this translation I would carefully check back with the other partner to ensure that I was expressing their experience fairly. Verification is even more important when working with people with ASD.

I quickly figured out that I had to encourage Cliff to locate feelings he had not even been aware he was having and help him speak up about these, especially when they were unspoken positive feelings. He was already quite good at showing his negative feelings with offensive remarks and obstructive actions. I had to enable Cathy to speak confidently about the feelings she was sometimes drowning in, but too frightened to speak up about. Many of these feelings were negative ones, which she felt were taboo. She was already very good at giving Clive positive feedback when he did rally around and perhaps only too prepared to forgive him when he hurt her. I soon learnt that both ignoring Cathy's despair or resonating and empathizing with it were counter-productive. If I ignored it, she would become frozen in it. If I empathized, Clive would switch off. However, if I acknowledged Cathy's despair and challenged it, she would respond extremely vigorously, with anger and numerous good arguments, engaging profoundly with a search for solutions. Cliff would also become very engaged, though a little bit frightened of Cathy's vehemence. I showed Cliff, by example, how he might use his ability to be challenging in a more sensitive and humorous way. He began showing more and more sensitivity, initiative and humour as a result, because he could now see a pathway towards communication that he felt able to use. Here is an example of one of their exchanges in therapy.

Cathy [weeping]: I feel like giving up. It's no use. It's been decades of suffering and it doesn't get any better. He will never see what he is doing to me. I just want to throw myself off a cliff.

Cliff [gruffly]: I have no idea what you are talking about.

Cathy [sobbing]: You see, he just pushes me over the edge.

Emmy [smiling]: He is just a rude so and so, who is making your life impossible and you are totally at the end of your tether and he still doesn't get it.

Cliff [triumphant]: But what is there to get?

Emmy [encouraging]: Yes, Cathy, what is there to get! You really need to spell it out. The tears are not doing the job. You have got to reach this man and tell him, straight out.

Cathy [angry]: You think it is easy, do you? I have put up with this for years and I can't cope with his indifference and rudeness any longer. Do you really think he will make an effort to be sensitive to me?

Emmy [turning to Cliff]: Well, will you, Cliff? Will you make that effort for your wife, the wife you love more than anything in the world?

Cliff [looks scared now]: Of course I will.
  [Silence]

Emmy [to Cliff]: Well, tell her what you need to know, Cliff. Reach out to her.

Cliff [hesitant]: What are you crying about?

Cathy [eyes to heavens]: You should know. I have told you often enough.

Emmy [to Cathy]: You need to tell him straight, Cathy. Don't expect him to play guessing games. Cliff is in good faith here. You just need to learn to communicate together.

Cliff [shy and genuine, smiling at Cathy]: I really haven't got a clue.

Cathy [to Emmy, sounding relieved, stopping crying]: Perhaps I have not realised how to get through to him.

[Emmy nods and invites Cathy with a hand gesture to keep talking, but to address herself to Cliff.]

Cathy [to Cliff, some tears still dribbling down her cheeks]: I really need to know you care about me when I am upset. Do you want to find out what it is about, or is it just a bother to you?

Emmy [jumping in before Cliff can put his foot in it]: It is just a bother to him, but he wants to find out. [Turning to Cliff]: True?

Cliff [looking dazed and relieved]: Well, it is not really a bother either, I just don't understand it. But yes, I do want to find out, if that's possible.

Emmy [to Cathy]: Is it possible?

Cathy [to both]: Of course. I want nothing more.

Cathy then started telling Cliff about an event that happened last week, which he had completely forgotten about but which had stuck in her mind as she had felt completely destroyed by the way he had behaved in front of one of the children who was visiting. Cliff had no idea what he had done wrong and was crestfallen as he carefully listened to Cathy's story, now pouring out as the tears had poured out of her before. Cliff then was genuinely confused about exactly where he had gone wrong and was grateful when I pointed out that what Cathy had wanted was for him to speak respectfully of her rather than dismissively. He had no idea that what he had said was inappropriate. He knew not what was required. To him it had just been a bit of small talk and he had said what he thought his son might have expected him to say about his mother, who he was not on good terms with. Cathy, with further encouragement, was able to explain how she thought that their son perceived her in this bad light, precisely because of the way in which Cliff spoke of her badly to the children, regularly. Cliff asked me what he should have said. I asked Cathy to tell him. She said that it would have been nice if he had felt able to say something a bit more positive. I said (and illustrated this with some objects on the floor): look what you did, Cliff: you lined yourself up with your son, leaving Cathy standing alone on the other side. What she needed was for you to join her on her side and speak together to your son, showing him your loyalty to your wife and his mum.

Cliff [surprised]: You felt left out?

Cathy [exasperated]: Yes, of course I did. I always do. You never see it.

Emmy [calming]: Cliff is learning, Cathy. This is new.

Cliff [sincere and contrite]: I really want to find out how it works. I am trying to get it.

Cathy [softly]: It would be so good if you could understand and take my side, for a change.

Cliff [softly]: But how? What do I do? What did you want me to do?

Cathy [confused]: Well, not be so rude about me.

Emmy [affirmative]: You mean, you wanted him to say something nice rather than unkind about you.

Cathy [smiling at me, with surprise]: Well yes, that would be novel, if that is not too much to ask.

Emmy [enthusiastically joining with her]: Or better still: physically move over to where you stood and put his arm around you, saying: 'I love your mum, you know'.

Cathy [weeping softly]: Oh, that would be marvellous.

Cliff [tearful too]: I could do that. Is that what you want, then?

[Cathy nodding vigorously. Cliff looking sheepish.]

Emmy [moved]: Why don't you try it now?

[Cliff gets up and embraces Cathy. They are both deeply moved. It is as if a barrier between them has dissolved.]

Each time I encouraged them to face their challenges rather than to avoid each other the situation would unfold in this way. They made various new agreements, like having certain days where they would go for a walk together, or go to the pub together, or meet the children more often and stay on the same side when talking to them. Gradually they got better at speaking to each other, though they still claimed for a long time that they needed me as translator and arbiter of their thoughts and feelings. Sessions usually started with finding out what had gone wrong during the period since the last session and what Cathy was stewing over, then I had to encourage Cliff to uncover his sympathy with Cathy and express it ever more directly. After a while it became possible to turn the tables on them and start by asking Cliff what had gone wrong and for Cathy to explain it to him if he wasn't quite getting why it had gone wrong. So, slowly they learnt to be a therapist to the other, with me still modelling a stronger way of doing this when necessary. It was wonderful to watch them reach a mutual sense of understanding at those times and to feel with them the tangible release of waves of love between them. Once they connected they would need few words to find this love for each other and they would be quite delighted with hugs, which I encouraged them to give each other.

The therapy ended with each of them doing drawings of how they had been in the world as individuals when they met, how they had been as a couple, first when things were difficult between them and then how they were in relation to each other now and where they wanted to get to (Figures 13.1–13.7). This served for them to see for themselves how far they had come and to remind them of where they were going.

They agreed that Cathy's picture of what they were aiming for was a good one (Figure 13.8), though it was Cliff who noted that they were still not looking at each other even in this one! Perhaps, they both thought, that would be alright.

Figure 13.1   Cliff

This is Cliff's picture of himself when he met Cathy. His comments were that he was a loner and had been rather caught up in his own world and was very grateful that she wanted him.

Figure 13.2   Cliff and Cathy before therapy

This is Cliff's picture of when things weren't working out in the marriage and he felt that Cathy was tearing at him all the time.

Figure 13.3   Cliff and Cathy after therapy

This is a picture of how Cliff felt they had become as a couple after some years of therapy. He emphasized the fact they were holding hands, since there was a connection between them now. I pointed out they were still not looking at each other.

Figure 13.4 Cathy

This was Cathy's picture of herself before she met Cliff, with many bubbles of confused thought and angry spikes coming out of her: this was to show the inhibitions and her lack of ability to get on with people, she said. She noted there had been no mouth, as she was never sure what to say or not to say.

Figure 13.5 Cathy and Cliff

This was Cathy's drawing of meeting Cliff. Neither of them have a mouth as they were not good at talking to each other. Her spikes are now going in rather than out and her thought bubbles have gone.

Figure 13.6 Cathy before therapy

This is Cathy's picture of when things were going wrong in the marriage and there was always too much going on inside her head and she was unable to understand or communicate about it. The red arrows are attacks from Cliff on her with her inner space being invaded. At the time she thought he was evil and wanted to harm her.

Figure 13.7   Cathy and Cliff after therapy

This was Cathy's picture of how she and Cliff were now. They were now whole people rather than just heads and had other people around them. Though Cliff was still too close to his telly and computer screens, she had her plants and books and was glad he now was polite and tried to show his affection for her.

Figure 13.8   Cathy and Cliff's ideal future

This is the agreed picture of Cathy and Cliff in an ideal future world, with children and friends more closely around them, holding on to each other tightly and focused on the same things, smiling and feeling happy to be together. They agreed they wanted to be companions, without smothering or bothering each other. They felt much more confident in themselves and with each other.

Conclusions

In working with couples with ASD it is important to be prepared to do more than normal translating of how each partner is in the world and experiences the other person. It may be equally helpful to give concrete pointers to where misunderstandings are coming from and show a different path forward to each partner. This is about teaching partners to anticipate each other's sensitivity and pain and leap ahead for them, rather than leaping in (Heidegger, 1978 [1927]) or criticize them for it. In the above example, Cliff needed to understand that Cathy was sensitive and fretted greatly over his non-verbal communication, which made her nervous. She thought he was glaring at her, making 'that face' at her, and presumed he was plotting some aggression towards her, when actually he meant nothing by it and was unaware that he often came across as sarcastic and condemnatory. The 'face' was a mask he put on when in doubt and afraid. It did not mean he was angry or evil.

Once he felt understood and accepted as not meaning harm, he accepted very easily that Cathy needed support from him and that his love was crucial to her. All of this had to be spelled out to both of them, whilst constantly asking them to correct any wrong interpretations. They had to be able to own their way of being and explain it to each other.

Cliff quickly understood that he needed to make Cathy's physical and social world safer and that she actually needed him to protect her. He rose gladly to this challenge once he realized how easy it might be to earn her respect and gratitude and thus her affection.

Cathy needed to believe that Cliff really did not know what his impact on her had been and continued to be. Once she began to believe in his innocence, she became able to see that her disapproval of him was devastating to him and had the effect of making him want to withdraw from her. She was in the habit of making strongly critical remarks about his behaviour and was unaware that this had made him ever more defensive and inclined to seek his privacy.

Cathy and Cliff both accepted very easily that they were both entitled to being understood and supported and became eager to learn to do so for each other, with my explicit encouragement.

Once they had agreed to make it work together they were keen to use the sessions to explain their personal experience to the other, with the help of the 'interpreter' or 'referee', who could remind them of what the other had intended. They became much better at finding words to overcome the negative body language and non-verbal communication that had kept them separated and trapped in a negative spiral for so long.

Nietzsche described courage as the prime mover. It certainly was the therapeutic mover for Cathy and Cliff. When they faced their challenges with courage and began to tell each other what they really feared and really wanted from each other, they came close and learnt to love each other in a much deeper way. They began to work as a team and were then able to deal with communication with the children and third parties together, jointly as a couple. They learnt to stand together and support each other. They learnt to get the benefits of being in a loving, loyal relationship. In such a relationship one is prepared for any challenge, in the sure knowledge that it will be overcome by talking about it together and finding a way forward.

References

Heidegger, M. (1927/1978) *Being and Time*, trans. J. Macquarrie and E. Robinson, Oxford: Wiley Blackwell.

Tantam, D. (1988) 'Life-long eccentricity and social isolation 2. Asperger's syndrome or schizoid personality disorder', *British Journal of Psychiatry*, 153, 783–791.

Tantam, D. (2011) *Autism Spectrum Disorders: A Life-span Perspective*, London: Jessica Kingsley.

CHAPTER 14

Relationship Therapy with Blended Families

EMMY VAN DEURZEN AND SUSAN IACOVOU

> Blended: 'combined or mixed together so that the constituent parts are indistinguishable. Antonym of unblended'
>
> (Webster, 1913)

Blended families are a challenging and potentially rewarding new reality with which relationship therapists need to be familiar. Though blended families have existed for many centuries, they were classically related to the death of a parent and the remarriage of the remaining parent. These days blended families are usually the result of one or more divorces. More than half of all marriages end in divorce (most commonly when people are in their early forties) and half of these marriages contain at least one child under the age of sixteen (Office for National Statistics, 2011). With up to 80 per cent of divorcees remarrying (Bramlett and Moshet, 2002), and with similar statistics amongst cohabiting couples, families in which two married adults are the biological parents of all children in the family – the nuclear family model – are increasingly being replaced by a range of alternative family structures (Peuckert, 2008; Kapella et al., 2009). This chapter looks at blended families or stepfamilies — those families where siblings share only one or no biological parents.

According to Kreider and Fields (2005), the presence of a stepparent, stepsibling, or half-sibling constitutes a blended family. As Beier et al. (2010) point out, however, there are several different types of blended family (see also Steinbach, 2008):

- Simple stepfamilies with children from just one side (most commonly the 'stepfather-family')
- Complex stepfamilies with children from both sides and perhaps shared children as well
- Multi-fragmented stepfamilies with partners and children coming into the family from multiple divorces and/or deaths of one parent

These last two – complex stepfamilies and multi-fragmented stepfamilies – are often described as 'patchwork-families', a rather quaint term which often belies the reality of the experience of members of such families. Far from fitting or relating harmoniously, when children from previous partnerships are brought into new relationships and their families are blended, often against their own wishes, all members of such a new blended family face tensions that are so complex and relationships that are so challenging and complicated that they frequently falter and fail.

There is a growing likelihood that relationship therapists will work with blended families at the transition point between endings (previous marriages/relationships and previous families) and beginnings (new marriages/relationships and new families) (Carter and McGoldrick, 1989). During this time, previous hurts and losses must be grieved over and new strengths identified and utilized. Fresh ways of identifying, preventing and managing differences need to be negotiated, underlying assumptions clarified, and on occasions challenged, and a new more complex family format established and supported.

This chapter will consider what existential therapy can offer families in transition, focusing on the existential view of key aspects of human relatedness in this situation. It will consider experiences such as loss, choice, conflict and anxiety as existential challenges that can encourage awareness and deliberate living, transcending the original desire for comfort, continuity, safety and familiarity.

Key issues faced by blended families – an existential perspective

Although many of the issues identified in traditional nuclear families will also feature in therapeutic work with blended families, blended families are likely to experience the additional challenges that come from the throwing together of adults, children and young people with varying degrees of enthusiasm and commitment in an attempt to create a functioning family. Some of the most fundamental of these issues are considered below.

Grief and loss

> He who would learn to fly one day must first learn to stand and walk and run and climb and dance; one cannot fly into flying. (Nietzsche, 1995 [1885])

Nietzsche recognized the human tendency to throw ourselves at new situations – to demand much of ourselves and of others, often without acknowledging the fact that mastery is achieved through hard work. It is often wrongly assumed (particularly by the adult partners involved) that remarriage and the formation of a blended family will be a mostly positive experience. What can be forgotten in the enthusiastic rush to unite is that members of the blended family need to deal with the death of their previous families, as well as the birth of this new one (Bobes and Rothman, 1998), and have to find ways to handle the grief and loss that accompanies this process. Loss of family rituals and traditions can be felt keenly, particularly when remarriage occurs quickly after the disintegration of previous relationships. The partners themselves may fear acknowledging the loss of their previous relationship (and the vision they had for that family) and the children may feel that it would be hurtful to their parents to openly show their sadness and confusion. Even if old relationships didn't work well, at least the children knew how they worked and felt a degree of comfort from that familiarity.

So while partners celebrate their newfound love, both they and their children may be struggling secretly to process the pain of divorce and the loss, or at least changing reality, of previous family ties. An existential therapist will encourage the members of the blended family to face the death of possibilities occasioned by the break-up of their previous families with openness and honesty, acknowledging their feelings of loss frankly both to themselves and to the rest of the family and exploring ways through them. She will normalize feelings of sorrow and regret, resentment and anger, helping the clients to understand the centrality of loss in human existence and encouraging them to see the wisdom and strength that may come from confronting and understanding it fully. In doing so, the family members can be released from the isolation, tension and guilt that come from holding such feelings secretly, and can be helped to support each other in processing them.

Roles and responsibilities

> stepparents generally believe that they should play a more active role in parenting than do their stepchildren and, on some dimensions, than their spouses. (Fine et al., 1998: 290)

Another key issue facing blended families is the lack of societal norms for how the members should relate to one another (Gamache, 1997). It is the absence of these norms, say Ganong and Coleman (1999), that make the role that step-parents should take in parenting their stepchildren, for example, unclear and open to interpretation. While the role of mother and father are reasonably well defined by society, the role of stepmother is most often associated with the view from the realm of fairy tales (where invariably she is depicted as the evil, conniving, jealous villain of the piece) and the role of stepfather lacks even this derogatory clarity, remaining largely unexplored in popular culture apart from an assumption that stepfathers can be unreasonable, uncaring and even dangerously violent. Children often bring such unexamined fears to the new family and begin fighting against the situation from the outset. Yet, the vacuum of societal norms also creates freedom within which the members of the blended family can negotiate and determine their own roles, though this often proves difficult to manage without professional intervention. In the absence of even broad frameworks to guide their behaviour, step-parents may find themselves veering between different stances – 'best friend', 'replacement parent' and 'favourite uncle/aunt', for example – or trying to recreate the role they had in their previous family. If they fail to discuss their role with their partner, they may also find themselves in conflict over the stance they take on how to relate to the children. This can create divisive schisms that children find anxiety provoking, but nevertheless willingly exploit to their advantage.

An existential therapist will need to bracket her own values and beliefs in this area and act in a way that is unbound by fixed ideas as to how families 'should work'. She will encourage the parents to acknowledge that they are free to work together to redefine their roles within the new family constellation. These roles should not be determined by society, by the way things worked in their previous families, nor by the expectations of others within their new family. Instead they should aim for authentic relationships with the other family members, being true to their needs and desires, while respecting and supporting the needs and desires of the other individuals within the family. This will require ongoing exploration and negotiation in a spirit of curiosity and openness, something the existential relationship therapist can model during the therapeutic process.

Freedom and choice

> ... the individual is defined only by his relationship to the world and to other individuals; he exists only by transcending himself, and his freedom can be achieved only through the freedom of others. (de Beauvoir, 1986 [1948]: 156)

Central to existential philosophy is the concept of free choice (Macquarrie, 1972) – the idea that our lives do not consist of a predetermined series of events, that we can, within certain givens and limitations, choose at the very least the attitude we take to our circumstances. But our choices take place in a context of relatedness, as illustrated by de Beauvoir's quote.

When we enter into a relationship with another that results in the creation of a blended family, we act in bad faith if we talk about having chosen our partner but not their children. Acting in bad faith in this way we may deny our responsibility for creating a shared space in which all members of the blended family can co-exist, preferring to blame our partner for failing to bring his or her children 'into line'. We may also neglect the responsibility we have to choose for others, and not just for ourselves (Sartre, 2007 [1948]) – something that can be easy to do when 'the other' is a stepchild who is 'unreasonable, rejecting and demanding' and for whom we feel little love or care. Similarly the children in a blended family may disclaim all responsibility for the relationship with their step-parent, as long as they are unable to see and accept the choice they have in the attitude they take towards them. Existential therapy then needs to restitute the freedom and responsibility to all partners in blended families to enable them to acknowledge their ability to transform the relationship.

Sartre (2007 [1948]) points out that 'man is defined first of all as being "in a situation"', for example we cannot examine and understand the existence of an individual without examining his or her environment, biology, culture, etc. Existential therapy with blended families starts by taking as broad a view of the situation as a whole as is possible, rather than separating out one or more individuals in the family as scapegoats for the unsolved problems. Rather than colluding with attempts at shifting responsibility for difficult issues onto one member of the family, the objective is to free all members of the family to take responsibility for their own part in creating the context in which they will now co-exist.

The existential therapist will encourage her clients to find out how they might be acting in bad faith by denying their own responsibilities within this context. Failing to take this responsibility leads to a corrosive culture of criticism and blame in which scapegoating occurs and a member or members of the family take on the role of the 'family bucket' (Laing, 1964) upon which the rest of the family focus their anger and frustration. It is the therapist's role to help the blended family meet the challenge of creating and maintaining a flexible yet coherent identity as a family (Banker et al., 2004) in a way that does not take away the freedom or choice of any one individual within that family.

Conflict

> There is scarcely any passion without struggle. (Camus, 1991 [1955]: 73)

As this quote illustrates, Camus recognized the link between deeply held feelings and conflict. When one relationship breaks down and another is formed it is often difficult to manage the tensions that are created in relation to the old partnerships that continue to overshadow the new relationship. Conflict exists in all relationships, but blended families, where two families without shared meanings, values and beliefs are thrown together and have to negotiate a shared basis on which to move forward, in spite of reproaches and resentments, are a particularly rich source of controversy and conflict.

Many models of marital therapy emphasize conflict prevention, management or avoidance (e.g. Gottman et al., 1998; Jacobson and Margolin, 1979) and talk about anger as a destructive emotion (Parrott and Parrott, 1995; Hendrix, 1988). Contrary to some of these models, existential theory regards conflict as an inevitable feature of our relatedness, and conflict avoidance as not only impossible but also undesirable.

Members of blended families are confronted with a number of existential dilemmas and paradoxes, all of which may lead to conflict:

- how can I join this family yet retain my freedom?
- should I compromise some of my core values for 'peace' with my ex-partner/current partner/children/stepchildren?
- how can I let my old relationship go yet still acknowledge the importance of my previous partner as parent to my children?
- what are my responsibilities in relation to this new family and how can I meet them best?
- how should I balance my loyalty to my birth parents with the reality of my dependence on or relationship with my step-parent/s?

An existential therapist will help the members of a blended family to face up to the reality of life as being full of conflict and unease. The myth of the serene, eternally harmonious, 'happy family' will be exposed and realistic expectations established around the creation of the 'good enough' family, in which contention, collision and collusion are engaged with in a meaningful way and accepted as part of the hard work that is family life. The key to this is to encourage members of the new family to commit to a future where problems and conflicts are faced robustly and with fairness and respect for all concerned.

Boundaries

> A paradox arises: the only way to meaning in freedom is through boundaries. The only way that boundaries make any sense at all is through freedom. (Moustakas, 1995: 93)

Moustakas highlights the paradoxical, inter-dependent nature of freedom and boundaries. The creation of blended families involves the breaking of previously held boundaries around families of origin and the creation of new boundaries, including new members and excluding previous members. Often members of the new blended family stay in contact with the old family of origin, which can complicate and confuse matters further. Children may share residence between their family of origin and the new blended family, and have to learn to move in and out of different relationships with different boundaries. These challenges to the freedom of the individuals within the new blended family need to be negotiated if boundaries that hold but do not constrain them are to be established and maintained.

The lack of clarity over shifting, multiple, boundaries can create what Boss and Greenberg (1984) have described as 'boundary ambiguity' where family members are unclear as to what constitutes the boundary of their family (who is in and who is out of the core and wider family systems) and find it difficult to understand what is expected of them or what to expect of other family members.

The role of the existential therapist in this scenario is to work with the blended family to help them to define clear boundaries around themselves as a family and to identify shared, explicit frameworks in which to operate where it is clear to everyone which challenges to these boundaries are acceptable (and will merely flex the boundaries) and which challenges are unacceptable (and likely to breach agreed boundaries). As Moustakas points out, paradoxically, we require boundaries if we are to recognize and benefit from our freedom. This is true not only for children but also for adult members of blended families, all of whom will benefit from clearly delineated, shared, boundaries and the mutual understanding of how they can help themselves and each other to create a sense of safety and trust within the new family.

Truth, values and meanings

> When we are dealing with human beings, no truth has reality by itself; it is always dependent upon the reality of the immediate relationship. (May, 1994 [1958]: 27)

May's stance on relatedness acknowledges the fact that our existence is fundamentally contingent and groundless and accepts that there is no such thing as a single truth or one reality. As there is no universal meaning of life that everyone can subscribe to, one of the tensions of existence is that we are challenged to find meaning in an essentially meaningless world. To make sense of our world, we need to develop a worldview, which contains our 'truth' about our world and our place in it, and yet we need to accept that this is just a personal truth and that other people have their own, equally valid, personal truths. The coming together of blended families challenges family members to confront the reality of the personal truths of others – about us, about relationships between partners and between partners and children and about our parenting. Blended families are an exercise in reflective living, but not everyone immediately realizes this.

The existential therapist will work with members of the blended family to recognize that within the constant pull between their own truth, values and meanings and those of others, they are challenged to negotiate and build an element of shared truth, a collective, cooperative sense of meaning, around which the family can unite. This requires family members to demonstrate an 'openness to the world' (Heidegger, 1949) that will allow explicit understanding and acceptance of differences while also encouraging recognition of a common purpose and vision.

Anxiety

> Whoever has learned to be anxious in the right way has learned the ultimate. (Kierkegaard, 1986 [1844])

In the context of all the issues and challenges faced by blended families, it is not surprising to note that anxiety is a common feature of their experience – anxiety about how and if the new family will work; anxiety about how the new relationship will affect each parent's relationship with their own children; anxiety on the part of the children about how their relationship with their new step-parent(s) will affect their relationship with their own parent(s) (both the one joining the blended family and the one left out); anxiety as to how step-brothers and sisters will get on together; anxiety about discipline, shared rules, ways of living together, priorities, finances; anxiety about changing identities.

An existential therapist will emphasize the importance of seeing anxiety not as pathological or threatening but as a signpost or guide to areas in our life that need our attention. As Kierkegaard highlights above, the challenge is to be anxious 'in the right way' – to recognize our emotion and heed its cry, taking steps to respond to our anxiety with curiosity and fortitude. The existential therapist will also help family members to achieve a level of comfort around being in a state of 'not knowing'. They cannot know, for example, if their blended family will eventually work in a way that is acceptable and sustainable for them. Living with uncertainty like this is an existential skill that an existential therapist can help individuals to develop. The existential therapist will also reassure the clients, however, by reminding them that openness to the potentiality of each individual in the blended family and the potentiality of the family as a whole is a stance that will give them the best opportunity of creating a working, collaborative family unit.

The case illustration below demonstrates the issues discussed so far and raises some further issues in relation to working with blended families.

Case illustration

Background and initial interaction

George and Ruby were in a relationship that had started four years previously and they had recently 'tied the knot', as they called it. George was fifteen years older than Ruby and in his early fifties. He had three grown-up children from his previous marriage. His wife, Ailsa, had died of lung cancer seven years previously and he had been very close to his children during his late wife's illness and after her death. He had two daughters, Lydia (27) and Louise (25), and a son Max (20). George had had a number of unsatisfactory short-term relationships since his wife's death, before meeting Ruby. Ruby, 39, had been in a live-in relationship with Ray, a teacher and the father of their now six-year-old son, Anton.

Ruby and George had fallen desperately in love with each other after meeting at a professional business fair, where each of them represented a different company selling the same product. It was clear that they had a very strongly developed joint narrative about their initial meeting and liked to remember it and take strength from it. They had been competitors who had started out by chiding each other as they had vied for new customers in the exhibition hall. Over after-show drinks with a number of other colleagues, and whilst still surrounded by lots of other people, they had flirted and stared at each other and had both felt an intense and strong attraction. George described this in his first session as having realized almost immediately after meeting Ruby that he did not want to spend any time with any other woman ever again, as Ruby was the one. Ruby described the situation as that of falling head over heels in love and becoming obsessed with George, in spite of the fact she felt terrible confusion and was reluctant to give in to temptation. She felt it was George who had persuaded her to betray and abandon her partnership with Ray. George, she said, had just seemed completely certain that they had to be together. He simply had not taken 'no' for an answer. She clearly took a lot of pride in this, though still wondering whether she ought to be punished for being loved by him and for having deserted Ray. George said that although he knew Ruby was committed to Ray and at the time had a two-year-old son, he had not hesitated to woo her and win her over. He knew from Ruby that Ray had had many affairs and he simply thought Ray did not deserve someone as wonderful as Ruby. He also felt he could be a better dad to Anton than Ray would be. Ruby was in two minds about this, on the one hand scandalized by George's self-assurance and on the other hand taking succour from his open hostility to

Ray, whom she clearly felt very hurt by. George had been generous towards Anton and treated him the same as his own son Max, but Ruby often disagreed with George's paternalistic educational practice. This became even more of an issue as Ruby became pregnant with George's child.

Ruby described her falling in love with George as a dangerous and scary experience rather than an exhilarating one, as George did. She had had a fairly good relationship with her partner Ray until she had realized he had frequent affairs. She found out about this when she was seven months pregnant with their son and she was appalled, but for the sake of their son had tried to forgive him, hoping it would stop after Anton's birth. She felt she had tried hard to win back Ray's commitment to her and although she was at first dismayed that she was tempted to have an affair herself, she soon gave into George as she realized he was serious about her and prepared to marry her and raise Anton. She suppressed her feelings for George for as long as she could, but caved in after being pursued relentlessly by him for six months. Even so the whole experience still left her feeling dazed and guilty. She said George had 'swept her off her feet'. She and George both agreed that the story illustrated how George was being bestowed with the main responsibility (and thus also guilt) for what had happened. Ruby said that she eventually gave in to George and filed for divorce. She took Anton with her and moved in with George just months before they got married. Somehow none of what she had done chimed in with her own idea of who she was. It helped her in the therapy sessions to realize that she had lost her own sense of agency and identity. When Ray began to persecute her and give her a hard time over the divorce, she felt more and more guilty for taking Anton away from him. This made her doubt herself. In the session she became aware that she had started, at this time, to lose her confidence, feeling she had become a 'bad' person, having previously always seen herself as a 'good' person. Anton would cry and scream for his dad each time Ray took him out and though she knew Ray set him up to do this, she still felt terrible about it. Meanwhile George introduced her to his daughters and son. He had told her that they were fantastic children and that he was tremendously proud of them (two were studying at university at the time while Max was doing his final exams). The children had been his best support after his wife died, up to the moment Ruby had come into his life. His two daughters did not take to their new stepmother very enthusiastically. Ruby was only half a generation older than they were and they were dismissive about her and thought Anton, who had been used to a very libertarian household, a spoiled brat. Max, their brother, was ok with Ruby initially, but gradually seemed to take his sisters' side more and more and once he too was in university had begun to undermine Ruby's relationship with his father as well. George and Ruby agreed on these points, but Ruby sounded very blaming of the children, whereas George was full of understanding about his children's difficulties. It was important to find a neutral way of describing the situation and arrive at a narrative they both recognized.

After a hasty marriage, in order to force everyone to accept the new situation, their romantic union was constantly under pressure from the demands of the various children. This is where the disagreements about what had happened began to become obvious. George felt that Ruby had not understood at all what was needed from her in relation to the girls and Ruby felt that George was far too set in his ways and was imposing his vision of the ideal family on her and Anton. She also felt George did not protect her from his daughters' onslaughts. She felt able to tell off Max when he was unkind to Anton, but could not touch Lydia and Louise, as George would automatically rise to their defence. She grew very dispirited when Max also became a problem, and with some probing it became clear that she felt she had lost Max's support because George was so ready to take his children's side. The therapy allowed them to begin thinking about the very concept of 'taking sides' and to see that there was actually only one side to take now: that of the new blended family. She and George argued about the best way of dealing with all this on a daily basis. These disputes had grown into terrible scenes and endless mutual reproach. When they came for therapy, both George and Ruby felt completely out of control with the situation and were at their wits' end.

The joint sessions of therapy started with them both regretting the loss of the perfect relationship they had once had together. They needed to grieve for their past families but also for the new happy family they had initially hoped they could create. Ruby said she often thought of the days when George was pursuing her, before she had left her partner, Ray. She also harked back to being with Ray, and Ray was still very much part of their new life, as he frequently came to see Anton, especially when George was not at home. George was most upset about all the unnecessary complications that had been created since he had married Ruby and he was very unhappy about the open arrangement with Ray. He wanted Ray to meet Anton only outside of the home. Ruby argued that it was important for Anton to feel that his dad was part of the new family in some way. She agreed when the therapist pointed out that she seemed to hang on to Ray as if he was another of her children and as if his presence could be a counterweight to that of George's children, who often came to stay and were then in the majority. George utterly rejected the notion that Ruby was trying to hang on to her support system. He took the view that his children were perfectly civil with Ruby and that he, George, was now Anton's dad and that Ray should stay away. George said that he had never realized what hell a family could become when people were not happy with its new constellation. He felt his old family with his late wife Ailsa and their three children was a perfect example of how things should be. Any reference to his past family immediately enraged Ruby, who would make snide remarks like: 'Oh, yes, sure, your perfect little family and your wonderful wife! Poor Ailsa, who was so happy and obedient that she died of a lack of oxygen.' Unsurprisingly this would anger George, who would storm out. He felt desperately torn between his children and his new wife, who now was pregnant with their baby, a girl, Lily, who was born four months later. The birth interrupted the therapy for some six months and while they had expressed the hope that Lily's birth might solve their problems, it actually exacerbated them considerably.

They had come for therapy because of Ruby's pregnancy as they felt they owed it to their unborn child to try and create a good atmosphere at home. They both said that if it were not for the pregnancy they would have already given up on their second marriage. George hoped that with the arrival of the baby Ruby would find the security she had been lacking. Ruby said she hoped that once their core family consisted of just George, herself, Anton and the new baby, things would settle down. There were only two therapy sessions before the birth and they were pretty much about information gathering and some initial formulations of a joint story. When the couple returned six months later, they felt things had gone from bad to worse. George felt that his daughters were being kept out by Ruby and Ruby felt that on the contrary the girls had become incredibly possessive of their dad and were practically staying in the family home non-stop, ignoring her and Anton, while making a fuss of Lily. She already regretted having given their daughter another name starting with L (something requested by George), since somehow the girls seemed to think this meant Lily belonged to them rather than to her. It was, she said, as if the daughters wanted to steal her baby from her and play at happy families with dad. She reproached George for going along with this and noted that Max had hardly visited since the birth, since he did not feel he wanted to have any part in any of this either. She also felt that Anton was being crushed by the situation and since George was now no longer allowing Ray into the home, Anton had begun to spend longer away with Ray, leaving Ruby feeling bereft and worried she was losing him.

When asked what each of them wanted from the therapeutic work, George said he wanted to find a way for his children to be able to accept his new wife, if that is what would return peace to his home. Ruby gave him a dirty look when he said this and remarked that this would never happen, as long as George favoured his eldest daughter Lydia over anyone else in his life and as long as he let her get away with bad behaviour. George said she should not criticize him as long as Anton threw the kind of temper tantrums he did. His own son Max had had a temper problem at 2 but would never have been allowed to carry on as Anton did at the age of six. There was a sense of continuous warfare in that first session after the baby was born and a profound feeling of despair. Ruby said she wanted to get clarity about whether it was worth persisting with the marriage. She was so unhappy that she was considering leaving with Anton and Lily and going to live somewhere else, as a single parent. George remarked that there was no way they were going to settle down into a peaceful household if Ruby kept threatening and complaining.

The therapy

Through separate and joint sessions George and Ruby had to begin the long process of becoming clear about their own feelings, beliefs, values and reactions to each other before they were able to reformulate these reactions and responses as a series of existential concerns with which they could enlist the other's help and support. They gradually began to formulate their personal concerns and dilemmas, first alone, then with the other in the room and silently witnessing their personal work.

George in his personal sessions needed to start by going over the past. He began to realize he had only just begun the grieving process for Ailsa and that in some ways his daughters Louise, but mainly Lydia, reminded him terribly of his late wife, who he had very much loved. He felt both protective of his children (including Max, but especially of Louise and Lydia) and deeply drawn to their need for him. He wanted desperately to be available to them and recreate the family atmosphere that had been lost and he could not initially see why this was a threat to Ruby. George also realized that he had hurt his daughters' sensitivities when he had hopelessly fallen in love with Ruby and that they had become very jealous of him and envious of Ruby. They had been around far more since his marriage than they had been before. He accepted that they were fighting Ruby and making life hard for her sometimes. He even used the word 'spiteful'. He regretted very much that they did not seem to like Ruby or get on with her, but thought it couldn't be as bad as Ruby thought it was, for otherwise the girls would not be coming home so often. He also thought it was marvellous that his daughters loved Lily so much and it pained him that Ruby did not take pleasure in his daughters' help with the baby. He wished very much that Ruby could accept their offers of babysitting so that he and Ruby could go out together. He had really no idea how he was hurting Ruby by his ostentatious love for his late wife and their daughters. He could not conceive of paternal love being perceived as a threat to the love of a couple.

Ruby in her personal sessions needed to cry a lot. She had suppressed so many feelings and she was utterly confused and fed up. She felt so many things and just could not keep track of it all. She was sad, angry, upset, jealous, envious, anxious, competitive, disappointed, exposed, confused, but above all determined to protect Anton and Lily. Her current regrets were mostly about having had to give in about Ray no longer being allowed to visit Anton in the home. She was acutely aware that she was living in what used to be George's old family home and that she had no say over it. She realized she had given up on her own authority, only to deeply resent this and accuse George of bullying. On the positive side she was besotted with Lily and felt terribly protective of her, feeling a deep love and great pride and pleasure in her daughter. She sometimes just wanted to close the door of the nursery and keep everyone else out. She repeatedly mentioned her worry that one of the girls might harm Lily out of spite and she totally mistrusted their apparent delight in Lily. When she was reminded that Lily was their half sister, she said she feared they did not see it like that and saw Lily as their own daughter with their dad. She sounded very sad, realizing the enormity of what she had said and falling tearfully silent thinking about it. Had George married her to make her like one of his daughters? Was she not a second wife but more like a fourth wife? That is how it felt, she said. She was also very worried about Anton, who now belonged even less in the family than before. He was being pushed out towards Ray. Max, who had got on with him rather well, had now made himself scarce and since Ray was no longer allowed to visit, Anton had started pulling away towards Ray.

He had said to her that now that mummy had a new baby girl and George did not want daddy to come around, perhaps he should go live with daddy instead. This, Ruby said, had broken her heart. It felt as if she had lost so much more than she had gained. Where was George in all this? Did he understand any of her pain?

All of these existential anxieties and changing identities were brought out into the open and the partners were encouraged to speak honestly with each other about their personal pain. In this initial process they were helped to respect their own and each other's life struggle and not to argue but rather to seek to convey their most deeply felt yearnings, sorrows and aspirations to the other. Of course they also had to learn to listen and attend to the other without immediate condemnation. In doing so, with their therapist's guidance, they began to respect each other's intentions and warmed to each other's predicament and outlook and gradually began to realize they had a common objective: to overcome the contradictions and misunderstandings and create a place of safety in their home. They both craved this security more than anything and could easily agree on its desirability. So, with the therapist reminding them of this fundamental value each time they lost sight of it, they learnt to negotiate with each other about the priorities they wished to establish their lives around, together, and as a new family. They realized they needed to dare to re-structure their lives and instead of pandering to everyone else's needs and sensitivities, act firmly and coherently as a couple and as joint parents. They agreed that none of the children should be allowed to dictate priorities. They would always agree priorities together first and take each other into account no matter what, so that whatever they decided would be based on an agreed stance. They were surprised to find how easy it was for them to come to a shared worldview, with a little encouragement and reminder of the values they had separately expressed as holding dear. They both wanted to create a home where there was peace and where each of them felt respected and able to feel loved and taken into account. So, their first commitment was to their personal sense of safety and peace, their second commitment was to each other, their third commitment was to the two youngest children, Anton and Lily and their fourth commitment was to the facilitation of the independence of the three grown-up children. Each issue they discussed and each decision they had to take had to be seen through those lenses rather than being approached from a confusion of conflicting impulses and reactions. Primary considerations should always be considered before secondary ones and so on. It was an easy new structure from which to live. They practised in the sessions and whilst needing a lot of prompts and reminders at first, they began to apply this way of talking to each other at home as well. They learnt how important it was for them to speak the truth with each other, air their fears, worries and resentments and to trust each other to take account of these. They created a daily space in their lives to listen to each other and to make value-based decisions, for which a foundation had been established in the sessions. They learnt to be robust and trusting in their exchanges, rather than vulnerable and afraid. They learnt to squarely face up to the consequences of the complex life conditions they had opted for and to stop hoping that everything would be easy and that other people would behave in ideal ways. They were pleasantly surprised to find that the children responded very favourably to the new atmosphere in the house.

The role of the existential therapist

As this case illustration shows, the existentially informed relationship therapist, may face a myriad of challenges when seeking to unravel the complexities of relationships that exist in blended families. However, being prepared to face up to the conflicts and supporting all members of the family equally whilst being flexible and open to possibilities, allows new possibilities to arise. Therapists need to learn to bracket their own cultural values and emotional assumptions in order to stop the blaming and start the process of mutual respect that comes from everyone being allowed to express their position. Existential therapy can help members of blended families like George and Ruby's to accept and work with conflict, anxiety, role ambiguity and disappointments by facing all these facts of life squarely and seeing the problems as situational rather than as the consequence of personal faults. In reminding couples of their responsibility in setting the tone for the entire family we can help them face the contra-dictions and sometimes terrifying realities of their new lives. Therapists can help couples to create a new centre of gravity and a new worldview that can inspire a commitment to working things out rather than resenting difficulty. The existential perspective is very powerful in such situations as it provides a strong philosophical stance, which posits the vital importance of accepting difficulty whilst making room for difference and disagreement. The existential therapist puts things back into a wider context, and encourages each partner to describe their experience, translating this experience so that it can be under-stood by the other. Once partners have learnt to be attentive to each other's way of experiencing the world, the existential method can then show the way forward by cutting across the complications and elucidating shared values and purpose. It clearly states that life does not have to be easy or rosy and that it is possible to thrive in dire circumstances if these are met with courage, clarity and commitment to a worthwhile joint project. George and Ruby, with the vigorous help of their existential therapist, were able to successfully negotiate their way to a shared understanding of how their joint life could be imbued with new meaning. This allowed them, step by step, day by day and year by year, to establish a working, dynamically stable family in a new home – a place where they both felt able to settle into safety, learn to love each other properly, and cherish their complex, combined, gradually blending family. This provided their children with new role models: not those of chaos and conflict, but those of overcoming and understanding and of commitment to love.

As Buber reminds us:

> the inmost growth of self is not accomplished, as people like to suppose today, in man's relation to himself, but in relation between one and the other. (1988 [1965]: 61)

References

Banker, B. S., Gaertner, S., Dovidio, J. F., Houlette, M., Johnson, K. M. and Riek, B. M. (2004) 'Reducing stepfamily conflict: the importance of inclusive social identity', in M. Bennett and F. Sani (eds), *The Development of the Social Self*, New York: Psychology Press.

Beier, L., Hofäcker, D., Marchese, E. and Rupp, M. (2010) *Existential Field 1: Family Structures and Family Forms, Working Report – Summary (April 2010)*, available at: http://www.expoo.be/sites/default/files/kennisdocument/Summary_Family_StructuresFamily_Forms.pdf.

Bobes, T. and Rothman, B. (1998) *The Crowded Bed: An Effective Framework for Doing Couple Therapy*, New York: Norton Professional Books.

Boss, P. and Greenberg, J. (1984) 'Family boundary ambiguity: a new variable in family stress theory', *Family Process*, 23, 535–546.

Bramlett, M. D. and Moshet, W. D. (2002) 'Cohabitation, marriage, divorce, and remarriage in the United States', National Center for Health Statistics, *Vital and Health Statistics*, 23 (22).

Buber, M. (1988 [1965]) *Between Man and Man*, London: Routledge.

Camus, A. (1991 [1955]) *The Myth of Sisyphus: And Other Essays*, London: Vintage.

Carter, B. and McGoldrick, M. (eds) (1989) *The Changing Family Life Cycle: A Framework for Family Therapy*, Boston: Allyn and Bacon.

de Beauvoir, S. (1986 [1948]) *The Ethics of Ambiguity*, New York and London: Citadel Press.

Fine, M. A., Coleman, M. and Ganong, L. H. (1998) 'Consistency in perceptions of the step-parent role among stepparents, parents, and stepchildren', *Journal of Social and Personal Relationships*, 15, 811–829.

Gamache, S. (1997) 'Confronting nuclear family bias in stepfamily research', *Marriage and Family Review*, 26 (1–2), 41–69.

Ganong, L. and Coleman, M. (1999) *Changing Families, Changing Responsibilities: Family Obligations Following Divorce and Remarriage*, Hillsdale, NJ: Erlbaum.

Gottman, J. M., Coan, J., Carrere, S. and Swanson, C. (1998) 'Predicting marital happiness and stability from newlywed interactions', *Journal of Marriage and the Family*, 60, 5–22.

Heidegger, M. (1949) *Existence and Being*, Chicago: Henry Regnery.

Hendrix, H. (1988) *Getting the Love You Want: A Guide for Couples*, New York: Holt Paperbacks.

Jacobson, N. S. and Margolin G. (1979) *Marital Therapy: Strategies Based on Social Learning and Behaviour Exchange Principles*, London: Routledge.

Kapella, O., Rille-Pfeiffer, C., Rupp, M. and Schneider, N. F. (eds) (2009) *Die Vielfalt der Familie*, Opladen: Barbara Budrich.

Kierkegaard, S. (1986 [1844]) *Fear and Trembling*, London: Penguin.

Kreider, R. M. and Fields, J. (2005) *Living Arrangements of Children: 2001*, Current Population Reports, P70-104, Washington, DC: US Census Bureau.

Laing, R. D. (1964) *Sanity, Madness and the Family: Studies in Existential Analysis and Phenomenology*, London: Tavistock.

MacQuarrie, J. (1972) *Existentialism*, New York: Penguin.

May, R. (1994 [1958]) 'The origins of the existential movement in psychology', in R. May, E. Angel and H. F. Ellenberger (eds) *Existence*, Northvale, NJ: Jason Aronson.

Moustakas, C. E. (1995) *Being-In, Being-For, Being-With*, Northvale, NJ: Jason Aronson.

Nietzsche, F. (1995) *Thus Spoke Zarathustra*, New York: Modern Library.

Office for National Statistics (2011) *Divorces in England and Wales 2010*, London: Office for National Statistics.

Parrott, L. and Parrott, L. (1995) *Saving your Marriage before it Starts*, Grand Rapids, MI: Zondervan.

Peuckert, R. (2008) *Familienformen im sozialen Wandel*, Wiesbaden: VS Verlag für Sozialwissenschaften.

Sartre, J.-P. (2007 [1948]) *Existentialism and Humanism*, London: Methuen.

Steinbach, A. (2008) 'Stieffamilien in Deutschland. Ergebnisse des Generation and Gender Surveys 2005', *Zeitschrift für Bevölkerungswissenschaft*, 33 (2), 153–180.

Webster, Noah (2013) *Webster's Revised Unabridged Dictionary Version*, C. & G. Merriam Co. Springfield, Mass.

CHAPTER 15

Working with Violent and Abusive Relationships

MARTIN ADAMS AND MARK JEPSON

Introduction

Relationship violence is one of our most pressing social problems which has many adverse physical and emotional consequences, yet despite forty years of research, it remains a considerable theoretical and therapeutic challenge when working with couples. For the therapist working with relationship violence, there are significant problems in determining both the nature of the problem and the appropriate intervention. We suggest here that an existential approach to relationship violence and abuse, based on a philosophical approach to relationship conflict, provides a useful complementary approach to existing modalities.

In this chapter we use the classification proposed by the British Crime Survey (Walby and Allen, 2006) in which relationship violence includes both non-sexual domestic violence – bullying, psychological abuse, the threat of force, and the use of force and sexual violence – rape and attempted rape, together with less serious forms of sexual assault and stalking. It is important to note that this includes the everyday but nonetheless damaging examples of abuse such as constant denigration, criticism, ignoring and undermining.

We will first review some of the research into relationship violence to show the range and diversity of theories, empirical studies and interventions, we then position an existential view of relationship violence, explore some of the ethical issues around working with relationship violence and the main elements of an existential approach, and conclude with a case illustration.

A brief review of current literature on relationship violence

In the UK in 2005, over 150 men and women were killed in incidents of domestic violence (Walby and Allen, 2006). Internationally, incidents of relationship violence were found to occur in between 25 per cent and 50 per cent of intimate relationships (World Health Organization, 2005). Although generally thought of as being perpetrated by men on women, the

191

level of women's violence towards their male partners is the subject of some dispute. While some studies have found equivalent levels but different forms of violence between men's violence towards women and women's towards men (for example the meta-analysis by Archer, 2000), others have found that in a significant minority of cases the perpetrator is female and the victim male (Smith et al., 2010).

Research into relationship violence and treatment has taken a number of directions. One of the dominant research strands derives from sociological feminism. Bograd (1988) and Walker (1989), for example, propose that relationship violence is one of the ways men enforce the patriarchal power to which they feel entitled over their partners. This view forms the basis of the Duluth Intervention Model (Domestic Abuse Intervention Programs, 2010), which prioritizes women's safety, holds men to account for their actions, emphasizes the importance of preventing men from repeating violence, and aims to change men's behaviour through re-education. However, the results of outcome studies (for example, Dunford, 2000; Feder and Dugan, 2002 and Babcock et al., 2004) suggest that the Duluth Model is no more effective than other interventions in reducing levels of relationship violence. The theoretical model on which the Duluth Model is based has also been challenged, for example by Straus and Gelles (1990) and by Archer (2000), amongst others, who proposed that the sociological feminist account provides a partial account at best of relationship violence.

A second strand of research derives from attachment theory (for example, Downey and Feldman, 1996; Kesner et al., 1997) and suggests that perpetrator violence is correlated with a heightened need for reassurance, and a failure to manage separation anxiety in insecure attachment. From this approach, therapeutically the aggressor would therefore need to be helped to address unresolved childhood trauma and attachment issues (Cunningham et al., 1998; Sonkin and Dutton, 2003).

A third strand seeks to identify the thoughts and feelings that underlie the problematic interactional cycles that go on between people and connect them to the emergence of relationship violence. Therapeutic interventions based on this approach include relationship or family counselling involving both partners (Holtzworth-Munroe et al., 1998).

A fourth strand explores violence *per se*. Fontaine (2007) describes two contrasting types of violence: instrumental violence and reactive violence, both of which have been found to characterize different types of relationship violence (for example, James et al., 2002). Instrumental violence is characterized by low levels of affect and the ability of the perpetrator to control their anger before becoming violent. Reactive violence is characterized by its immediacy and impulsivity and the aggressor in these cases finds it more difficult to contain their anger. These important findings suggest that therapists should not treat all relationship violence as being of the same character.

Another strand of research emerged from social learning theory and proposes that early experiences of relationship violence are replicated in adult relationships. Some studies (for example, Jewkes, 2002; Ehrensaft et al., 2003) have shown support for this view, although they have not accounted for why only some children who are exposed to violence go on to become violent themselves, or why some adults who have been violent within relationships have no early exposure to relationship violence. Therapeutic interventions based on this strand tend to be based on cognitive-behavioural techniques to address core beliefs and associated behaviours.

A final research strand investigates the experience of the victim and perpetrator, and suggests that there are a number of different types of relationship violence based on individuals' motivations and intentions. One of the most important typologies of relationship violence was developed by Johnson (2006) who proposed that the conflict inherent within relationships is key to both differentiating types of violence and also to the experiences of victims and perpetrators. Johnson (2006) proposes three sets of experiences of relationship violence based on the way conflict is managed within the relationship: *intimate terrorism* describes the use of violence as one of the tactics employed in trying to take general control within a relationship, *retaliatory violence* is violent resistance to previous violence, and *situational couple violence* emerges out of more general and escalating relationship conflict. Other research (for example, Holtzworth-Munroe and Stuart, 1994, and Dixon and Browne, 2003) supports the view that relationship violence should be viewed as a multi-type phenomenon.

Qualitative and phenomenological research into experiences of relationship violence point to the fact that there is a wide range of different experiences that may be associated with these different types of violence. For example, research by Cavanagh et al. (2001) suggests that male perpetrators may make sense of their violence by blaming their partner and denying their own responsibility, while the victims may attempt to take some control within the relationship by adopting the paradoxical position of accepting responsibility for the violence done to them (Burman, 2003: 84). However, prolonged relationship violence may result in 'feelings of powerlessness, helplessness, and hopelessness' (Burman, 2003: 85) in which ambivalence and dissociation from the relationship may provide the person with a self-protective detachment from the reality of their violent relationship that serves to deny or minimize the traumatic experience (Dutton and Hemphill, 1992).

These various strands of existing research suggest that relationship violence might not be considered as a single, unitary phenomenon, but instead be understood as a number of different types of violence each with its own different characteristics and etiologies and associated with different experiences for perpetrators and victims. As Briere and Jordan (2004: 1261) suggest, therapeutic assessment and treatment for domestic violence should be geared towards the particular types of violence, and the specific experiences of those involved.

An existential perspective on relationship violence

How should we position an existential approach to dealing with relationship violence, given this current state of theoretical and therapeutic plurality? An existential approach to relationship violence provides a distinctive, philosophically derived view, allowing us to position specific research findings in the context of a more fundamental view of the nature of conflict within human relationships. An existential view of relationship violence is consistent with many of the major empirical research strands we have already described, providing added depth to our understanding of this phenomenon.

An existential approach to relationship violence starts from a philosophical standpoint, from which human problems are viewed in the context of the basic givens of the human condition. According to Sartre (1973: 26), one of these givens is that 'existence comes before essence'. This means that the fact that we are (our existence) is more basic to us than what we are (our essence). We come into being (into existence) and then our life task is to make something (our essence) out of what we are given. Existentially all that is certain is that we are born and that we will die; what is uncertain is that which we choose to do with the space in between. We have the autonomy and responsibility for the choices we make, and how we conduct our lives (Warnock, 1970).

Existentially, our lives are permeated by unsolvable dilemmas and paradoxes. Human relationships take place in the social world (Deurzen, 2010) and one of the dilemmas of the social world is that we are forever torn between our need for individuality and our need to belong. We are at the same time individuals who live a life that no-one else can fully understand or experience, but also need to get on with others so as not to feel isolated. As Heidegger (1962) argued, we are both separate as individuals, and also 'beings-in-the-world' who derive meaning and identity from our connectedness to others. The desire for connection provides emotional security while our essential difference from others preserves our individuality. For Fromm, this dilemma between individuality and connectedness generates an inevitable anxiety, suggesting that 'it is the experience of separateness that arouses anxiety, indeed it is the source of all anxiety' (1957: 15). One of the key ways we structure our choices throughout our lives is in the ways in which we choose to deal with this dilemma of individuality and connectedness within our relationships.

An existential view of relationships therefore is predicated on the proposition that relationships are necessarily unpredictable because we all make choices that affect both ourselves and others, and it is this unpredictability that generates anxiety for us. Existentially, we all have the responsibility and freedom to make choices about our lives. While our own freedom to choose gives us a sense of personal agency, it is other people's freedom to choose that makes them exciting; Sartre (2003) calls this Being-for-Itself. Moreover, the closer we get to another person, the more this excitement turns to anxiety as we realize that the other person's choices cannot be predicted or controlled, particularly when these choices have an impact on us. If we fear being taken over by the other person, perhaps by the other wanting to gain more connectedness in the relationship, this will threaten our sense of individuality. If we fear being abandoned by the other person, perhaps by the other choosing to express more of their individuality, this too will be felt as threatening. In this sense both other people and our relationships with them are inherently unpredictable and sources of anxiety because they threaten our desire for appropriate closeness or individuality. Both Buber (1958) and Sartre (2003) said that we seek to manage our anxiety within relationships by trying to reduce our sense of relationship unpredictability. One way in which we can achieve this is by treating individuals as objects, because objects cannot make choices and so our relationships with them are less unpredictable than those with people, who do of course make choices. Sartre (2003) described this process of making them into objects as turning the other into a 'Being-in-Itself'. In this view, our relationships permanently fluctuate between enjoying the freedom of the other to choose, and our desire to manage and lessen the anxiety associated with this freedom by treating the other as an object.

Sartre (1962) and Cannon (1991) described a number of different relational strategies we use to manage the unpredictability of relationships by trying to circumscribe the other's freedom and right to choose. One strategy involves assuming a position of dominance in which we attempt to overpower or to control the other and thereby circumscribe their freedom to choose. Submission is a second strategy in which we give ourselves up to be controlled by the other, thereby circumscribing our own freedom to choose. A third strategy is to avoid the conflict and isolate ourselves from relationships. These strategies of dominance, submission and withdrawal are seen as problematic from an existential perspective because they variously involve us 'taking responsibility for things one has no responsibility for, and denying responsibility for things that one does have responsibility for' (Deurzen and Adams, 2011: 19).

Within a relationship, both individuals may attempt to manage their own anxiety about relationship unpredictability using strategies of dominance, submission and isolation. This leads to particular combinations of dominance, submission and isolation within the relationships, in which specific combinations of strategies lead to different sorts of conflict between individuals over the impingement of their individual freedoms. For example, we may be submissive in response to the other person's attempts to dominate us; we may seek to dominate the person who is trying to dominate us; we might attempt to dominate the person who intends to leave the relationship when we don't want them to go, and so on. In each of these scenarios, violence and abuse might be used to resolve the conflict, and enforce our dominance, submission or isolation. We may become violent as we try to make someone do what we want them to do, we may abuse someone when they try to control us, we may lash out when someone threatens to leave us. From this perspective, violence and abuse can be seen as tactics employed within strategies of dominance, submission or withdrawal.

However, Sartre (2003) suggested another way of dealing with the anxiety and unpredictability of relationships that is consistent with the rights of individuals to choose. This approach starts by acknowledging the freedoms and choices that individuals should properly exercise. Conflict, therefore, can be addressed through cooperation, in a both/and dialectical way, in which we acknowledge the rights of ourselves and of the other, together. However, this approach rests on finding the ability to tolerate greater degrees of unpredictability and anxiety as we allow and encourage the other to make choices and decisions about their life, even if those decisions might be painful for us. This more cooperative approach is when intimacy with another is felt to be freeing and not constraining, and although more challenging, it is also more fulfilling since it acknowledges both partners' autonomy. This both-and solution can be summarized as: 'I have the responsibility to do what I want in a world of others, but so does everybody else and it works best if we take each other into account' (Deurzen and Adams, 2011: 63).

The objective for existential work with relationship violence is to find other means for the couple to manage relationship conflict without recourse to violence and abuse. From this summary of an existential view of relationship violence, we might draw four implications for therapists about how to achieve this aim whilst working existentially.

1. Ensuring client safety

All therapists have an obligation to consider and manage the ethical dimensions of working with relationship violence before, during and potentially after therapeutic work. A *sine qua non* for this working with violence is client safety, it is impossible to overvalue the importance of client safety in working with relationship violence. When considering working with relationship violence:

- Therapists have an ethical obligation to assess the risk of the therapy and to consider the consequences of engaging with couples where there is violence, risk of violence or ongoing abuse of any sort.
- The therapist needs to ensure that clients are aware of the nature, purpose and potential consequences of therapy, and also that both partners make an informed decision to participate.
- The risk to client safety is also rarely static during therapy, for example, there is likely to be an increased risk of violence if the attacked person indicates their desire to leave the relationship. The therapist therefore constantly needs to monitor the risk of violence throughout the therapeutic process.
- Insights gained by clients through the therapy process about their partner's fears and vulnerabilities may be used against them as a way of dominating or otherwise abusing the other, the therapy can become unsafe if that which is disclosed in the sessions is subsequently used within the couple. The therapist needs to assure himself that the work with the couple will not put either of them at increased risk of violence and abuse. Consideration might be given to working with individuals rather than couples where violence is a feature of the relationship.

All therapists will have their own views of how relationships should work. Managing these so they inform rather than contaminate the work can be particularly difficult. One of the key skills of existential practice is the ability to bracket our own views in order to better understand the lived experience of the client(s). In bracketing, the therapist becomes aware of the ways their own assumptions always influence their understanding. These assumptions are then put aside to be examined in greater depth at a later stage (Deurzen and Adams, 2011). The therapist does not judge or evaluate the relationship violence, but instead adopts a participant-observer position that helps both clients to reflect on how they have lived in their relationships so far, and how they would choose to do so in the future in accordance with their chosen values.

Therapists working with relationship violence can often find it difficult to assess the associated risks by themselves. Developing empathic relationships with both clients to allow an understanding of their lived experiences carries with it the associated difficulty of standing back and evaluating the risks to either or both of the clients. It is important to review the safety of working with particular clients through a supervision and review process to develop a more balanced assessment and management of the risks involved in the therapy.

2. Modelling respectful relationships

One of the key roles for the existential therapist is to create a relationship between therapist and client(s) that models respectful, responsible and cooperative relating and which emphasizes the importance of respecting the rights of ourselves at the same time as those of the other. This involves the therapist in seeking to understand the choices and actions that the other has made (even if that includes abuse and violence) whilst neither agreeing or condoning them. At the same time the therapist must make clear that each client must take responsibility for their actions, and that violence in relationships is unacceptable. This is a difficult line to tread, but existential couple therapists should show understanding for each partner's plight without condoning any form of bullying, abuse or violence. The therapy session itself will demonstrate alternative ways of dealing with disagreements and conflicts within the safe environment of the therapy session. The therapist does not allow any acting out or violence during therapy and demonstrates a more effective way to communicate.

3. Exploring the clients' relational approach

An existential approach to working with relationship violence is rooted, as with other existential therapies in the experience of anxiety (Spinelli, 2005). As we have seen, an existential view of relationship violence is grounded in the anxiety about the unpredictability of relationships as we address the dilemma of our need for individuality balanced against the need to belong. One aspect of the therapeutic work is to understand how the individuals have sought to address their needs for individuality and belonging, both in the current relationship, and more generally across other relationships and in other parts of their lives. Have they generally looked to have more independence in relationships, or do they seek closer connections? This helps provide a context for understanding the nature of a couple's relational dynamics.

In the context of the relationship itself, the work is to explore the ways in which both people in the relationship negotiate their own anxiety, and how strategies of dominance, submission or withdrawal might be used in an effort to manage their anxiety about unpredictability. Couple therapy allows individuals to hear the experience of the other, to understand the consequences of their actions, to understand the effects of not making choices, and to explore other options for taking responsibility for their behaviour in the context of the needs of others. How individuals make choices in their lives, both the choices they make, and the choices that they perhaps fail to make. How they have responded to the choices of the other, and the extent to which they respect the choices made by the other. How their choices have affected both themselves and others. How both partners have influenced one another.

4. Challenging the clients' relational approach

The focus for existential therapy is on helping individuals to take responsibility for individual choices in the context of the choices of the other. The objective for existential work with relationship violence is to find ways for a couple to manage relationship conflict without the use of violence and abuse. It is predicated on helping individuals to take responsibility for those choices that they can take, not taking on responsibility for things that are beyond their scope.

A critical part of working with relationship violence involves challenging clients with the ways in which they have tried to manage conflict in the past. This may be done in a number of different ways. One technique is to discuss particular incidents of violence in detail, exploring the choices that were made, the other choices that were available but not made, exploring the possible consequences, and whether a situation could have been dealt with in another way. This inevitably raises questions about freedom of choice, and responsibility for actions and opens possibilities for future behaviour, for different ways of making choices, and for different types of relationships.

The challenging might involve exploring the implicit assumptions on which the violence and abuse are based. For example, someone may become violent as a way of stopping their partner going out with their friends because they fear the other will leave. Exploring these implicit assumptions may show the paradoxical effect that the outcome the perpetrator feared (being left by their partner) becomes more likely because of the way they tried to control that fear; becoming violent. Greater understanding of ourselves, and why we behave as we do allows greater insight and more informed, better, non-violent decisions.

The therapist might also at this point use disconnections in exploring and challenging the way individuals are in relationships. For example, 'How do you make sense of saying that you love your partner, and yet you are violent towards her?' or 'How do you reconcile saying you respect your partner, and yet he feels that you constantly abuse him?' Challenging in this way helps to bring more coherence to our thoughts, feelings and behaviours.

The objective for existential work with relationship violence is to find other means for the couple to manage relationship conflict without recourse to violence and abuse. An existential approach to relationship violence starts from the therapist's ethical responsibilities for client safety. Within the therapy process, the therapist aims to find other ways for clients to manage relationship conflict by first exploring the nature of the client relationship and how conflict has been managed in the past, then through a process of sensitive challenge identify opportunities for making different, non-violent and non-abusive decisions to manage conflict. Underpinning this process, the therapist will model a relationship that respects the rights of all.

Case illustration

John and Paula came to therapy following an incident in which John had hit Paula following a particularly intense and difficult argument. Both in their early thirties, they had been together for five years and had lived together for four years. They had both been disturbed by the violence and wanted to understand why it had occurred and whether their relationship could continue. The work consisted of thirty weekly sessions with a male therapist, over a twelve-month period.

In accordance with the protocol of the agency regarding relationship violence, both John and Paula were given separate confidential assessment interviews following their initial assessment session to allow for an informed judgement of client safety.

Assessing the risk of working with couples where violence is a feature has produced a wealth of literature and is worthy of a chapter on its own. Some argue (Island and Letellier, 1991) that couple therapy is never appropriate where violence is a feature, because it may serve to bolster a pattern of coercion and control within the relationship. Others argue that, under specific circumstances, couple work might be possible. The work of Johnson (2006) proposed that not all domestic violence is the same, and that therefore the decision on whether or not couple work should be undertaken in these circumstances depends in part on the type of relationship violence that has occurred. Holtzworth-Munroe and colleagues (1997) suggest that prerequisites for potentially successful couple treatment would include:

- the violence not fitting a pattern of abuse and control
- the violence only happening once, perhaps twice (separated by a long interval)
- the batterer taking responsibility for the abuse
- a clear set of terms under which therapy would be ended being agreed (to include any 'relapse' into violence, or the use of manipulative efforts to control).

Couple counselling may then help elucidate an understanding of the dynamics that led to the violence and provide a 'safe place' to discuss difficult and anxiety-provoking topics. Research suggests that couple therapy within this group is effective providing the above conditions are present (Brannen and Rubin, 1996; O'Leary et al., 1999; Horowitz and Skiff, 2007).

In this case, after a supervisory review and risk assessment, it was agreed that John's violence did not fit a pattern of abuse and control – it was a one off, and he took responsibility for his violence. He and Paula agreed the conditions under which the therapy would end, and it was agreed that relationship therapy could proceed in light of these understandings. From their individual interviews John and Paula seemed equally committed to the work and they both gave informed consent to participate in the therapy. Apart from the two individual sessions, all the work was done with both of the partners present.

For the therapy to work, it was also important for the therapist to remain phenomenologically neutral – to be aware of his own reactions to John and Paula and to remain even-handed in his response. For example, although his own value system led him to feel that couples should generally stay together, he needed to bracket this to ensure that this did not influence the work.

At the start of the work the therapist's priority was to create an environment where both John and Paula could feel safe talking about issues that had previously felt very unsafe including being able to hear and not judge the other's experience of the violence. The initial sessions were taken up with understanding both the history of their relationship and their personal history, not only to allow them to build confidence in the therapeutic relationship, but also to hear each other. It transpired that they actually knew little about each other's backgrounds, for example Paula did not know about John's painful childhood memories of watching his parents fighting and eventually divorcing and John did not know about Paula's childhood in a tight knit and controlling rural environment.

One of the first tasks in working with relationship violence is to enable both partners to take realistic responsibility for their actions and the consequences. Existentially, the therapist needed to note the various ways both John and Paula placed responsibility for their actions on themselves, their partner, other people and sometimes the therapist. One of the aims of existential therapy is for people to understand what they are evading and denying and so to be able to take greater responsibility for their decisions and actions. By doing so they discover their own authority and capacity for change.

Both John and Paula came to counselling feeling very confused about the way their relationship was going, and also about the occurrence of violence. They were confused about who was responsible. Although they blamed each other, they also felt guilty and ashamed about the part they had played in the deterioration of their relationship.

John blamed Paula because, from his point of view, the problems began with Paula failing to give him the reassurance he needed, making him increasingly anxious and frustrated. As the therapy progressed John began to realize that his violence came out of his fear of being abandoned and his inability to tolerate this fear.

Paula blamed John because, from her point of view, John was both needy and controlling, and this led her to become increasingly secretive. Paula tried to reduce her feelings of being smothered by John's needs by withdrawing from him. For her, withdrawal was associated with her past experiences in which separation from others was the only way to gain autonomy. As the therapy progressed she began to see that her withdrawal made John more anxious.

This escalating dynamic led to a vicious circle, in which John's pursuit of Paula to gain reassurance led her to withdraw from the relationship to protect herself from her fear of being smothered, which in turn increased John's anxiety about abandonment, generating a greater need for and greater insistence on reassurance.

The latest incident occurred when Paula refused to deny John's accusation of her having an affair. He described how he 'saw red' and, to his subsequent distress, hit Paula.

They described their long pattern of highs and lows, which included two brief separations. As John began to take responsibility for his actions, and started to understand more of what lay behind his behaviour within the relationship with Paula the therapist suggested that John and Paula, who were still living together, set aside some time between the sessions to talk to each other about any current issue and to try to listen without judging. It was suggested that they take it in turns and only do it for as long as it was comfortable. They initially found this very difficult, but were able to persevere throughout the work.

This middle part of the therapy was challenging not just for John and Paula, but also for the therapist, because both clients wanted him to take sides against the other. Also, because of his own experience, the therapist found it easier to see John's side, and used supervision to enable him to bracket his assumptions and remain even-handed and phenomenological so that both John and Paula would feel able to describe their experience in detail and feel heard.

One of the recurring points of contention within the relationship was about the attribution of blame. For John it was terrifying to acknowledge that Paula might choose to leave – he could not believe that she would freely choose to stay with him. Paula was frightened that John would take away her hard won self-sufficiency and the only option she allowed herself was to cut off from him. Neither was able to accept the other's basic autonomy and freedom and although John resorted to physical violence, both of them attempted to manage their own anxiety by constraining each other's freedom. Gradually, John was able to own and describe not only his expectation that Paula would get fed up with him and leave, but also his worry that expressing his need of her would make her want to go anyway – she would not be sufficiently interested in him to care. He discovered that his jealousy, which scared him, was linked to his fear of abandonment. As the therapist modelled acceptance in understanding John's fears, Paula was able to hear how he was feeling and John felt more able to express his fears. In turn, this acceptance enabled Paula to explain her anxiety about being controlled and her frustration at John's increasing suspicion, and the way her feelings created her need to spend more time away from him. As they began to take account of each other, they also grew to take responsibility for their own views and how these inadvertently led to the very thing they feared. John grew to understand how his helplessness over his parents' acrimonious divorce led to his expectation of abandonment. Paula grew to recognize that she associated intimacy with being controlled, and that led her to become overly self-sufficient, needing but not trusting John.

They grew to understand that they were drawn to each other because of elements in the other that reminded them of qualities they desired but did not have. John was attracted to Paula's apparent self-sufficiency and Paula was attracted to John's apparent ability to trust. Such was the emotional ambivalence of their respective sensitivities to these issues that it meant that the best solution would be a period spent apart. This was in fact first suggested by John and meant they both had to work through and come to terms with the loss of what they hoped the relationship could have been.

At the start of the therapy, they were both struggling in their different ways with the question of how to have a close relationship with another person. They both faced the same existential dilemma, of being torn between the need for individuality and the need for a sense of connection with someone else. From solving this by perpetual conflict, they moved to realizing that they were equally but differently responsible for what had happened between them.

The therapist's part in the interaction was to model the dialectical principle of listening and accepting two different experiences of the same relationship, while working phenomenologically and bracketing his own responses. By doing this, he was able to facilitate the discovery of another position that both honoured and augmented the experiences of both John and Paula, such that both could acknowledge the experiences and choices of the other. This in turn allowed them to come to a new perspective on the values, rules and principles of how they wanted to live their lives.

Conclusion

Although existential theory and practice in relation to working with relationship violence is somewhat underdeveloped, it can, however, generate powerful insights that can complement other approaches, especially in relation to the nature of freedom and responsibility in relationships.

One of the major objectives for working existentially with relationship violence is to help manage inevitable relationship conflict without recourse to violence and abuse. This should of course only be undertaken when safe and ethically appropriate. The objective is to work with both partners to understand their lives as they have lived them, help them reflect on what has happened and enable them to determine how they would like to live in the future in accordance with their chosen values but without violence and abuse.

References

Archer, J. (2000) 'Sex differences in aggression between heterosexual partners: a meta-analytic review', *Psychological Bulletin*, 126, 651–680.

Babcock, J. C., Green, C. E. and Robie, C. (2004) 'Does batterer treatment work? A meta-analytic review of domestic violence treatment', *Clinical Psychology Review*, 23 (8), 1023–1053.

Bograd, M. (1988) 'How battered women and abusive men account for domestic violence: Excuses, justifications, or explanations?' in G. Hotaling, D. Finkelhor, J. Kirkpatrick and M. Straus (eds), *Coping with Family Violence: Research and Policy Perspectives*, 60–77,Thousand Oaks, CA: Sage.

Brannen, S. J. and Rubin, A. (1996) 'Comparing the effectiveness of gender-specific and couples groups in a court-mandated spouse abuse treatment program', *Research on Social Work Practice*, 6, 405–424.

Briere, J. and Jordan, C. (2004) 'Violence against women: outcome complexity and implications for assessment and treatment', *Journal of Interpersonal Violence*, 19, 1252–1276.

Buber, M. (1958) *I and Thou,* trans. G. Smith, Edinburgh: Clark.

Burman, S. (2003) 'Battered women: stages of change and other treatment models that instigate and sustain leaving', *Brief Treatment and Crisis Intervention*, 3 (1), 83–98.

Cannon B. (1991) *Sartre and Psychoanalysis: An Existentialist Challenge to Clinical Metatheory,* Kansas: University Press of Kansas.

Cavanagh, K., Dobash, R. E., Dobash, R. P. and Lewis, R. (2001) ' "Remedial work": men's strategic responses to their violence against their female intimate partners', *Sociology*, 35 (3), 695–714.

Cunningham, A., Jaffe, P. G., Baker, L., Dick, T., Malla, S., Mazaheri, N. and Poisson, S. (1998) *Theory-derived Explanations of Male Violence against female Partners: Literature Update and Related Implications for Treatment and Evaluation.* Ontario: London Family Court Clinic.

Deurzen, E. van (2010) *Everyday Mysteries: A Handbook of Existential Psychotherapy,* 2nd edn, London: Routledge.

Deurzen, E. van and Adams, M. (2011) *Skills in Existential Counselling and Psychotherapy,* London: Sage.

Dixon, L. and Browne, K. (2003) Heterogeneity of spouse abuse: a review, *Aggression and Violent Behaviour*, 8 (1), 107–130.

Domestic Abuse Intervention Programs (2010) 'The Duluth Model', available at: http://www.theduluthmodel.org/.

Downey, G. and Feldman, S. I. (1996) 'Implications of rejection sensitivity for intimate relationships', *Journal of Personality and Social Psychology*, 70 (6), 1327–1343.

Dunford, F. W. (2000) 'The San Diego navy experiment: an assessment of interventions for men who assault their wives', *Journal of Consulting and Clinical Psychology*, 68 (3), 468–476.

Dutton, D. and Hemphill, K. (1992) 'Patterns of socially desirable responding among perpetrators and victims of wife assault', *Violence Victims*, 7 (1), 29–39.

Ehrensaft, M. K., Cohen, P., Brown, J., Smailes, E., Chen, H. and Johnson, J. G. (2003) 'Intergenerational transmission of partner violence: a 20 year prospective study', *Journal of Consulting and Clinical Psychology*, 71 (4), 741–753.

Feder, L. and Dugan, L. (2002) 'A test of the efficacy of court-mandated counselling for domestic violence offenders: the Broward experiment', *Justice Quarterly*, 19 (2), 343–375.

Fontaine, R. G. (2007) 'Toward a conceptual framework of instrumental antisocial decision-making and behavior in youth', *Clinical Psychology Review*, 27, 655–675.

Fromm, E. (1957) *The Art of Loving*, London: Sage.

Heidegger, M. (1962) *Being and Time,* trans. J. McQuarrie, Oxford: Blackwell.

Holtzworth-Munroe, A., Bates, L., Smutzler, N. and Sandin, E. (1997) 'A brief review of the research on husband violence', *Aggression and Violent Behavior*, 1, 65–99.

Holtzworth-Munroe, A. and Stuart, G. L. (1994) 'Typologies of male batterers: three sub-types and differences among them', *Psychological Bulletin*, 116 (3), 476–497.

Holtzworth-Munroe, A., Smutzler, N. and Stuart, G. L. (1998) 'Demand and withdraw communication among couples experiencing husband violence', *Journal of Consulting and Clinical Psychology*, 66, 731–743.

Horowitz, S. H. and Skiff, D. (2007) 'Historical evidence for couples' treatment for partner violence', *Family Therapy Magazine*, 7, 32–35.

Island, D. and Letellier, P. (1991) *Men Who Beat the Men Who Love Them*, New York: Harrington.

James. K., Seddon, B. and Brown, J. (2002) ' "Using it or losing it": men's constructions of their violence towards female partners', research paper, Australian Domestic and Family Violence Clearinghouse.

Jewkes, R. (2002) 'Intimate partner violence: causes and prevention', *Lancet*, 38097,1423–1429.

Johnson, M. P. (2006) 'Conflict and control: gender symmetry and asymmetry in domestic violence', *Violence Against Women*, 12 (11), 1–16.

Kesner, J. E., Julian, T. and McKenry, P. C. (1997) 'The application of attachment theory to male violence toward female intimates', *Journal of Family Violence*, 12 (2), 211–228.

O'Leary, K. D., Heyman, R. E. and Neidig, P. H. (1999) 'Treatment of wife abuse: a comparison of gender-specific and conjoint approaches', *Behavior Therapy*, 30, 475–505.

Sartre, J.-P. (1962) *Existential Psychoanalysis*, New York: Regnery Publishing.

Sartre, J.-P (1973 [1946]) *Existentialism and Humanism*, trans. P. Mairet, London: Methuen.

Sartre, J.-P. (2003 [1943]) *Being and Nothingness: An Essay in Phenomenological Ontology*, trans. H. E. Barnes, London: Routledge.

Smith, K. (ed.), Flatley, J. (ed.), Coleman, K., Osborne, S., Kaiza, P. and Roe, S. (2010) 'Homicides, Firearm Offences and Intimate Violence 2008/09: Supplementary Volume 2 to Crime in England and Wales 2008/09', *Home Office Statistical Bulletin*, 21 January.

Sonkin, D. and Dutton, D. (2003) 'Treating assaultative men from an attachment perspective', in D. Dutton and D. Sonkin (eds), *Intimate Violence: Contemporary Treatment Innovations*, New York: Haworth Press.

Spinelli, E. (2005) *The Interpreted World: An Introduction to Phenomenological Psychology*, London: Sage.

Straus, M. A. and Gelles, R. J. (1990) *Physical Violence in American Families: Risk Factors and Adaptations to Violence in 8,145 Families*, New Brunswick, NJ: Transaction.

Walby, S. and Allen, J. (2006) *Domestic Violence, Sexual Assault and Stalking: Findings from the British Crime Survey*, Home Office Research Study 276, Research, Development and Statistics Directorate, London.

Walker, L. E. A. (1989) 'Psychology and violence against women', *American Psychologist*, 44 (4), 695–702.

Warnock, M. (1970) *Existentialism*, Oxford: Oxford University Press.

World Health Organization (2005) *WHO Multi-country Study on Women's Health and Domestic Violence against Women*, available at http://www.who.int/gender/violence/who_multicountry_study/en (accessed 25 October 2010).

CHAPTER 16

Therapy with Couples Presenting with Issues of Addiction

SIMON DU PLOCK

Introduction

My approach to working with couples is distinct from my work with individuals. When I meet with an individual client my focus is primarily on the relational field which the client and I inhabit, and co-create. I am concerned to meet them via what May (1958: 37) has termed 'Here-is-a-new-person'. My aim in doing this is to encounter the other with the minimum of preconceptions and biases in order that I may model genuine curiosity and naivety about their way of being in the world. This optimizes the opportunity for the client to notice that another approaches their being with care and encourages them, in turn, to take their being seriously – May's (1958: 43) 'I-am' experience. This stance reflects Kierkegaard's attitude of encouraging people to become objective towards themselves, rather than becoming lost in subjectivity. Enhanced objectivity may assist clients to take renewed responsibility for making active choices to author their own life.

Clients frequently describe themselves as addicts, drawing terms from the language of the world of addiction that suggest they are in some sense 'ill' and not fully responsible for their lives – 'life' is something which happens to them, not something to actively shape according to their values. Human being is inevitably being in relation: as Cohn (1997: 45) expresses it, we are 'always and inevitably in a context with others'. It follows that couple therapy provides increased opportunity to work, since the relational world presented in the consulting room is far more richly textured.

Towards a model for working with couples with issues of addiction

The therapist's role changes when one or both clients present with an issue related in some way to addiction. The member of the couple describing themselves as an addict may resist exploring their way of being other than via the selective lens of addiction. Their partner may also subscribe to the notion that the 'addict' is defined by this label. One or both may seek 'treatment' to remove the addiction or help in symptom reduction or management. An ethical existential-phenomenological practitioner needs to be clear that they are primarily offering an opportunity to help the couple clarify their way of being in the world, rather than a specific treatment for addiction. It is helpful, though, to indicate that this clarity will enable them to proceed with more confidence, regardless of the direction they decide to take.

My practice is influenced by the movement in the British and North American literature on addiction in the past decade, moving away from concentrating on addiction as a state characterized by a sharp reduction of the capacity for voluntary behaviour in relation to specific substances (generally termed 'drugs'), towards the notion that people can get caught up in ordinary activities when those activities become invested with special meaning. Following Shaffer's (1994) contention 'anything can be addictive which powerfully and quickly and predictably changes how you feel', I view the addict as one who self-medicates. The addiction can be a substance or an experience; shopping, gambling or eating (or abstaining from eating) may equally fulfil this definition. The degree to which these phenomena fit the classical notion of addiction varies, but I find myself drawn to Walters' (1999: 10) definition of addiction as 'the persistent and repetitive enactment of a behavioural pattern' that includes four elements:

1. progression (or increase in severity)
2. preoccupation with the activity
3. perceived loss of control, and
4. persistence, despite negative long-term consequences.

Working with couples presenting with issues of addiction

I find the most facilitative way I can explore issues of addiction with clients in couple therapy is via the concept Spinelli (2007: 198) has termed 'the couple-construct'. This concept has grown out of his earlier notion of the 'self-structure' (1994: 348), which directs our attention to how each of us assembles, over time, a set of beliefs, values and aspirations about who we believe ourselves to be. An exploration of the individual's self-structure will clarify the role of the addiction in providing them with a sense of structure in their life that they might not otherwise have. A key element of existential couple therapy is the clarification of the extent to which these beliefs, values and assumptions about addiction are shared, or not, by both partners.

Much of my work with couples focuses on the particular ways in which their unique couple-construct functions to both open up and limit their way-of-being-in-the-world as a couple. I engage in this process of clarification with them not with the intention of helping them 'move on' in some way, but to enable them to engage as fully as possible with me so that we can all 'see what is there'. This is especially important with addiction where denial of a wide spectrum of ways to live can be a key feature. When both clients can genuinely see the way they have constructed their 'way-of-being-in-the-world' as a couple they may elect to modify it. This is not, though, to underestimate how difficult this is likely to be, nor the degree of support they may require from the therapeutic alliance: as Spinelli makes clear, the couple may decide to separate if they discover that their individual understandings of being a couple are too divergent.

I generally utilize the following template for exploring the couple-construct. Sessions are 75 minutes, rather than the 50-minute 'therapeutic hour' of one-to-one work:

- Session 1: I meet with the couple and we explore what brings them into therapy, and the extent to which the emerging couple-construct is characterized by fluidity or the rigidity that may signal issues of addiction.
- Sessions 2 and 3: I have individual meetings with each partner to explore their personal self-constructs and reflect on how these operate within the couple-construct.
- Session 4: I meet with the couple together and we reflect on the experience of the previous two sessions, and relate what was explored to their couple-construct.
- Session 5: I meet with the couple to clarify the extent to which their individual constructs and couple-construct remains the same or have changed, and to consider whether they wish to continue to work with me or leave therapy at this point.

During Session 5 I offer clients the opportunity to continue to work for a further cycle of five sessions. In this second cycle we use the first session to review their objectives for continuing in therapy.

In my meetings with each individual, I typically invite them to reflect on:

1. Their individual sense of who they are, what is important to them, what they hold to be fundamental to their identity and, where addiction is a concern, the extent to which it impacts on identity.
2. The same, but as they imagine their partner might respond to the question.
3. How their couple-construct supports and/or destabilizes their sense of self and what they hold to be important for themselves.
4. The same, but as they imagine their partner might answer the question.
5. As a result of this reflection, how do they feel about their partnership? What is their 'felt-sense'? Are they clearer about aspects that feel satisfying, and aspects where they might want to work towards making a change? If addiction is a feature of the partnership, in what ways is the relationship shaped by this phenomenon?
6. If there are areas where they might like to make changes, how do they feel this might impact upon the couple-construct? How do they feel this might change the quality of their partnership?

Case illustration: working with Tony and Pedro

I am always interested in how a couple negotiate getting into the room with me since it is indicative of how they function in the world more generally. In the case of Tony and Pedro, Pedro made the first move by emailing to ask if I had availability to see them 'as a matter of urgency'. They were seeking therapy, he explained, because their relationship of fourteen months had deteriorated dramatically over the last six, having previously been 'wonderful'. Tony was forty years old and Pedro was approaching thirty. They arrived exactly on time for the first session, Pedro saying as they entered that they were glad I was able to see them so quickly. It seemed clear that Pedro had done the planning for setting up this session. I welcomed them both, and invited them to tell me more. I wondered to myself whether Pedro would be the first to speak as he had initiated the contact with me, but instead Tony jumped in immediately.

> Pedro wanted us to come and see you as I have a problem which is really messing us both up and I need some help with it. Of course Pedro's right, I do need to change if we are to stay together. At the moment the way I am, the way I'm behaving, is putting such a strain on our relationship. It isn't fair to ask him to continue like this.

These opening words led me to speculate whether Tony had agreed to come to therapy in order to use it as a way of leaving the relationship. I wondered to myself what this problem which had got them into the room might be, and if it would turn out that both had problems, some of them shared and some not. It seemed a relief for Tony to be able to talk about 'his' problem – but I noticed that he seemed to be taking all the responsibility for the difficulties they were experiencing. This might be noble of him, but I was reminded of Sartre's example of the man who declares himself to be bad, or a thief, in order to excuse himself from responsibility – his is a bad faith response to the weight of responsibility since he gives himself an 'essence' – he is *only* bad, or a thief. In my work I have noticed people with addiction issues can describe themselves as 'only an addict' in a similar fashion. In response to an invitation to both to expand on their difficulties, Tony began to describe how he felt he had inherited an 'addictive personality' from his father who had been a smoker, a gambler (mostly 'the dogs') and heavy drinker – 'probably an alcoholic'.

He described how he got drunk regularly in his teens – it sounded as though he was attempting to drown his miseries by self-medicating – then found Ecstasy, poppers and speed freely available on the clubbing scene when he came out as gay in his early twenties. Alongside these 'recreational' drugs, he described himself as a bit a 'techy' and into gadgets and IT. 'I've always found it easier to get into my work rather than socialize. I always feel anxious with other people – I think they're like icebergs and you can't tell what's going on underneath. I know what I'm doing with computers.' I also noticed that Pedro was taking a back seat in our session – literally sitting right back in his chair. My fantasy was that Tony and I had an audience and I wondered if we would each receive marks at the end of the session – Tony for telling his story well, and me for solving his problem. Tony went on to describe how since Pedro had moved into his flat he had withdrawn increasingly into the room he used as his office, spending most of the evening on his computer. As he described it 'It's almost as though I'm not there for Pedro and he feels I'm rejecting him ... which is crazy because that's not my intention at all. For some weird reason my addict side seems to be coming up again and I can't control it.'

I wondered if what Tony had been talking about felt like it belonged to him and was not really about Pedro. I had a sense that Pedro saw this problem as 'alien', as external to their relationship, something that was coming in from outside and needed to be removed or eradicated. Pedro described walking into a bar and seeing Tony. 'Our eyes met and that was it – it was fate! We both knew straight away that "this is it" '. Tony agreed: 'We were absolutely drawn to each other. The first few months were like a dream. We were constantly together – it was wonderful.'

In reality they were, in fact, often apart – both had busy careers. But this made meeting up again all the more exciting. And then six months ago they decided to live together. As we were coming to the end of our time I offered some feedback on what I thought I had heard them each say, asking them to correct me on any aspect of this since the most important thing was for them to hear each other and my perspective might help them to do this. I had a sense that there was much more that Pedro might want to share about himself and his relationship with Tony. I reflected that I would be interested to explore with them what they wanted from being in a relationship, and the extent to which they shared a common vision. I said it seemed to me that they had different backgrounds and cultures, and that these factors could be significant in informing their perspective on what being a couple meant, and bringing this to the surface might be very helpful. So they had already shared a lot with me, and might choose to explore further if we decided to contract for further meetings. I noticed they had to some extent been talking to me rather than to each other, and I wondered if they shared this sense.

They agreed that I had understood what they had said, and Tony said that he felt a great sense of relief just to get his feelings out into the open. Pedro said it helped him to hear Tony's point of view and he said there was indeed a lot that he could say too. Both agreed they needed to communicate better and had been holding back but now they had a safe place to talk they would try to share more with each other. They agreed to contract for four more sessions and left looking thoughtful.

Reflecting afterwards on my time with Tony and Pedro I had the notion that Pedro was a disapproving adult busy trying to bring Tony round to correct behaviour. The image came to mind of a parent (Pedro) bringing a rebellious teenager (Tony) to an authority figure such as a teacher (me) for guidance. I decided to hold this in awareness for the next session.

Sessions two and three

I met with Tony first. He described how working freelance in IT he spent much of the day sitting at home in front of a computer screen, and in the evenings would spend hours more trawling pornographic websites for – as he described it – 'sexual release'. 'You have no idea how bored and stressed I get working from home. And it's all there at the touch of a button. Why wouldn't I use it?' I was interested to note that Tony had not previously been this specific about the nature of his Internet use, and I wondered if this was a secret that he kept from Pedro. I also noted that he talked about it as though he had little agency and I suggested we explore this in more detail. He responded by telling me about an insight he had had as a result of the sessions:

Tony: I realize I was seeing myself as the problem. Me being an addict. But Pedro's part of it. Things got difficult when we moved in together. Up till then I was coping fine . . .
Me: What was different when Pedro moved in?
Tony: Pretty much everything, really. A lot of it good, of course. But I'm like a delicate mechanism that normally runs ok, but I have to take care of it and if things get too stressed something goes!
Me: When you describe being like a 'delicate mechanism' you smile as if to say 'It's ok being like this', maybe you're even quite proud of being this delicate mechanism?
Tony: Well it feels a bit silly too – I mean look at me, I don't exactly look like a delicate mechanism do I? But inside I am. And I have to keep things balanced and ticking.
Me: I don't know if this makes sense, but I'm just thinking that drugs or the Internet provides the oil that keeps you running smoothly?

A key part of existential therapy with couples where addiction is a feature is to identify the purpose the 'addiction' has for the couple so that it can be seen as something with a value rather than a meaningless illness or condition requiring expert treatment. Tony agreed that his 'addictions' had a purpose and described how he had built a successful career and had found a balance which enabled him to have 'some sort of balance that allowed you to "do the addict" things and still fulfil my IT contracts. The two sort of fit together, because I don't get a lot of human contact with my line of work and the other stuff I got on line sort of compensated. And it kept me out of the bars and so I did drugs less'.

As he talked it became clear that, as he expressed it, he had managed his addictions pretty successfully in the past, and in fact had not necessarily seen them as a major problem in his life. We realized that his addiction was situational, in that he used different substances and activities to structure his world at different times in his life and in response to what was available at the time. We also noted his current addiction had a purpose – while Pedro felt that Tony's behaviour was symptomatic of a 'condition', his choice of sexual content on the Internet functioned to remove him from sexual intimacy with his partner. Tony described feeling his space invaded:

> I want intimacy but I'm a bit scared of it too. But I feel like I'm letting Pedro down. He's ten years younger than me and he wants us to be full-on.

Tony felt Pedro wanted the physical side of their relationship to be as intense as it had been when they first met, but he felt this was a demand on him.

Tony: Maybe it sounds daft, but sex isn't so important to me these days. It's like I've got my man, I don't need to prove myself day in, day out. He should know we're solid.
Me: But as I hear it, you aren't exactly 'there', you take yourself off somewhere behind a closed door where he can't reach you. And the place you go seems to be at least to some extent about sex.
Tony: Fair comment, I hadn't thought of that. It's as though the closer Pedro gets the more I hide.

I wondered if he had shared any of these feelings with Pedro. He looked sad and said Pedro wouldn't understand: 'I'm afraid I have disappointed him. He thought I was perfect and I'm not.'

I wondered privately whether Pedro could tolerate having a partner who was complex and flawed, rather than the perfect image of a couple which he seemed to hold dear. I decided to try to explore this with him in the next session.

In my meeting with Pedro, he described how he and Tony had talked 'into the night' after Tony's individual session the previous week. Pedro said he felt they had talked more about their relationship than previously. He was initially ambivalent about coming to see me after their conversation.

Pedro: When he started talking it was like I didn't recognize Tony anymore. I thought: this isn't my Tony, he isn't like this.
Me: When you say you didn't recognize him...
Pedro: Well I mean we don't have secrets, at least I didn't think we did. And now I find I'm in the flat with him but not really *with* him. You know what I mean? It's like he's not who I thought he was.
Me: It feels like it's really hard for you to discover he isn't just the person you know, he has other aspects to him as well. And that's so difficult that you react by saying you don't know him at all.
Pedro: Yes, I guess partly out of anger.
Me: Anger about...
Pedro: Anger that what I thought was the case isn't. Like, I've been tricked.
Me: Has someone deliberately set out to trick you?

As we unpacked this more, Pedro began to wonder if he had tricked himself by holding an image of Tony and ignoring anything that did not fit that image. The image of a lover he outlined was someone who was strong, totally reliable, confident and sure of themselves. He valued these qualities because he felt they were not qualities he possessed himself. Pedro saw himself as merging in a love relationship: he and his partner would become one, and in this act of merging he would attain all the qualities he felt he lacked. Such objectification of the other may help to co-create and then sustain an addiction designed to resist the pressures of objectification. I wondered if Pedro had described his notion of being a couple to Tony, and if Tony held the same view. He replied that he had not talked about this since he trusted that his ideal partner simply would share the same perspective: to make it explicit would be to acknowledge that this might not be the case. I reflected that his image of the couple (his couple-construct) seemed quite static. It was as though two pieces of a puzzle fitted together to make a whole, but what came next? Was he on a journey with Tony, and if so might that journey include engaging with differences that were not obviously complementary? Was there room for struggling with difficulty in his view of being a couple? This led us into a detailed discussion of Pedro's family of origin in rural Spain. As he talked he was able to see how he had constructed an image of romantic love in response to the relatively harsh conditions in his family. Leaving his small community for a foreign city, and creating an identity as a gay man had been both exciting and frightening, and he needed a 'perfect' relationship as proof that all this had been worthwhile. It seemed to me that Pedro had adopted a somewhat rigid, what Sartre (1958 [1943]: 597) refers to as a 'mineralised', position, regarding what it meant to be a couple.

Session four

Though they had been remarkably insightful when meeting with me individually I wondered to what extent they would be willing and able to do this *together*. As it turned out, I should have had more faith in their motivation since they announced on coming into the room that they had already begun to compare their ideas about being in a relationship. Tony and Pedro were shocked, but also pleasantly surprised, to discover in the course of our few sessions that they did not know each other as well as they had thought. This led Tony to wonder if he had really seen Pedro, or instead had assumed what Pedro wanted in a relationship without checking with him. If the latter, it seemed that he was holding Pedro at arm's length. Might this be because he was operating with a sense of self according to which he was destined to disappoint anyone who got close to him? Did he even feel substantial if he let go of his 'addict' identity? Was this an exciting possibility for the future?

Tony: It feels strange now to see how I was using addiction to push Pedro way.
Me: Can you say that directly to Pedro?
Tony: [Looking at Pedro] Sure, like I say it feels strange.
Pedro: [Looking at Tony] Well, that doesn't make it any better for me – how do you think it felt to be pushed out of your life just when we were supposed to be most together?

Tony: OK, you're angry, but then I was scared to be so close so I went to what I know and addiction is what I know.

Me: Pedro, I can see you want to come right back, but first can you say what you just heard Tony say?

Pedro: I heard him say he couldn't bear to have me close.

Me: Tony, is that what you said?

Tony: No, that's not it. I said I would love nothing better than to have you close but closeness scares me so I've always gone to my addictions when it came up.

Me: What did you hear then Pedro?

Pedro: I heard he wants me closer and he's scared of closeness.

Me: Right, of closeness, not of you. It's different.

Pedro: That makes me feel more hopeful, less attacked. I can work with 'scared'.

Tony [smiling]: So I'm not your ideal?

Pedro [laughing]: Don't kid yourself – maybe you never were.

Had Pedro really seen Tony, or had he much of the time been trying to fit him into his pre-formed, sedimented image of what a lover should be? Could he tolerate getting close to somebody who did not fit this sedimented image? Pedro said he felt frustrated with himself that he had not been able to see how difficult it might be for Tony to live with him and had, instead, assumed any problems were due to his addiction. He felt he had fallen short of his own image of an ideal partner. When working with couples where addiction is an issue I find that there is often a tendency to use the 'addiction' as the explanation for any difficulties; it is important in the therapy to question this lazy stance and allow problems to surface as what they actually are. In the process difficulties can be understood as part of the complex and rich texture of relationship. Tony initially heard Pedro was frustrated with him, but in the course of clarification was able to hear that Pedro was struggling to move to a more flexible, less sedimented, position.

Could they create a couple-construct that embraced the sense of self which each held individually, while providing a safe place to explore new ways of being, both individually and as a couple? Tony and Pedro talked directly about this and it emerged that they both felt more optimistic about their chances of staying together and wanted to work on this further. I raised further questions towards the end of the session: could their current position be the beginning of a journey rather than their destination? Might romantic love be translated into something more substantial if 'tested' in response to the reality rather than the fantasy of a partner? Could this hold its own satisfactions?

Session five

I met with Pedro and Tony to consider the extent to which their individual constructs and couple-construct remained the same or had changed as a result of clarifying together their previously unspecified positions on the couple-construct in the previous session. I noticed that they now talked to each other as often as they talked to me. They seemed more relaxed with each other, but in our conversation they said they were now no longer sure whether they would stay in their relationship or whether they would part. It seemed that in the course of our meetings they had begun to gain greater self-knowledge about their motivation for becoming a couple and had set aside many of the illusions they had previously held about each other. While they felt this was valuable, the cost was that they were no longer in the same place individually or in relation to each other. Pedro summed it up:

Pedro: I don't feel quite the same person. In fact I'm not sure what I do feel – except I know I feel unsettled.
Tony: That's right, it's as though we are seeing differently and we don't know how we feel about what we see.

I reflected that they did seem to be sharing *this* sensation at least. As Tony expressed it: 'I never realized the extent to which we were in this together. I know we both *said* we were a couple but we never saw *how* we were in a couple. It takes two to tango.'

At the end of the session they contracted with me to have five more sessions and continue to explore their situation.

Concluding reflection

I have outlined my way of working with couples presenting with issues of addiction in the hope that this may assist other existential-phenomenological practitioners to clarify their own approach in this area. In doing so, I have drawn on theory and practice with issues of addiction which I have developed over a number of years (du Plock, 2009; du Plock and Fisher, 2005). I am indebted to Spinelli (2007, 1997), for his investigation of the relational dimensions of the therapeutic encounter. My own approach in this area is grounded in the understanding that addiction is meaningful and serves a function for both members of the couple, individually and as a couple. It is only in the course of careful clarification of its meaning and function for both their self-constructs and their couple-construct that they can obtain a sense of agency which will enable them to decide whether they wish to continue or change their relationship to the phenomenon. My work with Tony and Pedro illustrates how such clarification, engaged with rigorously, provides an opportunity for both members of the couple to reach a deeper appreciation of their role in creating and maintaining the phenomenon of 'addiction'. Such clarification can enable the couple to generate a more sustaining couple-construct; it may also lead them to decide that their individual needs cannot be met within the couple-construct. In the latter case therapy offers the possibility to part on the basis of greater insight, which may provide a resource for future personal relationships.

References

Cohn, H. W. (1997) *Existential Thought and Therapeutic Practice: An Introduction to Existential Psychotherapy*, London: Sage.

du Plock, S. (2009) 'The world of addiction', in E. van Deurzen and S. Young (eds), *Existential Perspectives on Supervision: Widening the Horizon of Psychotherapy and Counselling*, Basingstoke: Palgrave Macmillan.

du Plock, S. and Fisher, J. (2005) 'An existential perspective on addiction', in E. van Deurzen and C. Arnold-Baker (eds), *Existential Perspectives on Human Issues: A Handbook for Therapeutic Practice*, Basingstoke: Palgrave Macmillan.

May, R. (1958) 'Contributions of existential psychotherapy', in R. May, E. Angel and H. F. Ellenberger (eds), *Existence: A New Dimension in Psychiatry and Psychology*, New York: Basic Books.

Sartre, J.-P. (1958 [1943]) *Being and Nothingness: An Essay on Phenomenological Ontology*, trans. H. E. Barnes, London: Methuen.

Shaffer, H. J. (1994) 'Denial, ambivilance and counter transferential hate', in J. Levin and E. Weirs (eds), *The Dynamics and Treatment of Alcoholism*, Northvale, NJ: Jason Aronson.

Spinelli, E. (1994) *Demystifying Therapy*, London: Constable.

Spinelli, E. (1997) *Tales of Un-Knowing: Therapeutic Encounters from an Existential Perspective*, London: Duckworth.

Spinelli, E. (2007) *Practising Existential Psychotherapy: The Relational World*, London: Sage.

Walters, G. D. (1999) *The Addiction Concept: Working Hypothesis or Self-Fulfilling Prophesy?* Needham Heights, MA: Allyn & Bacon.

CHAPTER 17

Working with Cultural or Racial Diversity in Relationships

JYOTI NANDA AND GOLNAR BAYAT

The process of co-authoring this chapter has highlighted for us in an embodied manner what we value in existential cross-cultural relationship work and how we meet the other in relationship. One of us is from India, the other from Iran. We are both women existential psychotherapists. The editors' invitation to us to co-author this chapter was our introduction. Our meetings by email have felt sensitive, respectful and authentic. There has been care and consideration for the other and openness to listening to the other and including the needs of the other, while expressing our own. It has highlighted our assumptions about the other, and the need to make space for the other. We have both felt heard and supported kindly by the other. It is within such a relationship that this chapter has emerged, and within such a relationship that existential cross-cultural relationship therapy can most effectively take place.

The theoretical framework illustrated through the use of examples is written by Jyoti, followed by a detailed case illustration highlighting further emergent themes, written by Golnar.

The existential approach and cross-cultural therapy

Cultural sensitivity is one of the most highly valued themes in cross-cultural literature.

To quote cross-cultural therapists Johannes and Erwin:

> Cultural sensitivity requires that therapists should refrain from imposing their own cultural values on their clients. This is indeed an essential guideline and it is crucial for successful outcomes for therapists to encounter clients where they (the clients) 'are at', understanding, respecting and approaching the interaction from within the framework of their values, rather than endeavouring a unilateral force-fit into the therapist's or majority culture's frame of values. (2004: 332)

216

The call for cultural sensitivity in counselling reflects recognition of the damaging effects that psychological profiling, which does not take into account cultural context, can have on clients from minority cultures. Similarly, in couple therapy, trying to 'normalize', 'cure' and 'fix' couple relationships where either one or both partners are not from the majority community leaves one or both feeling alienated, marginalized, objectified and not understood.

Respect for difference and moving away from psychological profiling

A fundamental existential position is respect for difference and a strong opposition to assigning psychological labels to clients. Based on Husserl's adaptation of Brentano's notion of intentionality that recognizes the inseparability of subject/object (Husserl, 1962 [1913]) and Heidegger's (2003) notion of *Dasein* and the inseparability of self/world/other, the existential tradition recognizes that meaning is contextually and relationally constructed. Existential therapy is concerned with staying alongside the meaning of the lived experience of clients, and focuses on the clarification of the beliefs, values, attitudes that comprise their worldview (Spinelli, 2005, 2007; Deurzen, 2002, 2010). While recognizing that the very enterprise of therapy confers power to therapists by virtue of clients coming to them for help (Buber in dialogue with Rogers in Kirschenbaum and Henderson, 1990), the range of relational possibilities created between therapists and clients can move between what Buber calls 'I-Thou' and 'I-It' relationships (Buber, 1958, 2002; Friedman, 2003).

In 'I-It' relationships, therapists objectify, analyse and label clients. Clients are treated as objects to be repaired (Buber, 1958; Friedman 2003). On the other hand, 'I-Thou' relationships are inter-human relationships, subject-to-subject relationships, relationships in which there is confirmation of the uniqueness of clients by therapists. Such relationships facilitate inclusion of clients, and open possibilities of healing and restoring connection with others (Buber, 1958, 2002; Friedman 2003). The effects of what Buber calls 'love' in an I-Thou encounter between R. D. Laing and a woman labelled paranoid schizophrenic show their power of transformation in restoring connection between the two (Cannon, 2003). How vital then, is the I-Thou relationship stance in multicultural couple therapy, if therapist and clients are to share an understanding of what the couple relationship feels like.

When there are three in the room

While the existential approach is always relational, the dynamic of three in the room brings the existential approach into its full strength.

In existential cross-cultural couple therapy, based on Buber's (1958, 2002) notion of inter-human encounter 'between' people, we believe as existential therapists, that the cultural worldviews 'between' therapist and each partner, whether 'emic' (client's cultural perspective) or 'etic' (therapist's cultural perspective) are in constant interaction with one another and may change.

Therapists need to bring an embodied awareness (see 'body-subject' Merleau-Ponty, 2002 and 'felt sense' Gendlin, 2003) of their own emerging reactions and responses in relation to each partner and the couple's 'inter-relational realm of encounter' (Spinelli, 2007: 200). This can inform therapists of the quality of the therapeutic encounter with each partner, and with the couple's relationship holistically, highlighting differences and similarities in their world-views and assumptions. Recognizing their own assumptions and consciously *bracketing* them (see 'epoché', Husserl, 1962; Spinelli, 2005), therapists then have a better chance of facilitating a dialogue between the couple that enables each partner to speak to and hear the other as directly as possible. Thus therapists facilitate clarification of the meanings, intentions, stances, beliefs and values in each partner's worldview in relation to the other (Spinelli, 2007), and help the couple who are 'reconsidering the values they live by and their experience of their interpersonal reality' (Tantam and Deurzen, 2005: 131).

Marcia and Peter seek relationship therapy. They met as international students, got married and now have three children. Marcia is Spanish. Peter is Polish. Their relationship difficulties started after the children came. Marcia now misses her life in Spain and feels a sense of isolation, is tearful and dejected. She stopped working to be a 'good' mother. Peter has a well-paying job in England where they live. He finds it hard to cope with Marcia's tearfulness and lack of warmth for him now, and their relationship is spiralling down. He works hard for the family. He expects her to be happy to be a part of his life.

A safe therapeutic space where the therapist embodies 'inclusion' of both partners becomes the crucible in which the therapist focuses on their inter-relational encounter, and where both Marcia and Peter find the courage to speak to and hear each other.

What Marcia was unable to express earlier, she is now able to tell Peter. She recounts the torment of her changed identity, from a working woman to a stay-at-home mother, her guilt at feeling this way, her loss of confidence in going back to the work place again, her loss of financial independence, and feeling vulnerable in a position of dependence on Peter. Themes of power and dominance emerge in their relationship. Peter is able to hear Marcia's distress being expressed 'between them within their relationship' rather than her distress being situated *within her*. He can hear how his arbitrary financial decisions for the family leave Marcia with a sense of loss of her autonomy and choice, and feeling an unequal partner in the relationship. What might easily be described as Marcia's postnatal depression, *causing* the couple's relational difficulty, can be seen existentially as being *co-created* within the realm of the relationship *between* Marcia and Peter and as a changed situation after the children came. It can be seen as a response to her changing being-in-the-world with others rather than residing intra-psychically *within her*.

Equally, Marcia could also see how her inability to express her relational needs adequately, and her withdrawal from Peter left him feeling rejected, alienated, lonely and resentful. Their inter-relational interactions had affected each other, resulting in their relationship spiralling downwards.

In this example, irrespective of the culture of therapist and each partner (with three different cultural perspectives in interaction with one another), therapist and both partners could relate to the emergent themes of conflict.

Within an existential cross-cultural relationship frame, conflict in relationships is a given because of difference. Sartre (1944) famously stated, 'Hell is other people'. Strasser and Randolph (2004) draw from Sartre's philosophy on conflict, free will and choice as the core of their mediation model. While every human interaction is in itself a conflict, and we are doomed to be in conflict, our actions are not predetermined – we have choice and free will (albeit within limitations) in terms of our attitude to these determining tendencies of conflict within any situation.

Marcia and Peter are gently challenged by the therapist to recognize that they have choices in how they respond to these conflicts within their relationship. Both recognize how each had left the other feeling excluded, distancing themselves from the other, thus co-creating and feeding a cycle of resentment.

The recognition of the presence of impermanence, change, uncertainty and existential anxiety is a fundamental existential therapeutic stance (Cohn, 1997; Deurzen, 2002, 2010; Deurzen van and Arnold-Baker, 2005; Heidegger, 2003; Nanda, 2009, 2010; Spinelli, 2005, 2007). Marcia and Peter realize circumstances change. Identities change. Relationships change. They are in the process of becoming, and are not fixed. Change and impermanence give rise to anxiety. Their experience of distress points to the implicit temporal recognition of life passing by, and feeling less meaningful within a deteriorating relationship between them.

The existential notion of time – that the present contains the past as it looks to the future (Heidegger, 2003) – challenges us to step out of being a victim of past circumstances, and choose to take responsibility for constructing meaning in our life and giving it direction. The reflective stance of existential therapy opens us to possibilities while recognizing human limitations (Heidegger, 2003; Deurzen, 2010).

Through the therapeutic process, both Marcia and Peter recognize the need to address and renew their relationship. Both recognize what it might mean to lose the other, and what each means to the other. Peter is able to tell Marcia that all the money he makes would lose all meaning if it were not for Marcia, and her contribution in his life, in their home and with their children. Peter's appreciation of Marcia moves her to tears – this time tears of a different kind. Now they can *feel* for each other again in their relationship. Peter's words of appreciation could have fallen on deaf ears, but they didn't because the partners had started opening to each other and hearing each other again.

This co-created therapeutic experience between therapist and both partners, in which each partner experienced 'inclusion' from the therapist and could speak to and hear the other, opened possibilities for each to include the relational needs of the other. They now had the choice of consciously nourishing their relationship in the recognition that their well-being was interconnected.

Each also discovered their habitual ways of relating, which surfaced in their encounter with each other. Marcia discovered how difficult she found expressing her needs in most relationships, including with Peter. Peter recognized how often he dictated terms to others – including Marcia – expecting them to obey.

While Marcia and Peter were from two different European cultures, and the therapist was from a minority Asian culture, what they shared with each other was the experience of living away from their home countries and residing within the same majority culture, a familiarity with Western culture in a broad sense, and the shared human existential conditions. The therapist's ability to enter into an inter-human encounter with each partner and facilitate a dialogue *between* the couple within their *inter-relational* encounter, opened for them possibilities of fresh understanding and new ways of relating.

The challenge of conflict of cultural values

When strong emotion arises for therapists in relation to cultural difference in basic values between therapist and clients, it requires acknowledgement. I feel challenged when a male partner takes on a domineering position within a heterosexual couple relationship based on religious/cultural views that dictate that the woman's place is at home while his partner wishes to experience the greater freedom available within the majority cultural perspective. How may we maintain empathy for the male client and resist siding with the female client?

While we have the choice to *bracket* our assumptions, we also have the choice to express *mutuality* (Buber, 1958). In acknowledging my discomfort in the immediacy of the encounter, I say, 'I am a woman, and here I am, not at home but working with both of you, what is that like for you?' In this way our different beliefs and attitudes can stand disclosed, while creating space for further clarification of meaning. Theoretically, this intervention draws from Buber (Buber, 2002; Friedman, 2003) recognizing that 'the self emerges in "dialogue" with others' (Nanda, 2006: 345).

In confronting the couple with my 'otherness', a different possibility for a woman's role when they are from a minority culture is made explicit. It would however, be important to ask each partner how they experience being with me, so each partner has the space to express how they feel – whether marginalized or not. In this way the unspoken can be acknowledged to explore how this intervention affects their *inter-relational encounter,* and therapist/couple relationship in this meeting of emic/etic views.

Culturally matching therapists/clients

The discourse around cultural matching of therapists/clients arose in response to the painful effects of objectifying clients with difference within a majority community. This is seen in the strong and passionate voice of cross-cultural therapist Derald Wing Sue.

Rather than educate or heal, rather than offer enlightenment and freedom, and rather than allow for equal access and opportunities, historical and current practices have restricted, stereotyped, damaged, and oppressed the culturally different in our society. (Drawing from Herlihy and Corey, 1996: 196, in Johannes and Erwin, 2004: 330)

In a similar vein, Pederson (1991, 2000) and Sue and Sue (1999) assert that it is the presence of therapists' unaddressed underlying cultural assumptions that discourages cultural minorities from using the mental health services.

Consonant with this view, the philosophical underpinnings of existential cross-cultural relationship therapy advocate that therapists examine their underlying cultural assumptions in therapeutic encounters and cultivate cultural sensitivity.

While there are both advantages (Alladin, 2002; Gim et al., 1991; Lin, 1994) and disadvantages (Alladin, 2002; Vontress et al., 1999; Sue et al., 1996) of culturally matching therapists/clients, where there is therapist cultural sensitivity the advantage of cultural matching is considerably reduced (Coleman et al., 1995; Sue and Sundberg, 1996). Cultural difference may even be an advantage (Beck, 1988; Lambert, 1982), as another cultural perspective may enrich client perspectives. However, Laungani (2004) asserts that when clients who come for therapy have not assimilated into the majority culture at all or have very little exposure to the values of the majority culture, the very assumptions of counselling and meanings around context, time, space and boundaries can be brought into challenge as these may not be shared between therapist and clients. He reiterates, therapists need deep appreciation of, and sensitivity to, socio-cultural differences in the family relationships of minority client cultures, and need to move from a rigid psychoanalytical therapeutic model to a more flexible systemic therapeutic model if they are to see therapeutic success.

Existential cross-cultural relationship therapy is already a relational contextual model. It stays with the meaning of each partner, facilitating the clarification of meaning as each partner speaks to and hears the other, is respectful of context and values the humility to acknowledge that therapists can never fully understand the other. It values remaining open to being corrected and learning from clients.

In the instance where one partner is from the majority community and the other is from a minority community, a shared understanding of social and cultural meanings and processes within both cultures by a culturally sensitive therapist has the advantage of facilitating better understanding of the difficulties within their relationship. This is seen in the culturally sensitive case illustration that follows.

Case illustration

It was Mary who contacted the therapist to explain that she and her partner were experiencing relationship problems. She and her partner, Marwan, had previously attended two sessions of therapy, then he had refused to attend any more. Mary explained that she knew they could not carry on living the way they were, and she had chosen to contact me because she guessed that my culture was closer to her husband's, resulting in him being more willing to attend sessions. She also said that her partner Marwan had been convinced that the previous therapist who, like Mary, belonged to the majority community, had sided with Mary and not understood what Marwan had to say, contributing to the failure of the therapy. Mary was not convinced that the previous therapist had indeed sided with her to the exclusion of her partner, but was willing to seek out therapy with a therapist who was culturally different from her, and 'more similar' to her partner, to see if the outcome would be different. I noted the importance Mary (and Marwan?) attached to the yet unexplored phenomenon of 'more similar' and wondered how significant this phenomenon would be in the relationship between Mary and Marwan and I. I also stated my commitment to co-creating a space in which all three of us could participate with our differences and similarities heard, owned and respected.

During the first session I observed that Mary and Marwan related to each other by use of angry outbursts and repeated accusations. Upon inquiring if they had noticed their way of relating to each other Marwan informed me that he found such a conflictual way of relating 'heartbreaking', and explained that he would often withdraw from such conversations with Mary. Mary explained that Marwan's withdrawal made her panicky, and her anxiety took the form of angry outbursts. I encouraged each of them to take turns to tell each other and me what their preferred mode of relating to each other was.

Neither Marwan nor Mary answered my question. Either the question came too early for them to feel able to express their wishes, or they did not yet have any answers – or both.

It took a number of sessions before both Marwan and Mary could state how they preferred to relate to each other. Following the principles of existential relationship work Mary and Marwan were each encouraged to describe and clarify the assumptions, beliefs, limitations and biases that they each held, whilst exploring the various dimensions of their existence (Binswanger, 1968; Deurzen, 2002). Such exploration of their worldviews enabled each of them to listen to the other's deeply held and unspoken assumptions, which had remained obscured from each other's knowing of the other. As our sessions progressed it became clearer that Marwan had an expectation that, if Mary really cared for him then he would be 'understood' by her. Being understood was linked very closely in his mind with being cared for. It was something he dearly missed, something that the previous therapist had failed to do and indeed something he believed Mary repeatedly failed to do. Mary found Marwan's accusation that she did not understand him hurtful and anger-inducing – she felt she was dedicating more and more of her time trying to understand him but all she got in return was his withdrawal. Marwan's response to hearing Mary's statement was to gather his arms tightly and close his eyes. I saw him physically withdraw and noted Mary's look of desperation.

The connection Marwan had made between being understood and being cared for offered a significant opening into the expression of his private world-view (Deurzen, 2002). I recalled identifying an air of nostalgia every time Marwan expressed his longing for a way of 'being understood' that he now desperately missed. Marwan's tone of voice, choked with tears, often reminded me of my own past struggles with finding words to communicate the series of losses that I believed no one around me could understand, as they had not shared similar experiences. The more I felt that I could understand Marwan, the more I felt that I needed to keep open the space for 'not knowing' and 'not understanding too quickly' so that Marwan could be invited to make sense of his longing for the past and his frustrations with the present alongside Mary, who was so desperately trying to understand. The key challenge to Marwan was to find the words to tell Mary and me what exactly he meant when he spoke of 'being understood'. The existential enquiry he was being encouraged to engage with was to clarify assumptions and beliefs that were held in the realm of his private world (Deurzen, 1988) and access feelings, ideas and yearnings that he had not spoken of to his partner.

Marwan's search took him to a time before he had had to leave his country of birth to seek refuge in the UK. To a time when he believed there was not so much need for words. A time when the people he loved and who loved him were close enough to each other to know what was important without needing to ask or to tell. He explained how he missed such closeness, such effortless understanding. He explained the physical proximity between him and members of his family and between him and his circle of close male friends. He described how the physical closeness resulted in a form of knowing that did not require words – a place where he felt 'understood' and 'understanding'. In the UK, he said, things were different. Everyone wanted him to *say* all the time what he wanted. Everyone wanted 'words'. He found it particularly hard that Mary, the woman he loved, constantly asked him to say what he wanted, explain how he was feeling, explain what the matter was with him. How could Mary love him if she had to ask him all the time?

Mary's immediate reaction to Marwan's explorations was one of bewilderment, and she explained with anger that she could not understand what it was exactly that Marwan was talking about. My invitation to Mary to describe the importance of 'asking' in her relationship with Marwan helped open a window into a worldview (Deurzen, 2002, 2010) which was different from Marwan's. She described how at the beginning of their relationship Mary would often ask Marwan to talk to her about his past. She remembered them talking a lot but it seemed to upset Marwan, so at some stage they had stopped talking about his past. But what she was hearing him complain about *now* was not that they were not talking about the past but something new. What he was talking about now was about a way of 'knowing' and 'understanding' that she did not comprehend. She had always thought that if you care for someone you ask them how they are, you offer them the opportunity to explain, to say, to describe. What she heard Marwan describe now was new to her. She talked about how close she felt to her own family. How important they were to her, and yet what cemented their relationship was not necessarily the physical proximity and wordless closeness that Marwan was describing – Mary actually found such physical proximity claustrophobic – but the act of talking. Her earliest memories were ones in which she was talking with her mum or dad or her sister, memories of times when they would be letting each other know what their likes and dislikes were, what their hopes and aspirations were. Mary had always prided herself in having a close relationship with her family, one in which such intimate conversations between them were allowed and cherished. Mary's clear description of what she valued uppermost in a close relationship enabled Marwan to describe how unfamiliar he had found himself, and still did, with Mary's insistence on knowing what Marwan wanted, liked or preferred. He described how uncomfortable he had felt with having to focus on his own needs and wants as separate from what they as a couple may want. He was unused to being asked what he preferred, although he acknowledged that during the course of his relationship with Mary he had started to cultivate a sense of his own preferences and likes and valued the fact that Mary allowed him space to explore these.

Working in an existential way encouraging Mary and Marwan to explore the unspoken assumptions and expectations in each of their worldviews enabled each of them to better understand the experiences of the other's world of meaning, thus bringing them closer.

Many of our sessions were spent on opening up space for Marwan and Mary to find words to describe their cultural values, and recognize beliefs and assumptions regarding what constituted 'togetherness', 'love' and 'closeness'. They attributed different meaning to the same words and expected different behaviour to demonstrate love and affection towards each other. The idea of 'differentness' was visited in our sessions often and it became a springboard for exploring 'sameness' as well. As Mary and Marwan explored their respective worldviews further, their deeply held and differing values became more apparent. At the same time as each sat alongside the other whilst the other experienced and interpreted their worldview, a space for meeting was created which allowed each to enter and experience the 'meaning world' of the other. There were facets of what Marwan described, particularly to do with notions of honouring his family, duty towards his mother, obligation towards his unmarried sisters and commitment to economically supporting his siblings, that puzzled and infuriated Mary. At times such as this, when the gap between Mary and Marwan widened, the practice of existential therapy which requires the therapist to remain aware of her own assumptions, beliefs and biases whilst holding open the expressed worldview of both people in the room became particularly important. Those were moments when my cultural familiarity with Marwan's elevation of interdependence between his small family of Mary and himself and his greater family back at home, and my familiarity with Mary's elevation of the needs of her small family unit above all others, allowed me to hold the frame so that Mary and Marwan's differing definitions of what constituted 'family' could emerge into the forefront of their dialogue with each other. Similarly Marwan could explore what he meant by the 'coldness' that he experienced in his relationship with Mary and her family. Mary had heard this as an accusation and felt scolded by it but when explored it became clear that Marwan was referring to the absence of the close physical contact he had been socialized into and had come to expect as depicting 'closeness', which in turn Mary experienced as 'too close and intrusive' when she saw it amongst Marwan's family. Mary's description of her response to such 'closeness' enabled Marwan to explore with Mary other ways there were for him to express his abundant love for her, rather than feel rejected as he had done in the past. My familiarity with Marwan's frustration at needing words to explain multiple layers of loss also led us to explore his belief that words in a language other than his own could not possibly describe his real pain. Space was created for Marwan to identify his sense of loss regarding his ability to convey meaning in his mother tongue, and gradually within our sessions Marwan started using words in his mother tongue to convey his feelings and Mary became increasingly interested in learning more about the experiences they had stopped talking about, and more of the language that linked Marwan with his family and described his web of affectionate bonds.

Once Mary and Marwan were able to examine their uniqueness as cultural beings and how subtly different they were from one another, they could explore what it was that they wanted for themselves and from each other and negotiate the changing contours of their closeness and intimacy so that they could support each other better in their relationship.

The relationship that was established between Marwan, Mary and myself as their therapist illustrates a number of the benefits that the existential approach brings to therapeutic cross-cultural work, including:

- How openness to meeting the clients where 'they are' can lead to an opening into their respective worldviews.
- How respect for the uniqueness of each individual's worldview can facilitate respect for 'differentness'.
- How a respectful acceptance of 'differentness' can lead to a genuine 'I-Thou' (Buber, 1958) meeting that is grounded on the 'sameness' of the human condition shared by the clients and the therapist.
- How the therapist's awareness of his or her own values acts as 'ground' alongside which clients' worldviews can emerge into the dialogue.
- How the therapist's sensitivity to, and awareness of, possible issues arising from cultural difference can help hold a space in which a dialogue can unfold about all that is expected but not named in a relationship. The beauty of cross-cultural work is not when different people from different cultures act differently, but when the same act is differently experienced and conveys differing meanings.

Conclusion

Offering cultural sensitivity in existential cross-cultural relationship therapy is not an intellectual exercise; it is an expression of a way of being genuinely grounded in inter-human interactions. Such therapeutic encounters shed light as much on therapists' own assumptions, stretching their learning, as they facilitate space for the couple to review their worldviews, beliefs and values, bringing new ways of seeing self and each other in their relationship.

References

Alladin, W. J. (2002) 'Ethnic matching in counselling: how important is it to ethnically match clients and counsellors?' in I. S. Palmer (ed.), *Multicultural Counselling: A Reader*, London: Sage.

Beck, D. F. (1988) *Counselor Characteristics: How They Affect Outcome*, Milwaukee, WI: Family Service America.

Binswanger, L. (1968) *Being-in-the-World*, New York: Harper Torchbooks.

Buber, M. (1958) *I and Thou*, trans. R. J. Smith, New York: Harper and Row.

Buber, M. (2002) *Between Man and Man*, London: Routledge Classics.

Cannon, B. (2003) 'Sartre's contribution to psychoanalysis', in R. Frie (ed.), *Understanding Experience – Psychotherapy and Postmodernism*, London and New York: Routledge.

Cohn, H. (1997) *Existential Thought and Therapeutic Practice*, London: Sage Publications.

Coleman, H. L. K., Wampold, B. E. and Casali, S. L. (1995) 'Ethnic minorities' ratings of ethnically similar and European American counselors: A meta-analysis', *Journal of Counseling Psychology*, 42, 55–64.

Deurzen, E. van (2002) *Existential Counselling and Psychotherapy in Practice*, London: Sage Publications.

Deurzen, E. van (2010) *Everyday Mysteries: A Handbook of Existential Psychotherapy*, London: Routledge.

Deurzen, E. van and Arnold-Baker, C. (2005) *Existential Perspectives on Human Issues: A Handbook for Therapeutic Practice*, London: Palgrave Macmillan.

Deurzen-Smith, E. van (1988) *Existential Counselling in Practice*, London: Sage.

Friedman, M. S. (2003) 'Martin Buber and dialogical psychotherapy', in R. Frie (ed.), *Understanding Experience – Psychotherapy and Postmodernism*, London and New York: Routledge.

Gendlin, E. (2003) 'Beyond postmodernism: from concepts through experiencing', in R. Frie (ed.), *Understanding Experience – Psychotherapy and Postmodernism*, London and New York: Routledge.

Gim, R. H., Atkinson, D. R. and Kim, S. J. (1991) 'Asian-American acculturation, counselor ethnicity and cultural sensitivity, and ratings of counselors', *Journal of Counseling Psychology*, 38, 57–62.

Heidegger, M. (2003) *Being and Time*, Oxford and Cambridge, MA: Blackwell.

Herlihy, B. and Corey, G. (1996) *ACA Ethical Standards Casebook*, 5th edn, Alexandria, VA: American Counseling Association.

Husserl, E. (1962 [1913]) *Ideas: General Introduction to Pure Phenomenology*, trans. W. R. Boyce Gibson, London and New York: Collier, Macmillan.

Husserl, E. (1997) *Cartesian Meditations*, The Hague: Nijhoff (Distributors: Kluwer Academic).

Johannes, C. K. and Erwin, P. G. (2004) 'Developing multicultural competence: perspectives on theory and practice', *Counselling Psychology Quarterly*, 17 (3), 329–338, London: Brunner-Routledge Taylor & Francis Health Sciences.

Kirschenbaum, H. and Henderson, V. L. (1990) *Carl Rogers Dialogues,* London: Constable.

Lambert, M. J. (1982) *The Effects of Psychotherapy,* New York: Human Sciences Press.

Laungani, P. (2004) *Asian Perspectives in Counselling and Psychotherapy,* London: Brunner-Routledge.

Lin, J. C. H. (1994) 'How long do Chinese Americans stay in psychotherapy?' *Journal of Counseling Psychology,* 41, 288–291.

Merleau-Ponty, M. (2002) *Phenomenology of Perception.* New York: Routledge Classics.

Nanda, J. (2006) 'Knowing it in the body: "I-Thou" in therapeutic encounter', *Journal of the Society for Existential Analysis,* 17 (2): 343–358.

Nanda, J. (2009) 'Mindfulness: a lived experience of existential-phenomenological themes', *Journal of Existential Analysis,* 20 (1), 147–162.

Nanda, J. (2010) 'Embodied integration: reflections on Mindfulness Based Cognitive Therapy (MBCT) and a case for Mindfulness Based Existential Therapy (MBET) – a single case illustration', *Existential Analysis,* 21 (2), 331–350.

Pedersen, P. (1991) 'Multiculturalism as a generic approach to counseling', *Journal of Counseling and Development,* 70 (1), 6–12.

Pedersen, P. (2000) *A Handbook for Developing Multicultural Awareness,* Alexandria, VA: American Counseling Association.

Sartre, J.-P. (1944) *No Exit.* Original French title *Huis Clos.* Play first performed at the Théâtre du Vieux-Colombier, Paris, in May 1944.

Spinelli, E. (2005) *The Interpreted World: An Introduction to Phenomenological Psychology,* London: Sage Publications.

Spinelli, E. (2007) *Practising Existential Psychotherapy: The Relational World,* London: Sage.

Strasser, F. and Randolph, P. (2004) *Mediation: A Psychological Insight into Conflict Resolution,* London: Continuum.

Sue, O. W., Ivey, A. E. and Pedersen, P. B. (1996) *A Theory of Multicultural Counseling and Therapy,* Pacific Grove, CA: Brooks/Cole.

Sue, D. W. and Sue, D. (1999) *Counseling the Culturally Different: Theory and Practice,* 3rd edn, New York: Wiley.

Sue, D. W. and Sundberg, N. D. (1996) 'Research and research hypotheses about effectiveness in multicultural counseling', in P. B. Pedersen, J. G. Draguns, W. J. Lonner and J. E. Trimble (eds), *Counseling across Cultures,* 4th edn, 323–352, Thousand Oaks, CA: Sage.

Tantam, D. and Deurzen, E. van (2005) 'Relationships', in E. van Deurzen and C. Arnold-Baker (eds), *Existential Perspectives on Human Issues,* New York: Palgrave Macmillan.

Vontress, C. E., Johnson, J. and Epp, L. R. (1999) *Cross-Cultural Counseling: A Casebook,* Alexandria, VA: American Counseling Association.

A Developing Model of Existential Relationship Therapy

EMMY VAN DEURZEN AND SUSAN IACOVOU

Life is nothing without love. It is probably not possible to be entirely without love, although it is quite common to feel unloved. Even if we are not in a loving relationship, we still love something, perhaps a place, or an idea, a pet, ourselves, or even life itself. But we are quite likely to love at least one other person too. Of course this love may be one-sided and unrequited, or it may be deeply problematic or conflicted in some other way. But even so, there is usually some special person in our life, most often a parent, a child, or a partner, who means the world to us. We use the phrase 'to love' quite loosely a lot of the time and figure we know what it means. Yet to really love another person is probably one of the hardest things in the world. And there is clearly a huge difference between loving and being loved. Some people are able to do both with ease and others confuse the two, or confuse loving with wanting to be loved, or with needing another.

As the case studies within this book show, many people who come for relationship therapy are convinced that they are good at loving other people but that others fall short in their capacity to love them properly in return. But, as we have seen, things are never that simple. In the first place our love of another can be possessive or self-serving or it can be lacking in warmth or in expression. In the second place it is difficult to be open to the love another shows us, as the other may have a different way of expressing love than we would like. But expecting others to love us in the same way we do ourselves is to hamper and want to control the other's love rather than to receive it and reciprocate it. Learning to love and live with another person in a loving manner is one of the most challenging existential tasks we ever have to deal with.

As existential relationship therapists, we recognize that it is not an easy path to learn to love oneself and then to extend this love to others. Many of our clients remain confused about what it is to love and be loved and they continue to confuse love and need. Other confusions also arise; between love and liking, between love and friendship, between love and lust, between love and control, to name but a few. When people come to have therapy together because the relationship between them feels unsafe and unloving, they are trusting us with some of the most precious aspects of their being – their connections and relatedness to others – with all the fear, pain, hope and joy inherent in them. In this context, we have an obligation to tread with the utmost sensitivity, informed, where possible, by the accumulated wisdom of some of the world's greatest thinkers, and guided by a philosophy that recognizes that relatedness is at the very centre of human existence.

As this book shows, existential relationship therapists are uniquely placed to work with clients who are confused, disillusioned and dismayed by the challenges and demands that come from 'being-in-the-world-with-others' (Heidegger, 2003). It remains to us as editors to review the diverse contributions in this volume, where different authors have focused on different aspects of the relational conundrum, and attempt to pull the various strands together to sketch out a model of existential relationship therapy that holds together. The model of existential relationship therapy we have defined, drawn from the knowledge and experience of the practitioner-authors within this volume, is non-prescriptive and leaves much room for individual freedom of therapists and the relational partners with whom they work. It is founded on a commitment to liberation and autonomy and allows for systematic work, while leaving plenty of room for individuality and personal interpretation of what makes relationships loving and yet strong enough to withstand challenge and change.

You will note that the model contains no step-by-step instructions, and no rigid tools or prescribed techniques. As the work of the different contributing practitioners illustrates, the essence of successful relatedness is a willingness to start afresh, to see anew each individual partner and each relationship, to recognize that:

> The client you meet as therapist is the client who meets you. There is no client as such. If two therapists meet the same client, it is not the same client. (Cohn, 1997: 33)

We have no desire, therefore, to manualize the existential approach to relationship therapy, as this would only neuter it by removing one of its core strengths. It is not for us to suggest, for example, that relationship therapists should see clients individually first, or second, or only work with all members of the relationship present, nor to prescribe the 'appropriate' length of the therapeutic contract, nor to outline how client contact outside sessions should be managed. These, together with other procedural decisions, make up the therapeutic contract and as such are very much part of the way in which each individual therapist interprets her approach to working with couples. These things will be negotiated and will change to suit the needs of individual therapists/clients and the nature of the particular issues being faced within the relationship.

Having said this, there are clearly some common threads, some foundational or core beliefs or assumptions that inform the work of every existential relationship therapist. These deserve to be captured in an explicit summary and together they form a model consisting of:

- a method of exploration and questioning designed to return us to 'the things themselves' (Husserl, 1999)
- theoretical underpinnings drawn from centuries of philosophical thinking
- attitudes commonly held by existential relationship therapists
- stances taken by clients undergoing existential relationship therapy
- key therapeutic tasks or aims of existential relationship therapy
- a focus on the tasks, challenges and paradoxes of life.

This model is described in more detail below.

A methodology of exploration

> ... phenomenology in the therapeutic setting encourages a focus on people's lived experience – how they encounter the world, how it appears to them and what it means to them. (Deurzen and Iacovou, Introduction to this volume)

As we outlined in our introductory chapter, therapists using the phenomenological method are better able to stay with their clients' experiences, as they appear to the client, and are less likely to allow their own biases, preconceptions and experiences to flavour the client's story. By bracketing their own responses and reactions, encouraging the client to describe rather than interpret their experiences, and taking care not to make assumptions about what is more, or less, important in the client's story, the existential relationship therapist helps to reveal the world of each individual partner and shows them how to map a detailed, dynamic picture of their relationship. The therapist then carefully validates this picture and, in an atmosphere of openness and curiosity, helps the clients to explore their particular way of relating. As a result of this process, the costs and benefits of the way in which each partner relates to the other become clear, and alternative ways of relating are brought into the light for consideration.

As we saw in earlier chapters, the phenomenological approach is particularly useful when working, for example, with sexual issues, or when dealing with clients with different cultural or racial backgrounds, or with relationships where one or both partners is on the autistic spectrum or struggles with addiction. In all these cases, phenomenology enables the therapist to remain open to a wide range of meanings even when their clients' experiences or ways of expressing themselves are well outside their own.

While noticing and bracketing their emotional and intellectual responses to clients, to their stories and even to the individual words they use, the existential relationship therapist also has the opportunity to go beyond the phenomenological attitude and express mutuality (Buber, 1970) or even to work in ways that mitigate against dominant cultural paradigms, challenging and questioning assumptions.

Theoretical underpinnings

While the writings within this book indicate that the phenomenological approach is the methodological foundation of existential relationship therapy, it is clear that this methodology is informed, supported and given authority by a comprehensive and consistent body of theory. The most central elements of this theory are captured below.

Normalizing not pathologizing

> ...the therapist seeks to set-aside their preconceptions and stay with the client and their own meaning making process. (Langdridge and Barker, Chapter 12)

Building on the curiosity and openness to meaning inherent in the phenomenological stance, existential relationship therapists oppose and resist the assigning of labels to clients, recognizing such labels as socially and culturally biased. This stance follows the radical approaches of Laing (1962), Szasz (1974) and Foucault (2006) in which psychological labels are recognized to be vague, arbitrary and open to interpretation and, importantly, as significant barriers to therapists and clients seeking to relate to each other as individuals in search of understanding.

Relatedness as a central aspect of existence

> Existential practitioners believe in the relational nature of being; we are always in relation with others. (Lewis, Chapter 8)

Existential philosophers have shown individuality to be secondary to relationship. Buber's I-It and I-Thou ways of being may refer to different modes of relating but they show up that there is no I without either an It or a Thou. Kierkegaard's crowd, Nietzsche's herd and Heidegger's inauthentic falling in with others are examples of the way in which we set out as part of a multitude rather than as individuals. Levinas showed the Other to be a primary category rather than a secondary one. Relationships are elemental and inevitable, as we can never be fully separate from others, in the same way in which we can never live without a physical world to dwell in. Even when we are on our own our thoughts and feelings are marked by their reference to others. The fact that being with others is a challenge that none of us can avoid has deep implications for understanding human relationships. We are in a sense at the mercy of others, for being part of humanity is as essential to human beings as breathing. This means that relationships cannot just be seen as commodities or as temporary events that we can take or leave. On the contrary relationships and the way we live them are utterly defining of who we are and what we become. We are interrelated rather than separate.

Embodiment and sexuality

> ...an embodied awareness...can inform therapists of the quality of the therapeutic encounter with each partner, and with the couple's relationship holistically, highlighting differences and similarities in their worldviews and assumptions. (Nanda and Bayat, Chapter 17)

Existential therapists recognize the fundamentally embodied nature of human existence. It was Merleau-Ponty (1962) who most famously emphasized the inseparable nature of mind and body (disputing the Cartesian view that they are separate features of our being). We are our bodies, we interact with others through our bodies and it is through our bodies that we make sense of the world. Our embodied experience has as much to tell us, therefore, about how we relate to ourselves and to our partners. Sexuality is part of this embodied being-in-the-world and therefore is also ever present in our interactions with others. There is massive potential in existential relationship therapy to make partners more aware of their embodied selves, as part of the way they experience their sexuality. The therapy will disclose previously unrecognized or unacknowledged aspects of both of the partners' relatedness and attunement to the world and of their physical attitude to this other person with whom they share their lives.

Intimacy and the authentic encounter

> Although 'intimacy' is a common word, true intimacy is, for many people, unknown. (Stadlen, Chapter 3)

The dialogical space between two people can be disorderly, uncontainable and fractious but it is only in the human encounter that we can experience the intimacy, honesty and trust that brings life into focus, reminds us of how good it is to be alive, makes us creative and clarifies our problems. Authentic relationship is founded upon love and desire lived in good faith, rather than on an escape from freedom and responsibility. Obviously authentic love must avoid the twin pitfalls of bad faith relationships – overemphasis on facticity and overemphasis on freedom. Interestingly many approaches to relationship therapy themselves founder on one or the other of these poles of bad faith. They either emphasize differentiation over commitment and togetherness – or security over freedom and risk taking. And while they have much to teach us about one or the other of these matters, what is unique about existential relationship therapy is that it recognizes and works with both, enabling partners to work with this constant tension dynamically for themselves.

Freedom, choice and responsibility

> Responsibility as connected to freedom is one of the universal existential givens in that, as humans, we are free and also responsible for our own course of actions in life, albeit within the finitude and facticity of existence. (Strasser and Clark, Chapter 10)

Authentic engagement reminds us that we are fully responsible for the way in which we choose to live our interrelatedness, or inter-subjectivity. Our freedom to choose (to which, according to Sartre, 1974, we are condemned) means that there are no absolute truths, no inherently 'right' or 'wrong' decisions, but rather a life lived in the uncertainty of liberty and choice, where everything is open to interpretation and where we must accept that our decisions are in our own hands (Deurzen, 2010). The theme of responsibility and reflection on our personal way of relating to others thus becomes a fundamental aspect of existential relationship work. No one can dismiss the problems in a relationship as 'just about the other', or as 'simply my partner's fault'. No matter how difficult the relationship or how impossible the other person may seem, there is always something to be learnt from being with another person and from understanding how we initiate and respond to difficulties.

Meaning, meanings and meaninglessness

> No longer believing in the same ideals and values generates a sense of isolation and loneliness as well as frustration, boredom and fear. (Savery, Chapter 7)

Existential relationship therapy always involves becoming more aware of who each of the partners in the relationship is and how they define themselves differently when alone or when with the other. This requires a tracing of the meanings that each partner in the relationship holds dear and an understanding of how such meanings are taken for granted and often remain unspoken. Hopefully this will lead to an exploration of how each partner can expand and grow and learn to create new joint meanings with each other. The process is one of comparing notes and learning to speak one's mind without fearing retaliation or loss of love. The therapist offers that kind of safety: the safety of knowing that each partner's deepest beliefs, experiences and yearnings will be equally valued and paid attention to, so that shared and not shared values and meanings can be spoken about and taken seriously. This, in turn, leads to an exploration of how existing tensions and differences can be discussed, accepted and worked with.

Anxiety

> Anxiety tends to reduce the likelihood of partner conflict being resolved and, unless it can be buffered by increasing support from the other partner, may lead to a long-term increase in conflict that can destroy the relationship. (Tantam and Deurzen, Chapter 13)

Relationships are inherently anxiety provoking and expose our clients to a number of risks, including that of being misunderstood, rejected or hurt in some way, being out of control and powerless to influence their partner, or being seen by the other in a way they do not like. Anxiety that is avoided or left unacknowledged can manifest itself in our clients' relationships as excessive neediness or suspicion and can lead to the anxious partner taking impulsive action, making snap decisions or to announcements or acting out in other ways to ameliorate or quell what feels to them like unbearable feelings. An existential therapist will emphasize the importance of tolerating and valuing anxiety, seeing it not as a threat or a sign of illness, but as an inevitable part of our existence, an existential given, and a signal that something in our life requires our focus, attention and energy.

Death, loss and suffering

> In the face of the inevitability of change, we can become more flexible and responsive to life's vagaries, instead of being bound by the dulling demands of the 'they'. (Weixel-Dixon, Chapter 6)

Through their suffering and pain, and the ultimate reality of their mortality, our clients have the opportunity to become aware of their limits and identify those ambitions that are outside their reach, whilst at the same time recognizing the areas in their lives in which they want to effect change. If they waste their energy trying to deny their finitude, or hiding from the contingency of existence, they risk becoming estranged from their lives, and may get caught up in the day-to-day minutiae, losing sight of the idea that life should be lived to the full in light of the fact that death is the end of all possibilities.

Even if we lived forever, we would still have to face the reality that we are finite in terms of our abilities and in relation to the reality of life's limitations. Every time we make a choice we lose the possibility of other choices – we cannot keep all our options open and we cannot choose not to choose. Existential relationship therapy helps clients to come to terms with the implications of death, loss, suffering and failure, both as they apply to their own lives as individuals and to their lives together in relationship. Couples frequently find that in becoming more realistic in their expectations of themselves and each other they open themselves up to being able to appreciate who they really are.

Time and space

> Existential therapists will emphasize the role various aspects of time play in our understanding of life. (Deurzen, Chapter 1)

The past is a time that may be gone, but it is tremendously important to understand its course and how it led to the present. The present is a time when we create a new narrative by understanding and exploring the givens that come from the past and from our actual position in the world. It is also where we learn to explore our possibilities. The future is time that is not yet here and that has many different potential guises. It demands of us that we consider how our actions and their consequences will pave the way to a new mode of being. The whole issue of temporality is woven through existential work and provides it with a leading edge. Existential relationship therapists aim to help those in relationship to understand the givens of their past, to share their 'here' and to identify a joint 'there', awash with possibilities, to aim for in the future.

Managing paradoxes, dilemmas and tensions

[Clients often face]...tensions that are so complex and relationships that are so challenging and complicated that they falter and fail. (Deurzen and Iacovou, Chapter 14)

The exploration of what it means to be in relationship and what it means to establish a bond of trust between two people, invariably exposes various tensions and contradictions – such as the tension between love and hate, which can be felt at the same time by partners – and challenges clients to accept these as part of the relationship. This requires them to face up to other challenges, like becoming aware of the inevitable conflicts between autonomy and communion or exploring the tensions between being alone and being together, between pursuing personal freedom and being dedicated to loyalty or between asserting individuality and relating with care to the other. Human existence is permeated by unsolvable dilemmas and paradoxes, and the dilemma of the social world is that we are forever torn between our need to be separate and our need to belong. Paradoxically, our desire for connection to others prevents us from complete isolation, but requires our capacity for aloneness. Our need to be different from others preserves our individuality but requires our awareness of similarity. Couples discover that it is not a matter of either/or in life and that there are lessons to learn on all sides. Paradoxes and dilemmas are the 'bedrock and fuel' of the work of the existential relationship therapist as it is through them that 'new purpose can be generated and sustained' (Deurzen, 1998: 2).

The inevitability of conflict

The Other is across the border of Me. (Leontiev, Chapter 2)

Another aspect of existential work with relationship is that it emphasizes the predictable conflicts and tensions of human existence. Rather than aiming for harmony and agreement, existential relationship therapists will recognize that relating is about commitment to resolving ongoing tensions and disagreements in such a way that all partners will feel they can contribute as much as they can learn from their being with another. Conflicts, then, are necessary and invaluable and challenge is every bit as important in relationships as harmony and peace. We encourage our clients to not be scared of conflict, but rather to be willing to approach it, get to know it and learn to work with it with courage, mutual respect and understanding.

The aims of existential relationship therapy

The use of the phenomenological method, together with the philosophy and theoretical underpinnings upon which existential relationship therapy is based, lead naturally to a set of aims or key tasks that are implicit to the model. Existential relationship therapy can:

● Encourage each partner to take cognizance of their own way of relating and the way in which this impacts on the other.
● Help clients to recognize the 'Otherness' of their partner and the necessity of true dialogue (with all its risks and challenges) if they are to enter the inner world of the Other.
● Uncover and soften entrenched existential worldviews that are blocking movement towards understanding, change and resolution.
● Identify possibilities for relationship other than those previously acknowledged and determine the costs and benefits and meaning of change for each partner.
● Develop a shared meaning and purpose in the relationship, or alternatively an appreciation that this shared meaning is not possible if each partner is to remain true only to their own individuality and life objectives.
● Create a climate where clients feel able to be courageous and to explore aspects of their relationship and their individual way of being in the world that may need to be witnessed and addressed, before they can engage and move forwards.
● Assist the development of clients as individuals, allowing them to take responsibility for themselves, to be authentic with others, and to acknowledge their own and their partner's anxiety.
● Offer the opportunity for clients to learn how to cope with occasions when they are challenged in their relationships by recognizing the potential such opportunities present for growth, intimacy and connectedness.

These aims are not meant to replace the clients' expressed objectives, but rather reflect the ways in which existential theory may positively impact on partners' ability to relate to each other, and indeed to their lives, in a more truthful, open and passionate way.

The stance of the existential relationship therapist

> Presence matters because the messenger is an important part of the message. A message is credible to the extent that the messenger is perceived as credible. (Wong and Wong, Chapter 9)

In addition to certain positive personal characteristics such as emotional maturity, the capacity for self-reflection and willingness to question the status quo (Deurzen, 2009), existential relationship therapists must have what Wong and Wong (above) describe as 'presence'. The writings in this book reveal at least some of the components of this presence:

● Skills and insights to manage the emotional polarities they and their clients experience.
● Personal strength and robustness to demonstrate how to be forthright, direct and courageous in respectfully confronting controversy and conflict.

- Ability to be even-handed and to recognize and resist partiality or special pleading and capacity to bring out and acknowledge the positions of each individual client fairly, without taking sides.
- Awareness of their own assumptions or biases about life, couples and relationships in general and a capacity for bracketing these to reduce their impact on the therapeutic process.
- Wisdom that comes from fighting their own battles with death anxiety, finitude, limitations and loss, leading to an attitude of genuine human compassion.
- Playfulness, humour and openness to the clients' stories and the ability to suspend judgement and relinquish control, flexibly following the flow.
- Resilience in dealing with serious life events without being incapacitated by them. This requires having learnt the hard way that it is usually safe to trust life to right situations, if people are willing to work their way patiently through them.
- Willingness to sit in the no-man's land of not yet knowing with clients who are lost and confused until they feel able to choose their own course of action, helping them to find their right way forward.
- Ability to identify and draw attention to the paradoxes, dilemmas, contradictions and differences that are apparent for each client and show the relevance both to the individual and the relationship in understanding their power.
- Capacity to challenge clients who are acting in bad faith either by denying their own responsibilities or by denying the limitations of the context in which they are situated.
- Necessary calmness and confidence to normalize feelings of anxiety, pain, sorrow and regret, and encourage clients to tolerate and learn from them.

The client in existential relationship therapy

> Existential therapy gives the opportunity for the client to notice that another approaches their being with care and encourages them, in turn, to take their being seriously. (du Plock, Chapter 16)

While we do not want to limit ourselves to working only with certain clients or client groups, it is important to recognize that not all clients will flourish in the kind of relationship therapy that encourages personal responsibility, authenticity and confrontation with existential givens like death and isolation. As Deurzen (2012) points out, clients can only engage fully with existential therapy (or any other therapeutic orientation) if they have confidence in its principles. This makes it essential for the existential relationship therapist to have a thorough understanding of the basic assumptions and foundational tenets that inform her work and to be willing to share these with prospective clients in simple terms.

The wisdom contained in the earlier chapters of this book points to the core characteristics of clients most likely to benefit from existential relationship therapy including their:

● Ability to explore their own perceptions and confront alternative ways of looking at the world despite the unease such examinations provoke.
● Willingness to consider their own worldview and the values and beliefs that make it up in order to open themselves to the worldview of the Other.
● Skills in managing conflict and negative emotions without engaging in destructive attacks on the Other.
● Openness to self-disclosure, dialogue and growth through deeper levels of interaction with the therapist and with their partner.
● Capacity to accept reality as it is without dressing it up or interpreting it as something it is not.
● Respect for their own freedom and the freedom of their partner, while allowing for the possibility of commitment, reciprocity and collaboration.

It goes without saying that most people initially lack in these qualities but discover themselves to be capable of learning and progressing. Existential relationship therapy has an educational and life training component, to free people up to learn new things about themselves and others and to master the art of loving dialogue and considerate living with an other. It is only if individuals continuously obstruct that process and persist with negativity or unwillingness to consider their own attitude that the therapeutic work may be judged to be impossible.

Conclusions

Taken in its entirety, this summary represents a tentative blueprint for existential relationship therapy. This blueprint is offered to all therapists who work with relationships, regardless of their orientation or training. What it confirms is that relationship therapy from an existential perspective aims at getting real about oneself and the other person we have chosen to live with. It is about seeing how relationship is our best bet for being confronted with conflict, with crisis and with challenges to our self-esteem as well as to our values, beliefs and illusions about ourselves. Relationship therapy is an eminently existential enterprise in this sense, as it always throws light on a person's predicaments and difficulties from different directions.

There can be no special pleading and no excuses: we have to face the contradictory images two or more partners hold about themselves and about each other, find the truth in each and come to a joint narrative, making sense of the whole story, in such a way that each has the freedom to be who they chose to become and to do so in a way that is caring of the self and loving of the other. If we succeed in this, even in a modest way, this is no mean feat. For people to learn from their seemingly insurmountable conflicts with each other is not just a worthy goal for couples in relationship, it is also a necessity for the future of humankind.

References

Buber, M. (1970) *I and Thou*, New York: Scribner's.

Cohn, H. W. (1997) *Existential Thought and Therapeutic Practice*, London: Sage.

Deurzen, E. van (1998) *Paradox and Passion in Psychotherapy*, Chichester: John Wiley and Sons.

Deurzen, E. van (2009) *Everyday Mysteries: Existential Dimensions of Psychotherapy*, London: Routledge.

Deurzen, E. van (2010) *Everyday Mysteries: A Handbook of Existential Psychotherapy,* 2nd edn, London: Routledge.

Deurzen, E. van (2012) *Existential Counselling and Psychotherapy in Practice*, London: Sage.

Foucault, M. (2006) *Madness and Civilization*, London and New York: Vintage.

Heidegger, M. (2003) *Being and Time*, Oxford and Cambridge, MA: Blackwell.

Husserl, E. (1999) *The Essential Husserl – Basic Writings in Transcendental Phenomenology*, ed. D. Welton, Bloomington, IN: Indiana University Press.

Laing, R. D. (1961) *Self and Others*, London: Pelican Books.

Merleau-Ponty, M. (1962) *The Phenomenology of Perception*, trans. C. Smith, London, Routledge & Kegan Paul.

Szasz, T. (1974) *The Second Sin*, London: Routledge.

Index